OVER THE D

EX LIBRIS
PACE COLLEGE
WESTCHESTER
PACE COLLEGE
OPPORTVNITAS
ARS COMMERCIVM CIVITAS
MCMVI
NEW YORK
PLEASANTVILLE, NEW YORK

BY THE SAME AUTHOR

Russia and the Soviet Union in the Far East

The Chinese Soviets

Eyes on Japan

Over the Divide

OVER THE DIVIDE

Impersonal Record of Personal Experiences

By VICTOR A. YAKHONTOFF

NEW YORK

COWARD-McCANN, INC.

1939

MANUFACTURED IN THE UNITED STATES OF AMERICA

Van Rees Press, New York

TO

VICTOR H. ORTHMANN

AND ALL YOUNGSTERS WHOSE FUTURE
DEPENDS ON WHAT THE ELDER PEOPLE
ARE DOING TODAY

ACKNOWLEDGMENTS

My warm thanks go to my old dear friend, J. Fletcher Smith, and my daughter Olga for reading the manuscript and making numerous valuable suggestions for improving its English and to Mrs. M. V. Yakhontoff for her encouragement.

THE AUTHOR

CONTENTS

INTRODUCTION

FROM time to time the friends of the present author have suggested that he write his reminiscences, but this was one thing he would never seriously consider doing. For in his opinion the experiences which had come his way, variegated and interesting though they might be—his life having been far from monotonous and dull—were in themselves of no particular significance to the public. This opinion the author has not yet changed. In other words, his present book is not an autobiography. It is rather *an impersonal record of personal experiences,* in which, to the sincere regret of the author, it has been necessary to employ the first person singular. But at the same time his aim has constantly been to remain in the remotest part of the stage, being heard merely as a narrator who, like the leader of the Greek chorus, is witness to the events described and to a minor extent involved in the action. His sincerest hope is that no one will find reason to accuse him of pose, parade, or self-magnification. But, as Arthur Schopenhauer said: "In doing accounts we make mistakes much oftener in our own favor than to our disadvantage; and this without the slightest dishonest intention." I kept that in mind while writing this book and have done my best to guard against it.

At the same time, this is by no means a history of our turbulent times. The author has no qualifications to undertake such a titanic work. He has simply attempted to project against these times the actual life of one individual, as an example of reaction to events. He will feel this effort justified if it attracts the attention of those numerous bewildered representatives of the privileged classes who are still so puzzled by the rapidly changing world in which they live, and are trying to find a way to cope with the problems which they have to face. Of course the book does not pretend to solve their problems, any more than it suggests "how to win friends and influence people." It is just the straightforward story of one man's reactions to such events as the war and revolutions through which he had to live, and of his attempt to find his proper place in the drama called Life.

One question in particular has been put to the author again and again on his lecture tours. "Why is it," his hearers and his hecklers ask, "that having been born into the so-called 'best society,' the choicest comforts, and the most enviable openings for a career, you elected to side with the common people against the elite, when confronted with the dilemma of making a choice?" The implication has always been that my choice was most irregular. I believe that it was the natural choice, and I hope that if the reader has the patience to read my pages to the end he will find that he agrees with me. In any event the choice I made was not unique.

Contemporary psychology holds that man's habits arise not from fixed instincts alone but are conditioned by environment, including the life of the society in which he lives. Consequently, as the environment changes, as new factors intrude, new theories are developed which force themselves on the attention of those who are not satisfied with a mere vegetating existence but are trying to live consciously, to understand the surrounding phenomena, and to contribute their share in shaping the future of the society in which they and their children must live. For people with active minds interested in social phenomena cannot fail to see that all old ideas and theories, having outlived their day, must gradually yield to more up-to-date conceptions. That is, apparently, the main reason why people belonging to the privileged groups so often appear not only in the role of advocates of reforms that seem contrary to the interest of their own class, but even as champions of the "under dogs." The Decembrists, who wanted a radical change in the political and economic structure of Russia in 1825, and so paid dearly for their convictions, were exclusively officers of the Imperial Army. All of them belonged to the landed gentry, and a number of them to the titled nobility. Prince Peter Kropotkin, a scion of one of the "best families" of Russia under the Czars, became a revolutionary for similar reasons. Count Leo Tolstoy, one of the world's greatest writers, was a "privileged" rebel, who demanded radical changes in the life, not only of his native Russia, but of the world at large.

Indeed, many Russian fighters for the betterment of the lot of the common people have belonged to the privileged classes. Such were Alexander Herzen, the publicist; Peter Lavrov, a colonel as well as a professor; Michael Bakunin, the apostle of anarchism; Nicholas Michailovsky, the writer; George Plekhanov, the Marxist scholar; and last, but by no means least, Lenin, and many of his coworkers. Of course, this was not a strictly Russian phenomenon. Men and women from the privileged classes all over the world have contributed incalculably toward the common good of their nations and humanity at large. The Count de Saint-Simon, who advocated a just division of the fruits of common labor, was as much an aristocrat as were Prince Kropotkin and Count Tolstoy. Robert Owen, the Utopian Socialist, was a wealthy merchant. The French Encyclopedists and many leaders of the French Revolution of 1789, like most of the Americans who framed the Constitution of the United States and the Bill of Rights, belonged to the privileged classes, too. So did Karl Marx and Frederic Engels.

Being privileged also in the educational facilities open to them, the upper classes in Russia and elsewhere have always had more leisure and better opportunity to develop leaders in the world of thought, including the social sciences. Those "intellectuals"—that is to say, those who rely on their mental capacities somewhat more than the average man—who advocated social changes, did it because they were thinkers, not because they were members of a class. But according to the definition of the term "intelligentsia," given by one of the outstanding figures in Russian sociology, Nicholas Michailovsky, only those intellectuals belong to this category who apply their knowledge to the good of society as a whole. In other words, social-mindedness seems to be a *conditio sine qua non* for admission into those ranks.

Clear thinking and intellectual honesty in drawing conclusions, important though they be, are nevertheless not enough. New ideas must be applied to life if the people at large are to derive benefit. Many people know more than they are willing to say, many understand more than they are able or willing to perform in order to promote common interest. Practical achievement, in short, entails a readiness to sacrifice one's immediate interests, and a willingness to fight for what one believes is the greatest good of the greatest number, and for real protection of one's inherent right to "life, liberty, and the pursuit of happiness."

All Churches, whatever the religion, whatever the denomination, emphasize in their teaching the greater duty toward others. So does ethics, independently of any cult. So did most of the philosophers. Something must be wrong in the application of such doctrines if they do not enable the individual to see beyond the narrow limits of self-interest, or the interest of his own family and group, or even that of his country when a problem arises concerning the race as a whole.

Human nature, unfortunately, is such that one readily forgets the grievances of another class, if they are not kept constantly before one's eyes through events, reading, and discussion. And at all times these stimuli must be potent indeed if mere social consciousness is to be translated into action. Concern for other people is one thing, but willingness to fight for the betterment of their lot is another. One can sympathize with the downtrodden, see injustice, realize the necessity for a change, and still remain aloof, taking no part in the struggle for procuring the desired change. Most people, unfortunately, follow this pattern, unless circumstances force them into the struggle itself.

Looking outside the limits of one's own class, learning more from books and personal experiences, understanding better, developing interest in social matters and appreciation of social values, one inevitably realizes that adjustments are necessary. Some people take the prospect calmly, if not even indifferently. Others weigh the chances for a change in their own lifetime, and, on deciding that the changes may not come so soon, especially if proper brakes are applied, resolve to continue on the old basis, without bothering about the future in which their children will live. Still others, like Kropotkin and Tolstoy, prefer to serve the future good of society rather than cling to the comforts which they themselves enjoy today.

Count Leo Tolstoy for years tried to harmonize his mode of living with his teachings. He opposed the keeping of wealth and living in luxury. His wife had other notions. She considered it her duty to provide for her children and therefore made the life of her great husband a misery of tormenting contradictions. She had her own way. The grand old man finally left his home in Yasnaya Poliana, and soon died at a lonely railway station away from his acquisitive family. The Countess kept the wealth. But Fate had the final word. The numerous children of the Countess were scattered all over the world by the Revolution and never enjoyed the advantages their mother strove to keep for them. Which was right, the Count or the Countess? Do we not know the answer now?

In Russia under the Czar, many of the writings of Leo Tolstoy and other great authors were banned as subversive. But even that which passed the censors was enough to arouse widespread interest in the lot of the other classes, to encourage independent thinking, and to point the way toward a better life for all. But something more was needed to translate social consciousness into victorious action. Wars which had exposed the inefficiency of the corrupt regime resulted in revolutions. Revolutions posed the question: "Old or New?" And still other events forced a final choice. What were these events? How did they come about? And what reactions did they bring? In these questions and their answers may be summed up the content of the present book.

OVER THE DIVIDE

Life is short, but truth works far and lives long; let us speak truth.

—ARTHUR SCHOPENHAUER, *The World as Will and Idea*

To love one's country (unless that love is quite blind and lazy) must involve a distinction between the country's actual condition and its inherent ideal; and this distinction in turn involves a demand for changes and for effort.

—GEORGE SANTAYANA, *Reason and Society*

CHAPTER I

THE BACKGROUND

(*Heredity and Environment*)

The epoch. Russia of the late nineteenth century. Ancestry. Judicial minds and rebels. Social life in Czarist Russia. Shocking lesson in sociology. Poor methods of making champions for the Monarchy. Schools. Press. Patrioteers. Cadet school. Comradeship. Pedagogues: good and otherwise. Summers in Moscow and on various estates. Wealth and egotism.

A BIRTH CERTIFICATE, issued in a church at Warsaw, states: "On June 12, 1881, a son was born to Major General Alexander Dmitrievich Yakhontoff and his wife, Lydia Pavlovna, both of the Orthodox Church, and on June 15 he was baptized and named Victor."

This child was born neither at a time of peace nor in a place blessed by serenity. It was an epoch rich in violence. All over Asia and Africa wars of aggression were being waged, while civil strife and unrest, and latent or open revolts, were brewing or breaking out in many widespread parts of the so-called civilized world.

In 1881 a Russian Czar, Alexander II, was assassinated by a group of young terrorists, which included no less a personage than Sophia Perovskaya, daughter of a Governor General of St. Petersburg, granddaughter of a Minister of the Interior, and a descendant of the Empress Elizabeth through a morganatic marriage. During the same year an American President, James A. Garfield, was shot and killed in Washington, D. C. The American crime may have been the isolated deed of an irresponsible fanatic. But the assassination of the Czar was nothing of the kind. It was the tragic culmination of a series of abortive attempts on the Imperial life, and of a long succession of revolutionary outbursts which found their cause in world trends and deep domestic grievances.

Some of the grievances dated back only to the Emancipation. Others were of a more ancient vintage.

It was in 1861, twenty years earlier, that the Czar Alexander II, known as the "Liberator of the Serfs," granted the long overdue reform, with which his name is associated. His chief purpose was, of course, to eliminate remnants of the feudal system. But, like radical instruments of change on a large scale, his reform was made the vehicle of abuse. The Czar was accused of allowing the landlords to cheat the peasants; for the latter had to pay unreasonably high prices for the meager parcels of land they received under the terms of the Emancipation. The effect thereby was to leave them to all intents and purposes at the mercy of the very landlords from whom they were supposed to have been freed. Such was one grievance; and it was in no way lessened by the fact that the standard of living of the rural population was close to starvation.

Among the industrial workers, likewise, conditions of life were extremely bad at that period, if one may judge by the number of strikes which, though illegal, were oft-recurring. At that time the number of industrial workers was rapidly growing. In the late seventies first workers' unions were organized. A number of revolutionary groups, furthermore, were active in the country, carrying propaganda to the toilers. A few of these—including the group known as "The Will of the People," to which Perovskaya and her companions belonged—advocated regicide and terror as a weapon in the struggle for the betterment of the lot of the masses. It is small wonder indeed that the Grand Duke Alexander, a cousin of the last Czar of the Romanov dynasty, wrote in his autobiography, *Once a Grand Duke,* about this period: "To say that we lived in a besieged fortress would be using a very poor simile. During war one knows one's friends and enemies. We never did. The butler serving morning coffee might have been in the employ of the nihilists for all we knew."

So much for agricultural and industrial discontent. But this was not all. Russia, being a conglomerate of nations, most of which had been incorporated into the Empire by force, had at that period to face a constant threat from separatist movements. She was, moreover, still on her march of expansion; for though her war with Turkey had come to an end in 1878 her conquest of Central Asia continued.

General Skobelieff and others were steadily adding new territories to the Empire. Along with the new lands, new nationalities were brought into the orbit of Russia; and these nationalities brought with them a fierce resentment of subjugation and oppression and the undying determination to regain independence.

Warsaw, the city of my birth, was one of the oldest and most pronounced centers of such separatist movement and smoldering revolt. After the three partitions of Poland [1] the outlying, or non-Polish, part of the ancient kingdom was annexed by the Russian Empire. Warsaw, the capital, had been occupied by the Russians in 1812, after the retreat of Napoleon from Moscow. Three years later the Principality of Warsaw was added, by the decision of the Vienna Congress, to the Russian possessions. For a time Poland was considered as a separate state under the Russian Czar as its King, but with a certain amount of autonomy. After two unsuccessful revolts,[2] designed to restore its independence, Poland was deprived of those privileges and became merely a part of the Russian Empire, governed by the Russians like any other province of their enormous country.

My father was one of the numerous officers assigned by the government to this work in Poland. Two months after my arrival in this world he died. The family of my mother never was quite reconciled to her choice of a "commoner," for he belonged to the nobility without a title. A graduate of the Demidov Lyceum—corresponding to an American college—he was a lawyer by training, possessed an unusually keen mind, and was making a brilliant career. By the time of his comparatively early death at the age of forty-six, he was already a general. But all this was not enough for the proud nobles, considering themselves aristocrats, who were the relatives of my mother.

Her father, Pavel Ivanovich Degay, an outstanding jurist of his time, was a Secretary of State and Minister of Justice. He was the descendant of a French aristocrat who had emigrated to Russia after the Revolution of 1789. Her mother was the daughter of General De Preradovich, friend of two Emperors, Alexander I and Nicholas I,

[1] In 1772, 1793, and 1795.
[2] In 1830 and 1863.

and a hero of the Napoleonic wars, whose portrait, now as before, hangs in the Winter Palace at Leningrad. When still fairly young, he led the Chevaliers Guard at the famous battle of Fère-Champenoise, described by Count Leo Tolstoy in his immortal novel, *War and Peace*. His wife was the Countess Miloradovich. On my mother's side also we were related to the Counts Ignatieff and Tolstoy, Princes Kochubey and Mestchersky; and in one way or another to a good many families of that class. In childhood, however, I never knew much about my genealogical tree, to the horror of my sisters, aunts, and other countless relatives. I never was impressed by it, never wanted to know any details of that sort, never believed that the exploits of my ancestors entitled me to any particular rights or honors. Apparently, I inherited this point of view from my mother, who, obviously, was a rebel, at least to the extent of opposing the too-rigid barriers between various strata of society.

Russia at that time had barely emerged from the feudal period and was divided in a rather sharp way between those who were *comme-il-faut,* the fashionable world, and the others, the *comme-il-ne-faut-pas,* or "common people." What was meant by the *comme-il-faut* has been sarcastically described by Count Leo Tolstoy in his *Childhood, Adolescence, and Youth*. To be *comme-il-faut* one had to speak good French, know how to dress, how to act under various circumstances, how to treat people of one's own class, and how to treat the "others." I remember once being reprimanded by my governess for speaking Russian when at the table. I ought to have spoken French "when the servants were present" in order to keep them out of "our" conversation. And this was explained to me when I was a kid of eight or nine years of age.

There were, of course, no castes similar to those of India, but there remained the snobbishness of those whose ancestors were famous one way or another, and who therefore were, or were supposed to be, economically independent, well-to-do, or at least in comfortable circumstances. If they considered their class as the elite, the *aristos,* they derived a certain justification from the past. For generations everything had been arranged to give them all the opportunities for acquiring knowledge and developing talent, if any. Naturally enough, this sheltered and easy-going life resulted in a good deal of degeneration; and as a class the Russian nobility was by now no longer a mine of such talents as are required for statesmanship. Gradually the advent of the middle class elements had become unavoidable, and more and more people, born out of the limits of the restricted "fashionable world" broke into the ranks of the government. But, still, those who belonged to the tiny layer on the top of this society continued to stick to their exclusiveness.

I learned about this "exclusiveness" when still of a tender age. My mother passed away when I was not quite five years old. Together with two of my sisters and a brother I went to live with a family of our mother's friends, who became our guardians. Soon I alone remained, for the other children were placed in boarding schools. We lived on the ground floor of a St. Petersburg apartment house. From the windows of my room I was able to see the court yard, and the merrily playing children. But I was not permitted to go out and play. I was told that these children did not belong to "my class." They were inferior; I was not supposed to have anything in common with them. But, once, when the guardian and governess were out and the servants far from my sight, I opened a window, and invited the nice kids, whose games I had enviously watched so long, to come in. So they did. It was a grand party. But, all too soon, the governess returned. My guests were ejected without ceremony, and I got a great scolding for my crime. I never was able to forget this little incident, and to this day I have not ceased hating snobbishness. Unconsciously, of course, I became at the same time interested in "social justice." And that no such thing existed in my country, I quickly discovered when I went to school.

Neither the search for truth, nor social justice were the main concern of the administrators of our school system—if these interested them at all. Those who were shaping plans for education in Russia at that time were of the opinion that its primary aim was to train personnel for the government and for leadership in various walks of life. A Minister of Education, one of the many Counts Tolstoy, had declared, for example, that "the high schools were not for the children of cooks," meaning that only the offspring of the privileged classes could expect to receive the more substantial kind of education. Another minister of "Public Enlightenment," Delianov, elaborated the same theme. Constantin Leontieff, the philosopher, suggested "freezing Russia for a while" in order to remove her from the "dangerous thoughts of the West." He advocated a specific culture, supposedly germane to the Russians as a Slavic nation, but apart from the Western culture of the rest of Europe. Pobiedonostzeff, the omnipotent Procurator of the Holy Synod, tutor and adviser of two Emperors, Alexander III and Nicholas II, was another advocate of this policy. He did everything in his power—and this was tantamount to the unlimited power of the Autocrat himself—to retard the cultural progress of the broad masses of the people, to check the civilizing influences of the West. The ridiculous assumption was that by keeping people in darkness it would be easier to cope with the tremendously aggrandized Empire and its enormous and heterogeneous population. As a result, over seventy-five per cent of the people remained illiterate.

The three cornerstones of the Slavianophiles, or those who opposed Westernization of Russia, were the Orthodox Church, Autocracy, and Nationalism. They continued to prevail and stubbornly to resist the advent of modern ideas, modern institutions, and the modern manner of living. Accordingly, the schools were supposed to prepare good champions for the Monarchy, pious sons of the Orthodox Church, and aggressive nationalists.

In this respect the work of the educational system was continued by the press and by the patrioteers. The few newspapers which existed were published at that time under a more or less strict censorship, exercised either by preliminary approval of the material to be published, or by severe punishment for anything already published and disapproved afterward by the authorities. The patrioteers, or the professional patriots, defenders of the regime that was expected to reward their zeal, were not wanting. Subsidies for this sort of patriotic work were distributed lavishly, if not always with results sought.

Trends were clear, but the means applied for attaining the desired ends very often were unavailing or inefficient.

My own school days commenced early. First I attended an institution which prepared one for entering a cadet school. Then followed the cadet school itself, and finally the military academy, similar to West Point in the United States.

At preparatory school I had a modest experience that served to increase my early doubts about justice. A boy of ten, with no ideas but those of chivalry and kindness, I offered a few flowers from the garden to the nurse attached to the school's infirmary. The result was that I was not allowed to go for my summer vacation. My tutor had caught me in this act of innocent gallantry and had disapproved violently.

In 1892 I entered the First Cadet School at St. Petersburg. The school occupied the site of the former palace of Prince Menstchikov, once the trusted lieutenant of Peter the Great. With many new buildings added, the palace had remained as a museum. Some of the buildings faced the Neva with its granite embankments; while across the wide majestic river stood the Bronze Horseman, monument to Peter the Great, the founder of St. Petersburg, with the cupola-crowned St. Isaak's Cathedral, built by Monferrant, towering behind. On either side of the monument rose the imposing buildings of the Senate and the Holy Synod, and the garden-encircled Admiralty. Next to the Admiralty stood the magnificent Winter Palace.

This panorama, always very impressive, was particularly alluring in the "white nights" of the summer. In June the sun, by reflection, continued to throw its rays upon this part of the earth even at night, painting everything in pastel tints, and thereby creating a dreamlike effect. In winter, of course, the Neva was icebound and teemed with sleighs and sportsmen. But even then the little bathhouse opposite our school continued to attract a few Spartans, whatever the mercury might say.

The First Cadet School was the oldest institution of the kind in Russia, and boasted among its alumni many of the greatest military heroes and civilian celebrities of the land. I liked the place. But its great attraction to me lay not in its surroundings, its historical associations, nor its educational facilities, but in the spirit of comradeship which existed among the cadets. This comradeship left with me the warmest reminiscences, and no doubt contributed much more toward the building of our characters than the formal instruction and discipline of the school were able to accomplish. Here was a world in itself, built up on cordiality and directed more by respect for truth than by established norms. Ignoring the high-sounding sermons of the elders, which smacked of hypocrisy, and with a discrimination respecting certain traditions, it was creating its own new code of behavior and social intercourse. To be sure we were never completely free from the influence of our families, but this influence, as is usually the case with boarding school children, was gradually waning.

As we all belonged to the privileged classes, with little variations in social and economic standing, we had no such disagreements as are apt to arise in the outer world. We all lived in the same dormitories, going home only for the week ends; we had identical intellectual food (which was never excessive); and we cherished more or less the same ideals. Our glorious country must be great under the benevolent rule of the Czar, our father; the Church is the guardian and disseminator of truth and the source of our moral strength; and we must at all times be patriotic, brave, and ready to sacrifice our lives for the good of the country. Such were our ideals.

Our teachers were of all categories, good, bad, and indifferent. In St. Petersburg, the capital, one would have expected the instructors to be of the best; but, as most of the desirable positions were sought by people who had "pull," the result was that not the best but the well-connected were commonly chosen. Besides, the cost of living in the capital was relatively high and salaries rather modest. Thus, many of the teachers had to seek for extra sources of income, with the inevitable result that some were overworked, and therefore physically unable to give their best to their classes.

The cadet schools, as we have seen, were designed not only to prepare youngsters for a military career, but to replenish a warrior caste. Practically all of the pupils came from military families. No tuition fees were charged, for this sort of education was offered as an additional compensation for services rendered to the Army by the parents. Hence the government looked upon all cadets as future military replacements, and saw to it that the curricula should not be so liberal as to encourage ambitions unconnected with the Army.

Almost every tutor was a military officer. Only a few civilians now remained from a short-lived period when these schools had not been specifically factories of soldiers. Fortunately, one of my own tutors was such a civilian—a most charming, cultured old gentleman, with a serious interest in education and a warm heart for his pupils. His successor for two years was a pet of the whole class. But later on this tutor was replaced by a typical profane drill sergeant, whose manners and rudeness were an object lesson in vulgarity. This fellow finally became Chief of Police in one of the largest cities.

As for the curriculum, it included little enough of social science. Instead, it was packed with mathematics, foreign languages, natural science, literature, and that variety of history which is concerned with the names of military heroes and monarchs, descriptions of battles and similar exploits, and pays little attention to the cultural development of a nation, its ideals and aspirations, and its social and economic problems. The summer vacations, naturally, opened up to us larger vistas. Then we could read more freely, and, perhaps, make wider social contacts. Thus, when we returned to school after the summer, we were always somewhat changed, and our mental baggage became more and more disparate. But always we remained children of the privileged class, with few worries, and the future certainty of a guaranteed career.

When I was eleven or twelve years old, I used to spend my summer vacations in Moscow with my uncle, an old general, in whose honor I had been named. My uncle was a kindhearted gentleman who adored me and did practically anything I wished, but I do not think he exerted any particular influence on my mental development. Later summers, however, were spent on the estates of various relatives and acquaintances, and here I had plenty of opportunity to observe the extravagant luxury of the Russian landlord and the indescribable misery of his peasants. True, food was occasionally offered to the needy, medicine was brought to the sick, and smiles—which cost nothing—were distributed to all. But my hosts and elders invariably seemed to be kindhearted, and they were good to me. Thus, my growing doubts about the equitable nature of the universe were intermittently aroused and dispelled. There were at least times when I had few qualms about accepting the dictum of our priest, who pointed out that the world had been designed by God Almighty, whose sole wish was to see everybody happy, and who might be trusted to know what was best for humanity at any given time.

But there were other times when my own experience could not fail to show me that everything was not based on justice, and that the conventional explanations simply would not do. Social differences were too extreme, misery and want were too obvious, and the behavior of some people was too shocking, to warrant acceptance of the comforting theory that this was all part of a divine plan. More and more I began to doubt, and more and more to read. I found that books had other explanations to offer for the causes of the strange situation which was puzzling me, and that these explanations were rather more convincing.

Fortunately for me at this time I had one aunt who was keenly anxious to develop my taste in literature. At first, of course, I had read chiefly because there were no children of my class near by to play with, and there was little else to do. Now, under the intelligent guidance of this aunt, who understood what to offer to a growing boy and in what order it should be offered, I became acquainted with the boundless wealth of the Russian classics. Pushkin, Gogol, Turgenieff, Tolstoy, Lermontov, and Goncharov—all these I read. And naturally for a long time I enjoyed their stories chiefly for the sake of the characters therein, admiring the heroes and sympathizing with the maltreated, with little or no thought of social implications. In literature, as in life, the abused and suffering were pitiable; but in literature, as in life, they continued to occupy the positions "prescribed by God." Whether this state of affairs could, or should, be changed was not for me to say. I may have had my doubts, but never did I attempt to find a remedy. Belief in the priest and his dictum was still far too strong within me. Indeed there was one time in the period of my adolescence when, impressed by the example of Aliosha in Dostoyevsky's *The Brothers Karamazov* and other similar characters in literature, I thought of escaping from the world's injustice by becoming a monk. Luckily, before I had a chance to enter a monastery, I began to think more independently and realistically.

CHAPTER II

CZARS AND THEIR SUBJECTS

(*Youth and the Old Regime*)

Death of Alexander III. Visit of the new Czar and Czarina. Story of the Romanov dynasty. The Smolny Institute for girls of nobility—years before it became the headquarters of Lenin. Li Hung Chang, the great Chinese diplomat. Youth and the old regime. Military Academy. Influence of the liberals. Bucolic naïveté of the boarding school life. The Boxer Rebellion. Grand Duke Constantin. Camps and maneuvers. Visits of the Czar. End of the school days. To Caucasia instead of the Guards.

WHEN THE Emperor Alexander III died in 1894, we, the cadets, were present at the funeral. It was an elaborate and pompous pageant designed to impress the populace, as, most likely, it did. But to such young children as ourselves it was a cruel ordeal. The weather was bitterly cold, and we were forced to stand in front of our buildings for hours and hours, awaiting the approach of the procession and the passing of that endless cortege. Regiment after regiment went by in gorgeous uniforms; numerous bands played funeral marches; courtiers of various ranks, from servants up to the highest dignitaries, marched by in plumed headgears; and strange medieval knights, representing Death and Life, contributed a last exotic touch to the spectacle. The favorite horse of the late Czar, draped in mourning, preceded the huge, gilded, and elaborately decorated hearse with its golden coffin bearing the embalmed body of the august monarch, accompanied by eminent pallbearers. It was followed by the Royal family, the foreign monarchs and princes, foreign envoys, the high ranking officials, and finally by an endless number of Court carriages bearing such celebrities as the older members of the Czar's family, and the ladies in waiting. Then came more soldiers, infantrymen and cavalry, passing soundlessly by; while even the artillery rattled but faintly on the snow-covered roadway, as if to underline thereby the mood of utter silence and meditation. It was a great spectacle, very impressive, indeed. But the frost was so biting that our limbs, inadequately protected by our Spartan garb, were burning and our faces were half frozen. Hence, we became wild with joy when it was over, and we were permitted to return to our warm dormitories. Contrary to the etiquette, we showed no signs of sorrow. And when afterward we were served, as an extra for the occasion, good cakes with our tea, we almost felt it was a holiday.

"The King is dead: long live the King." Alexander III was dead, and Nicholas II reigned in his place. Soon the new Czar came to visit us, and with him came his beautiful Czarina. We were elated at the event. The Emperor smiled and asked questions of no importance in the most friendly manner. Their Majesties visited our classrooms and finally came to the mess hall, where the Czarina, displaying a pronounced German accent, inquired of someone if he liked the soup. The Czar touched one boy's shoulder, and when he left, that boy tore off his epaulette, kissed it in ecstasy, and declared that he would treasure it as a priceless memento, for the rest of his life.

The visit was over. We had seen our Sovereigns. They had been most charming, most kind. We were captivated by their charm; we were prepared to love them affectionally, as a child may love its parents. This was not unnatural, for the Emperor was always pictured to us in the role of the "loving father," and our history books were crammed with tales about the glory of his House.

It was not until much later, and then only gradually, that I learned the true story of the Romanov dynasty. Attaining to supreme power early in the seventeenth century, after a long period of turmoil and confusion in which several changes of rulers occurred, the Romanovs were actually Czars of the landed nobility, to which they belonged, and by whom they were elected "by popular proclamation." It is true that the first of the Czars of this dynasty succeeded in restoring "order," though not without cruelty in putting down revolts of the peasantry; and it is also true that several of the Romanovs contributed to a glorious expansion of the Empire, while others, such as Peter the Great, introduced valuable reforms and led the country further along the road of progress. But they were the exceptions. Comparatively few were in any way solicitous for the welfare of their subjects.

Scandalous as were the stories of their personal lives, the Czars remained always the "most pious," the "most serene." Even we knew, of course, from our textbooks that Peter the Great had imprisoned in convents his sister Sophia and his first wife. His second wife, Catherine I, had been chambermaid to a pastor in Estonia, and was notorious for an insatiable thirst for liquor, which challenged that of Peter himself. But our textbooks failed to tell us, in so many words, that Peter had ordered his son, Alexis, to be executed in the fortress of Peter and Paul after putting him to torture with his own hands. Neither was it considered suitable to print the historic fact that Ivan VI, who was made Czar when still an infant, was imprisoned by his aunt, who became the Empress Elizabeth. Nor were we told that this wretched prisoner was assassinated in the fortress many years later when Catherine II, the Great, ascended the throne over the corpse of her husband, Czar Peter III, who was killed by officers of the Imperial Guard.

Certainly our textbooks did not make it clear to us that there were actually no more Romanovs on the throne, though the dynasty continued to be known under this name. The real House of Romanov became extinct after the death of the Empress Elizabeth, whose love affairs, numerous and scandalous, distinguished a reign marked by the wildest extravagance. When she died, some fifteen thousand dresses were found in her wardrobe, but hardly any money in the State Treasury. The House that reigned in Russia after her was that of Holstein-Gothorp. This dynasty was foreign to Russia: there was not a drop left of the Romanov blood.

Peter III was the first of the Holstein-Gothorp Czars. The fate of his heirs was far from happy. Paul, his son, was strangled in the presence of his son, who became Czar Alexander I. The fate of Alexander I remains an enigma which has intrigued many historians; for a legend insists that it was not Alexander I who was pronounced dead at Taganrog in 1825, but a Cossack. The Czar himself, so goes the tale, secretly left the palace and continued his long life as a hermit in Siberia. Most historians, however, do not accept this legend, which has no reliable basis.

As for his brother, Nicholas I, rumors persist that he committed suicide after the loss of the Crimean War. His son, Alexander II, was assassinated. The next in line, Alexander III, died, supposedly, from natural cause, though even this is open to doubt. His son, the last of the House, met in 1918 the tragic fate of Charles I of England and Louis XVI of France.

That such a thing might happen not one of us, in school, ever dreamed. We glorified our Emperor and all he stood for. Similarly, in the girls' schools for the nobility he was adored to the point of sentimentality. The most exclusive of such schools was the Smolny Institute, where both my sisters boarded. One of them had as classmate the present Queen Helena of Italy, then Princess of Montenegro. Not a girl in that school but was a daughter of a general, or someone of equivalent rank.

Sunday was a visiting day at the Smolny, and I used to go there to see my sisters for an hour or so, in a gorgeous ballroom, with immense portraits of the Czarinas and the Czars on the walls. There, at a graduation ball, I once saw among the guests of honor the famous Chinese statesman and diplomat, Li Hung Chang, who had arrived to represent his Emperor at the coronation of the new Czar. It was he who granted permission for a Russian railway through Chinese territory in Manchuria—a railroad later known under the name of the Chinese Eastern, and destined to play a sad role in future Russian history. For his approving contract for that concession the illustrious statesman was promised by Witte, then Russian Minister of Finance, a bribe of a couple of million rubles, of which actually he received only a part. On the occasion when I saw him in the Smolny Institute, this peer of the Celestial Empire demonstrated his oriental generosity by offering to all the girls of the graduating class lavish presents in jewels; but the gifts were at the expense of the hosts. The old fox was cashing in on the bribe offered to him by Witte for betraying his mother country.

Nobody present on this gala occasion could have had the slightest idea of what had to happen in that building two score years later. For this same Smolny Institute, where the daughters of the nobility had been educated since the time of the Empress Elizabeth, was to become the headquarters of the Revolution. From this very spot Lenin directed the armed uprising; and here he and his collaborators laid their plans for the new country of Soviet Russia. But we, in the cadet school, read little of revolutions in our history books; we never thought about the need to defend the Czar from his own people. It did not enter our heads that anything might happen to him. To us, all revolutionaries were criminals of the vilest type, not worth consideration.

Since the assassination of Alexander II there was no more "red terror": it had been replaced by a white one. Reaction was the watchword of the third Alexander's reign. Indeed, I do not remember ever having had in school a discussion about revolution and its perpetrators. In other words, we were interested in sports, had our little quarrels, pranks, and adventures, but no political interests. As for the possibility of a clash between different systems of government—well, in our world, there was no such question.

At the end of my sixth year, or one year before graduation, I was expelled. This was the work of that tutor who later became a Chief of Police. Scholastically I was always first in my class, but my behavior was not what this tutor considered as right. It is true that I was caught several times leaving school without permission, and, on a number of occasions I was reprimanded for various pranks. Time and again I was incarcerated for infractions of rules, and in particular for disrespect toward the tutor. He asserted that I was too advanced for my age, too independent in my judgments, and too insolent. I think he was wrong in his evaluation of my character. But it is true that I was extremely hotheaded, never knew how to control myself, and never hesitated to express my disapproval, often quite violently, of things I looked upon as being wrong.

My expulsion made no particular difference to finishing my schooling, for I succeeded in passing examinations with my class the following spring and received my diploma. But the experience left a deep scar: I had learned another bitter lesson about so-called justice. Subconsciously, perhaps, I was set to fight for justice, at first, no doubt, primarily for myself. But gradually and inevitably this selfish motive had to develop into one more general and altruistic. I think it did, though slowly and not without the pressure of subsequent events.

While still in the cadet school, I made plans to enter the Institute of Engineers of Communications. I never had any inclination for a military career. My teachers considered me exceptionally gifted in mathematics, and I wanted to become an engineer. But my relatives had their own ideas; they wished me to become an officer of the Army. This was in line with the family tradition; and besides, as a Russian adage puts it: "If one wants to be good-looking, one must become a hussar" (meaning to don a gorgeous uniform). My year out of the school, which I spent in the regiment where my elder brother was an officer, decided my fate. To please my relatives, who were grieved by my expulsion, I entered a Military Academy at St. Petersburg, and in two years I was an officer myself.

While in the Academy, I became friendly with a few students (junkers, as we were called), who came from the Kiev Cadet School well known for its liberal tendencies. Under their influence I had my first taste of political matters. That influence was far from revolutionary, but it did add new experiences, divert my curiosity, and start new interests. The topics of our conversations were mostly of a humanitarian character. Liberalism, not revolution, was the atmosphere in which these boys had been brought up. Classical literature, not revolutionary pamphlets, was their source of information. Russian literature, certainly, offered a great deal along these lines. There were such humanists as the literary critics, Belinsky and Dobroliubov, and to a certain extent the brilliant but erratic Pissariev. There were such writers as Gleb Uspensky, Pissemsky, and Pomialovsky, who vividly described the evils of contemporary society. There were such giants as Leo Tolstoy, Turgenieff and Dostoyevsky, all of whom in one way or another lamented the injustices prevailing in the Russia of their respective days. All this offered us a wealth of information, and an impressive arsenal from which to select our weapons in the fight for social betterment. What this might mean, what it could imply, we little understood. Our hearts burned with indignation; we wanted to see injustice rectified. That was all. We were still far from real knowledge of the causes of injustice, and the cures, if any. The most we looked for were reforms, reforms which the Czar, the loving father, we were certain would not refuse to grant when he learned the facts, which obviously were withheld from him by self-seeking courtiers.

How could we doubt the benevolence of the Czar? Again and again on his visits to the Academy he captivated everyone by his charming smile, by his soft voice, by his manners. Even then, when no longer little children, we continued to adore His Majesty. I, personally, felt lifted to the seventh heaven when, as first in the group, I had to make a report to the Czar on his visit to my class. I remember one rather amusing incident connected with one of these visits. When the Czar was leaving the building, a group of us escorted him to his carriage. When the latter began to move, one of my friends, a jolly Georgian prince, had in his boundless enthusiasm the impudence to ask the Czar to give him, as a souvenir, the ring that shone on one of the Imperial fingers. The Czar smiled and said: "I am sorry, but I cannot. This ring was given to me by my wife." It was a long time before our brave Georgian prince heard the last of this story.

In 1900 our attention was occupied for a while by events in the Far East. There was, we learned, a great empire called China, where some bad people, known as Boxers or the Big Fists, had started trouble against foreigners. The foreigners, Russia included, had decided jointly to restore order. Russian troops were therefore shipped to Manchuria and later marched on Peking, the capital of that neighboring country. But I do not remember hearing any voice condemn the acts of Russia, or of any of those other Great Powers, which were "restoring order" in China. We boys had no doubt that what the government did must be right. We never asked questions about the acts of the government. Was not the Czar its head? Was he not the righteous, loving father? Was not "the best of the churches," our Orthodox Church, blessing these acts? Were they not adding to the glory of Russia?

When in the later years I studied the Boxer Rebellion, that excuse for armed intervention in the affairs of China, I could not help asking myself how was it possible for students in a military academy, soon to become officers of the Army, to be so utterly ignorant about the march of an imperialism which was already heading Russia for her disastrous war with Japan, and all that the war brought in its wake? To be sure, it was not customary to read newspapers in the military school. Our officers made no efforts to enlighten us on current events, except as regards the victories of our troops on various occasions. And at such times, of course, they neglected to mention how utterly ignoble was this policy of aggression against an almost unarmed country. On the contrary, these acts were represented as the great exploits of military heroes. But the only really satisfying explanation I was able to find lay in the abnormality of boarding school life, and in the unreality of a world created in the desire to make out of us mute and obedient executors of an omnipotent, mysterious will.

For mysticism, so useful in fooling the uninitiated, surrounded most of us from earliest childhood through our years in school, where the priests contributed their part in discouraging free thinking. Mysticism of diverse origin continued to befog the minds of many; and often enough people lived under its spell up to their last breath.

The head of all the military educational institutions of that time was the Grand Duke Constantin, an uncle of the Czar, a poet of repute, a liberal, and a charming human being, but a mystic of a kind defying any rational explanations. He made one of the best Russian translations of the Shakespeare *Hamlet,* and played masterfully the leading role in that great tragedy when it was performed by a group of aristocratic amateurs at the Court Theater in the famous Hermitage art gallery in St. Petersburg. But, at the same time—as I was told by a cousin of mine who used to be his aide-de-camp and friend, he believed quite seriously in the existence of the devil—tail, horns, and all. And this was the man who was expected to direct the mental processes of the future officers of the Army, the defenders of Holy Russia! As a matter of fact, he did very little directing, for his task, like that of most of the Grand Dukes, was rather to see that nothing detrimental to the interests of the Royal family should happen in any branch of the government.

On the whole, this policy of fooling the dupes and supervising the potential villains seemed to work rather well. In the Army and Navy, at any rate, there were few skeptics. Excessive thinking was not the fashion. Merry living and easy going were the rule. Physical exercises provided beneficial fatigue; when tired by maneuvers or routine work in the camps, where we spent the larger part of each summer, we had neither the time nor the inclination to bother with the affairs of the "civilian world." Visits by the Czar, not frequent but always highly appreciated, provided us with fuel to keep our hearts burning for the "little father." Visits by the Grand Duke Constantin and other dignitaries made us feel close to the highest strata of the country. In addition, assignments to guard duty at the Winter Palace, and participation in parades there and elsewhere, may have served to impress many future officers with the grandeur of the Empire and the magnificence of the Imperial Court. They never gave me personally, however, the feeling that I was a servant of the Czar. I was a son of my country and an ardent patriot; but I never felt servile toward anyone, not even the Czar himself. But this did not make me any less loyal than another. And never in my future life, as an officer of the Imperial Army of Russia, did I do anything contrary to the oath we all had to take on receiving our commissions.

In 1901 our course of study was over. That autumn we were made first lieutenants and assigned to various regiments. In spite of the fact that my marks entitled me to first place in the class I was graduated as belonging to the "second category." This was because of a strange incident which occurred during the year and disqualified me from the honors earned by my scholastic achievements. When, at the beginning of my second and final year in the Academy, I was assigned as a noncommissioned officer in charge of my class, my classmates invited me for a party in my honor. We all had some drinks, as the officer on duty deduced (on our return to the school) from the gaiety of the group and their loud and too-animated conversations. Next day I was discharged from my "exalted" position and demoted to the second category. This was another stupid injustice, for I, certainly, was no drunkard, then or ever. The punishment, in any case, was altogether too severe for the alleged offense. I therefore embarked on a systematically carried-out rebellion; I did everything in my power to demonstrate my resentment, and did it in such a manner as simply to infuriate the officer in charge of my class. I spent a good many days under arrest and, never seeking reinstatement, ended my years at the Academy with highest marks in everything but conduct. As a result, I was prevented from receiving a commission in one of the regiments of the Imperial Guard, a commission for which I had otherwise all the required qualifications.

Instead of the Guards, I was assigned to my brother's regiment. Soon I was en route for Caucasia, to join him there and to begin my "independent" life.

Before me was the wide world, smiling with boundless opportunities, the enchanted world, intriguing by its mysteries, tempting by its untasted pleasures; the world free of tormenting doubts, free of worries, the world of happy youth, good will, and optimism.

CHAPTER III

CAUCASIA

(*Accumulation of Experiences*)

Caucasia. Its beauty. The story of its acquisition. Masters not interested in the aborigines, their language and customs, their aspirations. Caucasian princes and the common people. Forced Russification. My regiment. Officers and soldiers. Sheltered life and limited ambitions. Aloofness from reality. Camps. Strange adventure with a postman. Law in a new light. Teaching children as avocation. Various influences. Liberals and radicals. Political exiles. My group for study. A soldier and a Jew in it. Warning from authorities. Labor troubles in Batum. Stimulus for social-mindedness.

My regiment, the 79th Infantry, was stationed at Kutais, an ancient Transcaucasian town, built more than a thousand years ago, and still modernized only in the center. Ruins of a fortress, built in the early eleventh century, and the Galat Monastery, which dated back to the tenth century, if not even earlier, were picturesque monuments to the past. This monastery—famous for its Byzantine frescoes and ancient scripts of the Gospel in the Georgian language—was perched on a rock in a beautiful cleft on the mountains a few miles from the town.

To reach Kutais from the north you had the choice of three routes. One could go by the Black Sea, from Novorosiisk through Batum. Or you could travel by rail around the range of the Greater Caucasus, through Baku with its famous oil fields, and Tiflis, the capital of Transcaucasia. And finally there was the military highway for crossing the mountains on horses. I thought then, and still believe, that this Georgian miiltary highway is one of the world's most magnificent routes, so rare is its beauty and the grandeur of its mountain scenery. It goes through several ranges of the really majestic Greater Caucasus, the highest mountains in all Europe, by a series of mighty gorges including the Daryal Gorge, which has inspired many a poet and painter. It was near the Daryal Gorge that Demon whispered his seductive songs to Tamara in the beautiful poem by Lermontov, which served as libretto to Anton Rubinstein's opera. Furthermore, numerous myths of ancient Greece have Caucasia as a setting, and two, at least, are known to every child. Prometheus, who "took pity on the misery of mankind and stole fire from heaven, bringing it to mortals," was punished by being chained to a rock in the Caucasus. And the Argonauts, seeking the Golden Fleece, had as their destination Colchida, which is the Valley of the River Rion, on which Kutais is situated.

The history of Caucasia, that borderland between Asia and Europe, was forged by fire and sword in endless wars. The richness of this region has attracted conquerors from time immemorial. But the authentic history of Georgia, the largest of its states, begins only with its subjugation by Alexander the Great in 323 B.C. Then followed the Armenian, Hun, Persian, and Turkish hordes. Crusaders returning from Jerusalem used the country as a short cut to their European homes; and some of them, captivated by its wealth and beauty, settled there. Even today mountaineers may be found in Svanetia and Hevsuria who cherish large swords and armor handed down by Crusader ancestors. Here lies the explanation of the traces of the German language found in the dialect of Ossetia, a small district in northern Caucasia. With some eighty or more different nationalities and tribes inhabiting its expanse, this territorial link between Asia and Europe is indeed a veritable ethnographical museum.

Russian penetration of Caucasia dates back at least as far as the reign of Peter the Great, when Derbent, on the Caspian Sea, was captured from the Persians. This was in 1722. Half a century later, while at war with Turkey, Russian troops crossed the Caucasus and helped the Imeretians, who lived near the border of Turkey and owed a shadowy allegiance to the Ottoman Empire, to resist the Turks. In 1783 George XII, Prince of Georgia and Mingrelia, another little principality, put himself under the suzerainty of the Russian Czar, and in 1801, after his death, Georgia became a part of the Russian Empire. From time to time other districts were added, and by 1864 the last long and stubborn resistance by freedom-loving mountaineers was finally broken. The whole of Caucasia became a province of Russia, and a Russian Viceroy ruled at Tiflis.

At the time of the Czars Caucasia was virtually a colony. There, as elsewhere in the Empire, the old Roman policy of *divide et impere* was applied. Much was done to fan racial and tribal jealousies and enmities. Little was done to encourage cultural development of the "colony" along national lines.

It is illuminating to note in this connection that, although we were among Georgian people and had a considerable sprinkling of Georgians in the regiment itself, there was hardly a Russian officer among us who had the slightest thought of studying the Georgian language, or learning about Georgian customs and aspirations. We were the "superior" race, the conquerors. They must learn our language, not we theirs. Forcible Russification was the policy of this time. In schools and courts, in all official business there as elsewhere in Russia, the use of the Russian language was obligatory, whatever the inconvenience to the population. No wonder we had more enemies than friends! How could we expect the Georgians, Armenians, and other inhabitants to be really loyal to the Empire and to merge with their rulers? For only in a few minor respects did conquering Russia condescend. To encourage at least a semblance of loyalty in the upper classes St. Petersburg systematically flattered the most important of the innumerable Georgian princes by opening to them the doors of the "best society." But this failed to please the Armenians, a race with few titled gentry but many merchants and capitalists, some of whom played a considerable role in business circles according to their wealth. Another sop was the encouragement offered by the Russian government to Caucasians to enter military careers; and there were many officers, great and small, from all the subject nationalities and tribes. But little was done for the common people, mostly illiterate, miserably poor, and already badly abused by their own feudal lords. Their function was merely to supply taxes and cannon fodder for the armed forces of Holy Russia.

Naturally this Russification by force, this disregard of national peculiarities, this contempt for the cultural aspirations of all non-Russians, served only to intensify the Caucasian national spirit. In a few instances the separatist movement was quite aggressive.

The regiment to which I had been assigned was old and proud of its history. It had taken part in the long and bitter struggle with the Caucasian mountaineers and was credited with the capture of Wedeno, the stronghold of the legendary hero, Shamyl. And discreditable as the conquest of Caucasia may have been from some points of view, it was, certainly, no picnic. For more than twenty years the mountaineers had offered the most valiant resistance to the invaders, and the latter had been forced to shed much blood and to demonstrate real heroism before that gallant patriot, Shamyl, was rendered harmless. Many of the officers in the regiment were Russians (i.e. Slavic), and some of them were born in Caucasia and could still remember and boast of their "heroic" days. One such was my future father-in-law. His daughter, my future wife, was born in Wedeno, the former mountain fastness of Shamyl.

The ranks were largely filled with Georgians, Armenians, and representatives of other Caucasian ethnic groups. By far the greater number entered their military service, which was compulsory, without knowledge of Russian language. It was, therefore, no easy task to train them as soldiers and at the same time to see to it that they learned at least enough of the language to enable them to understand commands. And while relations between the officers and the rank and file, who were called in Russia of that time the "gray beasts," were possibly somewhat better in our regiment than in the Navy and certain other units of the Army, cruelty and contempt toward subordinates were not unusual. I saw once to my horror and disgust a young officer flogging his orderly with a savagery I would not have believed possible, even in punishing animals. When I expressed my indignation, he told me that before long I should be doing the same. Fortunately his prediction failed to come true.

Life in the regiment, especially that of the young bachelor officers, was centered in the officers' club. As in military circles everywhere, the emphasis was not on intellectual pursuits. A careless gaiety, coupled with a tendency toward heavy drinking and the inevitable accompaniment of song, was more typical. The guarantee of a lifelong, though underpaid, career, with very limited prospects, tended somewhat to create the illusion of a sheltered life. Ambitions were on promotion, which was generally automatic and dependent on no special efforts—and on the chances of a raise in pay. The latter was never adequate—indeed, the father of a large family could barely meet his needs. A first lieutenant, for example, received nominally an equivalent of some thirty-seven American dollars per month; and out of even this modest sum there were dues to be paid and deductions to be made for various social affairs in the club.

And so we lived among the Georgians with practically no interest in their life, with no interest in any life outside our own narrow circle. This fitted in perfectly with the intentions of the government, which preferred to keep the armed forces as far as possible from the civilian population, and hence from the contamination of dangerous thoughts and undesirable influences. There were, of course, some contacts with civilians, but mostly these were with the officials of other governmental services. With the local population, we had practically no contacts at all.

To me, the really pleasant phase of military life lay in the constant opportunity it afforded for the enjoyment of new surroundings. At least once a year the regiment went to camp; and maneuvers during the year held other possibilities for a change of scene. Usually our regiment spent the torrid season far from the regular headquarters, somewhere in the higher altitudes, away from the intense heat of the valleys. Thus, two of my summers in Caucasia were spent near Ahalkalaki, a small Armenian town in the Western Transcaucasia, high in the mountains separating Russia from Turkey. Our road through the passes was surrounded by snow-covered peaks, with slopes partly hidden by enormous evergreen forests. But below, in the valleys, the magnificent subtropical vegetation, the abundance of flowers, and the endless vineyards offered an ironic contrast to the poverty of the wretched villages.

The return from camp in 1903 proved eventful for me. When the regiment was approximately halfway to Kutais, something strange happened. I was riding apart from the column, having been instructed to catch the baggage train ahead and to prepare for the passage of the regiment. From the divide I saw the long line of heavy-loaded vans slowly descending toward the valley, and also a small mail coach speeding behind it. When the latter came close to the vans and found them obstructing the road, the constable who accompanied the mail got out of his carriage and, after an apparent argument, started beating some of the drivers. Now officers of the law, such as constables, were privileged persons; few dared quarrel with them, much less strike back. I hurried forward. But the horse I was riding did not develop the desired speed; and having no real whip, I made use of the cord to which the revolver is ordinarily attached. Soon I reached the quarreling group, and ordered the constable to stop the outrage and go on his way. This he did. I then returned to the regiment, related the experience to some of my friends, and never expected to hear of it again.

But one day, soon after our return to Kutais, I was summoned by the Colonel. He told me of a document, just received from Tiflis, in which I was accused not only of delaying the arrival of mail by interfering with its passage on the highway, but also of threatening with my revolver the postman and the constable who accompanied him. All this sounded ominous, because constables had only recently been introduced into Caucasia by the newly appointed Viceroy and were his especial pets. Interference with official work was bad enough. But threatening to shoot a postman and a constable on duty was a serious crime. What was I to say? I had little doubt that these men were late with the mail simply because they had stopped too long in some tavern; but how could I prove that their charges against me were lies? There were two to one, and the driver was, no doubt, on their side also. I knew nobody in the baggage train who could testify for me and refute their story.

Fortunately, I found a way to prove my innocence, at least as far as the revolver was involved. It so happened that on arrival at the last stop for the night before reaching our headquarters I had asked permission to leave the regiment and proceed to Kutais alone. My future wife was there, and I wanted to see her one day earlier. The permission was granted. But the way to Kutais crossed a forest known to be infested by brigands; it was not safe to go through it unarmed. Now up to the time of the World War I never carried a revolver; instead I used to keep a piece of newspaper to attach the cord which was part of the uniform. My fellow officers knew this, and naturally, when I asked somebody to loan me a revolver for this occasion, I got it. Here was the way out of my predicament. It was enough to ask those who had been present; they would be glad to vouch for me, and I should be spared standing trial for a really serious offense, of which I was innocent. The Colonel was satisfied. So were the authorities in Tiflis, and I escaped the decidedly unpleasant consequences which might have ensued if I had been unable to disprove the accusation. But I had a few hours of genuine anxiety. I realized what justice may mean under certain circumstances and understood that there can be hardly any guarantee against judicial mistakes.

In the winter months our working hours were easy. The very first year I was in the regiment I was appointed aide-de-camp to my battalion commander. This meant that I had practically no work to do at all, and more leisure than was healthy for a youngster. So I started teaching the children of my fellow officers; and this was not only a pleasant avocation but a good way to keep out of too many festivities and drinking parties. Drinking in Caucasia always was, and, I understand, still is, a glorified tradition. Good wines are plentiful and cheap, and the people indulge in them with gusto. But, good as they were, the wines of the country seldom satisfied our hardened Russian topers. They called for vodka, and consumed it in almost unbelievable quantities.

Luckily for me there were among the officers several really cultured gentlemen with interests beyond vodka. Their influence contributed a great deal toward my development. There were also some civilians, with whom I became friendly, who played a still more important part in molding my thoughts. Some of these civilians were liberals, others radicals. A few were even political exiles.

This group of exiles had charge of a large governmental vineyard at a near-by town of Kwirily; and their chief was V. Starosielsky, a highly educated man and a brilliant orator, born of a wealthy family of gentry. Eventually, at the time of the Revolution of 1905, Starosielsky was elected Governor of the Province of Kutais. But after the reaction he was not only dismissed, but forced to leave the country. He emigrated to France, where he died in poverty a few years later. Other members of this group were engineers, chemists, agronomists, and economists. All had suffered for their political convictions, which they did not hesitate to express.

As members of one or other of the two radical political parties which were outlawed by the government and constantly hounded, they differed in their programs and tactics. The Social Democrats, or the SD's, as they were called, considered themselves genuine followers of Karl Marx. They advocated concentration on the industrial workers, as politically more awakened, more capable of grasping the ideas of Marxism, and more accessible to the promulgation of these ideas. In their opinion, Marxism constituted the basis for the change in the political, social, and economic outlook of the country which they believed to be necessary. But the Social Revolutionaries, or the SR's, as they were called, preferred to work among the peasants, who represented more than eighty per cent of the entire population. The successors to the Narodniki, or Populists, the SR's followed to certain extent the Slavianophiles, that is to say the advocates of a peculiar Slavic culture, as opposed to the Westernization of Russia. They denied the need for Russia to imitate the West by accepting capitalism with its domination of machine industry.

The SR's strongly supported the heroic view of history. To them the masses were the raw material on which their leaders operated. Some of their philosophers developed to extremes this conception of exclusively gifted individuals, appointed by nature to foresee events and lead the rest of the people. Their opponents considered this overemphasis on heroes wrong and dangerous. They stressed, instead, the collective mind of the people. Though not denying the existence of superior minds, they looked upon them merely as the choicest in the mass, representing the mass, and expressing the ideas and aspirations of the people as a whole.

I attended only a few of their debates, which were somewhat above my head. I was not adequately educated then. But I was impressed by their learning and wanted to learn more. Similarly, I was impressed by the obviously high idealism, for which I heard they suffered. I considered them honest, reliable, and admirable; and I wanted to become like them. So I began to read more widely and systematically, and in due course formed a study group of people interested in the same subjects, namely economics, history, and sociology. I remember how, when reading H. T. Buckle's *History of Civilization in England,* I was struck by his declaration that officers of the Army and Navy never belonged to the intellectual elite; that they usually were poorly educated people, as the service did not require it to be otherwise. I wanted to disprove this contention. Anyhow, it was another stimulus for my interest in study.

My home served as a meeting place for the group. Little by little it expanded, and eventually even included one private, a well-educated Jew. To mingle with the privates in such a way, and especially to admit a Jew among the group of officers on an equal footing, was certainly irregular. But the others in the group raised no objections, and I, certainly, had no reason to oppose it. I had never met Jews socially before, but this one seemed quite agreeable. He had been abroad, had studied in a university in Germany, and was well read and pleasant. Of course I was used to hearing the word "Jid" applied to Jews, and even once used this expression in the presence of my new friend. He was shocked and told me so. I apologized, explaining that I did not mean to offend him, for the term was regularly used with no bad meaning in the circles to which I belonged. But from then on I, certainly, tried my best not to pronounce this word at all.

Our meetings were limited to the discussion of books read by various members of the group. The books were innocent enough: most of them were simply university textbooks, and none were illegal. Yet very soon the whole venture was forced to close. One day, while riding through the town, I met the Chief of the Governor's Council, who told me in a very friendly manner that authorities were frowning on these meetings at my home. They considered them undesirable and advised a discontinuance without awaiting an official ban. But the breaking-up of the group did not mean that no more reading was possible. On the contrary, my curiosity was awakened, and the desire to learn was only spurred.

Gradually, I acquired the reputation of being well read, and was asked occasionally to talk before the officers' club. Usually the topics assigned were of military interest. But once, on the occasion of the fiftieth anniversary of the death of the great Russian satirist, Nicholas Gogol, I was asked to give an appropriate commemorative discourse. While working in the library for my paper, I happened on some material that made me see the government in a new light. I discovered that when Gogol died the Czar's government decided to prevent any public demonstrations at his funeral, and suppressed all "undue" eulogies. Turgenieff, the great novelist, wrote an obituary for the newspapers in St. Petersburg, but the chief censor found it "subversive" and forbade its publication. Turgenieff then mailed the script to Moscow, where it appeared under the title "A Letter from St. Petersburg." The result was that the Emperor ordered Turgenieff exiled to his estate. Well, once upon a time I could have swallowed this kind of statement easily, without asking questions. But now it sounded rather odd. Why was it, I asked myself, that so many great men in Russia were censored, persecuted, and exiled? The fate of Turgenieff, compared with that of others, was mild. Dostoyevsky, the greatest of all Russian authors, was condemned to death, pardoned at the last minute, and exiled to Siberia. Another great man, Leo Tolstoy, was excommunicated by the Church, and many of his writings were never allowed to be published in Russia under the Czar. Chernishevsky was imprisoned in a fortress and eventually exiled to Siberia. Such an outstanding scholar as the historian, Vinogradov, was forced to leave Russia and settle in England, where he became Sir Paul Vinogradov. The great Russian scientists, Setchenov, Mechnikoff, and Kovalevsky all lived abroad, for the life in Russia was unendurable to them. The greatest of Russian poets, Pushkin, spent part of his life in exile, constantly hounded by gendarmes. There was definitely something strange about this system of government and society under which the greatest sons of the country were mistreated. Books told me more and more about this and similar happenings.

But books give no real knowledge of life. Life itself, with its boundless variety and innumerable shocks to self-complacency, alone gives real knowledge. Certain events, which I was to witness soon, were to open my eyes much more effectively and rapidly than any number of books.

One evening I received an order to leave at once with my battalion for Batum. There was labor trouble, I was informed when already on the train. The troops were being sent to keep order. It was the first time in my life that I had had to face a similar situation. I certainly had heard enough about "the internal and external enemies" of the country: this was one of the subjects of the so-called "literacy" lessons of the soldiers. Who the "external" enemies were, was easy to grasp. But who were the "internal enemies"? That was not so easy to answer, though the official explanation pointed to "students and Jews." That workers could be such enemies was not told to the soldiers for the very obvious reason that they themselves were workers or peasants, with relatives and friends among the workers.

I knew a few students already, and never thought of them as bad people; I found them usually well read, amiable, and devoted to the interests of the country and the nation. As for the Jews, I knew only a few among our soldiers, but had never found them very different from the rest. Of course I had heard from the priests that "the Jews crucified Jesus Christ," and from other people that they were "money-lenders." But having lived most of my young life in St. Petersburg, far from the "Pale" where Jews were allowed to live, I never met any outside the Army and had no opinion of my own about them. Similarly I knew little or nothing about the workers from personal experience. I simply never met them at close quarters. But from books I learned something about their grievances, and I was sure that they were not treated with complete justice.

Now we were on our way to Batum to keep order. What could it mean? What was the nature of the trouble? What were the workers doing? Why were troops needed? Briefly I thought about these things, and I fell asleep. Next morning we arrived at Batum. In formation we started from the railroad station to the town. The colonel in charge of our expedition explained to us, the officers, that he had decided to hold a drill on the main square of the town, in order to demonstrate to the population that additional military forces had arrived, and to give a warning thereby to all those who might be planning trouble. No trouble, however, occurred during the three days we spent in that sunny port, rich in subtropical flora, encircled by beautiful green mountains, and busy with incoming and outgoing ships under various flags.

I remember that on our first evening in Batum some of us officers were entertained by the director of one of the factories affected by the strike. Our host and his young and pretty wife were most charming in their hospitality. We had a splendid dinner with good wines, and after the repast our hostess played at the piano and demonstrated her vocal talents. It was a delightful evening. But did one of us consider, for a moment, the meaning of this hospitality? I for one, certainly, did not think of it as a sort of bribe to the defenders of the "victims" of the labor troubles. My conscience was clear, for I knew no better.

The "trouble" we came to break, as I have learned but recently, was the now famous strike organized by a certain Joseph Djugashvilli. I never heard his name then, and did not hear it at all until the Revolution of 1917. Who at that time could have guessed what this young Georgian cobbler's son, born at Gory, near Tiflis, was destined to become a few years later? For Djugashvilli, who led the strike, is the man known today to the whole world as Stalin.

All we were told then, however, was that workers, incited by "agitators," had left their shops and had demanded "unreasonable" changes in their working conditions and wages. Troops were needed to prevent violence. So went the story; and to what extent it was true we had no way of judging. But we certainly saw some of the strikers; and while they offered a picture of misery and despair, they hardly seemed like criminals. There was something obviously queer about the whole business. Something beyond the agitation by "bad men," was clearly involved. What? And how could one find out? Those were the questions I asked myself. I wanted answers more convincing and more complete than those supplied by the officials.

This experience at Batum greatly stimulated my social-mindedness. The groundwork for this had undoubtedly been prepared by my friends, and my curiosity had been aroused by the books they recommended. But, I repeat, one personal experience in meeting an acute social situation is more valuable than books and theoretical discussions combined.

The labor movement started in Russia later than in other countries; for the serfs were not emancipated until 1861, and it was about that time that industries patterned on the Western basis were first established in the Czar's Empire. By the end of the nineteenth century, however, a number of workers' organizations already existed. Most of them were illegal, as the government was opposed to labor activities of this kind. Nevertheless, strikes became quite frequent, in spite of the fact that they were usually suppressed with great cruelty.

Such early revolutionary groups as the "Will of the People" or "Land and Freedom" concentrated on the peasants. But as the number of industrial workers increased, the "Group for the Emancipation of Labor" came to life. It was founded in 1883 by Plekhanov, the great Marxist scholar, together with a few collaborators who lived in exile in Switzerland. About this time, too, a young man named Vladimir Ulianov was active among the workers' groups interested in Marxism at St. Petersburg, and by 1895 he succeeded in bringing these groups together into a League. This young man was Lenin.

By 1898 the nucleus of the Russian Social Democratic Workers Party was formed. But in 1903, during its Second Congress, held in London, this party split in two; one faction became known as Bolsheviks (meaning the majority), the other, as Mensheviks. Of all this, of course, I knew little or nothing before the strike at Batum; nor did I learn much more in the immediate future. It was not easy to get information on these matters. Nevertheless, by one means or another, I was resolved to learn about these movements and developments and understand their causes.

About this time a new star rose in the Russian literary firmament—namely, Alexis Peshkov, who later became known all over the world under his nom de plume of Maxim Gorky. His brilliant and fascinating stories about the "under-dogs," his warm and even affectionate descriptions of the Russian "hoboes," brought before me new characters, new situations. I was completely fascinated by this unfamiliar *milieu,* so remote from my life, from my surroundings, and the interests of the circle to which I belonged. In short, these new types depicted by the genius of Maxim Gorky were so human and so intriguingly interesting that I wanted to know more about them; and in the great talent of Maxim Gorky I found an additional stimulus for trying to get more information about the peasants living in misery, the workers struggling for the betterment of their lot, the occupants of the jails, and the political prisoners suffering in Siberia and the far north. It may sound strange, but some Americans knew more about this latter scandal than I did, for they could read George Kennan's vivid but shocking descriptions of the Russian prisons and the exiles in Siberia. We, in Russia, had no chance to read the Kennan stories, or anything like them in the Russian language.

My sympathy, however, still remained rather superficial; it was hardly more than sentimentality. Furthermore, my interest was still largely academic. It did not occur to me that the proper way to learn would be to see at closer range the injustices of which I was becoming more and more aware. It did not occur to me that I personally could help in any way. Not that I was afraid to help, or unwilling to change my mode of life. I simply never thought about the matter in such terms. Besides, I considered myself still far from adequately educated, and I wanted to get ahead in that respect. Many times, when the participation of university students in the revolutionary movement was discussed in my presence, I had heard people say that youth should first learn, and only after the end of their schooling take part in the political life of the country. I thought there was a certain sense in such reasoning. Anyhow, it seemed to fit me at that time.

CHAPTER IV

THE CRUMBLING EMPIRE

(*Learning from Books*)

Study reveals the country's weaknesses. The Monarch. The Church. The Nation. Peasantry and peasant revolts. The economic situation. Orgy of spending. General outlook. The international situation.

IN THE ENDEAVOR to acquire a better education than that provided by the Cadet School and the Military Academy, I decided to enter one of the War Colleges. My first choice was the Military College of Jurisprudence, but I was not sure that I could pass the examinations, which required a more profound knowledge of history and literature than I possessed. I therefore selected another one, the War College of the General Staff. The regulations allowed a whole winter free from any duties for those officers who wanted to prepare for the entrance examinations to any of the War Colleges. I availed myself of this privilege. By that time I had already collected a good-sized library of my own, and the officers' library generously bought quite a number of books I needed.

For almost a full year I studied, and learned several things which helped to give me a better understanding of the country's status. The Empire, with its three cornerstones, Monarchy, Church, and Nation, seemed definitely crumbling. The Czar was reputed to be a weakling, under strong influence of his wife. She was, after all, a foreigner, a German Princess. Both were mystics; and His Majesty's devotion to the Church was of a most peculiar character. He wanted divine guidance in his difficult task of ruling the enormous Empire; so at present he was interested in finding new saints to plead for him before the Almighty. Those who knew how to exploit this weakness advised the Monarch to order the Synod to proclaim as a saint a certain monk, Seraphim of Sarov. In 1903, Seraphim was canonized, in spite of the protest of the local bishop. The bishop was transferred to a remote diocese; but numerous courtiers and bureaucrats found in the recently discovered saint a means for currying new favors with the Czar.

Our State Church of that period, and its attitude toward all the other religions, denominations, and sects, offered a sad picture. The Russian Orthodox, or Greek Catholic, Church, with its Byzantine mysticism, the superstitions inherited from the pre-Christian era, was alone recognized. Its hierarchy, being paid by the Treasury, and hence dependent on the State, gradually became a servant to the Monarchical regime rather than a mediator between the believers and the Lord. Unlike the Roman Catholic Church, which claims a power superior to that of the State, the Russian Church was under the secular authority of the Czar. This subservience had been especially marked since the abolition of the Patriarchate by Peter the Great. Consequently it was not at all unusual to find priests and police closely working together against the people. This added little enough to the popularity of the clergy in the eyes of their parishioners. Indeed, it very definitely alienated them.

The upper classes visited places of worship mainly because it was fashionable to do so. A few, possibly, needed special dispensation for their behavior in view of the Gospel's parable about the camel and the needle's eye. There were, of course, also those who were deeply religious, pure in heart, and sincere in their piety; but these hardly represented a majority.

Commoners, on the other hand, went to church not only because their forebears had done so, but also because there they expected to find solace for their lives of hardship and suffering. With no expectation of any betterment in their earthly existence they clung to the advice of the priests to be concerned with matters of the soul and of life beyond the grave. Hardly ever did they go to church in order to see the priest. Very often they looked upon the latter merely as a greedy "taker," who must be paid for baptism, for weddings, funerals, and for holidays besides. Rare were the priests who were genuine friends of the poor.

The exclusive position created for the Orthodox Church made of it a large bureaucratic organization, extremely jealous of competitors. No other creed in the Russia of the Czars had rights equal to those of the highly privileged State Church. All the others were restricted in one way or another; and in this respect the Roman Catholic Church was hit the worst. It was not allowed to have more than a fixed, and very limited, number of edifices for worship; no more than the approved number of priests. Similar was the fate of the Armenian Gregorian Church, the properties of which were even sequestrated by the State in 1903.

Lutherans enjoyed a much better status, almost equal to that of the Orthodox Church. This was because the Imperial family was to a great extent of German origin, and though professing the Orthodox faith, as was required by law, remained sympathetic toward the Church of their ancestors and their living coreligionists in Russia. This all-around privileged position of the Germans was characterized by an anecdote about the famous General Yermoloff. When asked by the Czar Alexander I what he could do for this soldier in recognition of his exceptionally valuable services to the country, the General replied: "Could I not be made a German?"

Synagogues were merely tolerated. The mosques, though looked upon as loyal collaborators in keeping the faithful obedient to the regime, were never quite safe from the wrath of the government. But worst of all was the attitude toward the numerous minor sects. Many really fine people, such as the Dukhobors, the Old-Believers, the Molokans, and other sectarians, experienced all sorts of stupid persecution and cruelty. This policy was instigated by the Orthodox Church, with its hierarchy, and by the Procurator of the Holy Synod. Some of these dissenters were conscientious objectors to military service. They were quite willing to do their part in serving the country in any way but that of "killing human beings." The action taken against them was simply disgraceful. Banishment to Siberia and Transcaucasia, confinement in monasteries or prisons, scourging with Cossack *Nagaika* (Knut), and even such cruelty as the removal of children from their parents' custody, as in the case of the Molokans in 1897—all these were openly reported, even in the censored papers of that time.

I visited the Dukhobors while in camp near Ahalkalaki, and was deeply impressed by their puritan life and the considerable wealth they had amassed by hard work. Yet a great number of these people were forced by the attitude of the government to leave Russia and emigrate to the Americas. A number of Russian writers testified that most of the sectarians were people of high character, worthy of respect, and useful citizens. Their departure, certainly, was a loss to the country.

Among these persecuted religionists, many of whom were fanatics, the Imperial regime had, of course, plenty of enemies, or at least people who desired a change. Naturally, they wanted better treatment, more freedom, at least in religious matters. Actually among the sectarians, especially the Old Believers, there were always found sympathizers of the revolutionaries; and from them the latter received considerable material support for their activities. Many sectarians were wealthy, and sometimes even very wealthy, as were some of the Morozoffs and other leading merchants and manufacturers of those days, who belonged to various sects.

The regime itself relied, of course, on the armed forces, and on the bureaucrats, as well as on the Church. The population at large was supposed to be on the side of the Emperor; the peasants especially, for it was said that he was looked upon as the "little father." But already this was largely an illusion. It is true that most of the peasants had entertained the belief that the Czar was their friend. All their troubles, according to them, were due to the landlords, from whom the muzhiks had suffered directly for centuries, and to the bureaucrats, who were corrupt. Peasants had learned long ago that nothing could be achieved without bribing an official. But it was also true that this pastoral naïveté was rapidly giving place to new conceptions, or, possibly, to new suspicions.

A considerable percentage of the industrial workers of Russia in these days worked only a part of the year, returning to their native villages for the harvest or other seasons. A few among them had listened in the city to students, who were actively engaged in propaganda and agitation among the oppressed classes. So, returning to their villages, those socially conscious workingmen were instrumental in disseminating new ideas in the countryside too; and, as land hunger was acute in practically every village, there were always plenty of rustics willing to listen to these fellows from the city, who talked of better times. There were instances, of course, when peasants rose against these urban mentors, who were either simply beaten or reported to the police. This happened partly because the peasants were ignorant, mostly illiterate, and ever suspicious of plots against them; partly because the police and certain zealous patrioteers were busying themselves in misleading the peasants and rousing their wrath against the "self-seeking agitators." Nevertheless, little by little, more and more peasants ranged themselves in opposition to the State.

How bad were the conditions prevailing in the countryside in these days may be judged from a description given in his *Signs of the Times* by Saltycoff-Stchedrin, one of the best-known Russian satirists and an important official himself: "Why does our peasant go in bast shoes instead of leather boots?" he wrote: "Why does such dense and widespread ignorance prevail throughout the land? Why does the muzhik seldom or never eat meat, butter, or even animal fat? How does it happen that you rarely meet a peasant who knows what a bed is?"

Poverty, in short, was appalling; help from the throne was not forthcoming; and the government seemed wholly indifferent to the needs of the people. No wonder signs of growing discontent were piling up. But small explosions failed to impress the ruling classes. They stubbornly refused to take them as serious warnings of a coming catastrophe.

In 1902, following a wave of strikes in various industrial centers, the rural populace staged serious disturbances from the Ukrainian villages in the west up to the Volga region in the east. Manors were wrecked and often set afire. Grain and other stores were seized and distributed among the needy peasants. In scattered places the land itself was appropriated and partitioning begun. The government retaliated by shooting hundreds of peasants, flogging others to death, and imprisoning thousands more. The revolt, indeed, was crushed rather easily, as there was no proper organization among the peasants and no solidarity between the rural and urban parts of the population.

Such peasant uprisings were not new to Russia. In the past they had occurred and recurred more or less regularly, for injustice and abuses always existed, and even the famous patience of the muzhik would break down upon occasion. In 1606, for example, one Ivan Bolotnikov—a former serf who had escaped abroad and had now returned to his native land to rouse the downtrodden—marched a large number of armed peasants up to Moscow and laid siege to the city. During the siege, some of the detachments led by petty landlords who had joined the rebels betrayed their leader and deserted his ranks. Bolotnikov's army was forced to retreat and was soon defeated. The leader was captured and paid for the adventure with his life. Landlords put out his eyes and then drowned him through a hole in the ice.

It was in 1670 that Stephen Razin rallied the Cossacks on the Don district—that is to say, the free men who had fled from their masters and settled in the border lands—and led them "against the landlords and the corrupt officials, representing Moscow, who oppressed the people." For almost a year the army of Razin, growing in numbers as it advanced, joined by peasants and occasionally even soldiers, marched triumphantly along the Volga. But, finally, this peasant army was defeated by government troops. Razin was wounded and captured; sent to Moscow; and there executed with numerous followers. Another revolt was crushed and drowned in blood.

A rebellion on a larger scale was that led by Pugatchev, also a Cossack, in the reign of Catherine the Great. It broke out near the Urals, extended up to the Middle Volga, and was crushed in 1774 only after long and severe fighting. Pugatchev was captured, chained, put in a large cage, and taken to Moscow, where he was executed.

Cruel as were the measures taken by the government, they did not stop the recurrence of revolts. Lesser uprisings occurred periodically until the liberation of the serfs in 1861. Even this Emancipation—which left the land hunger of the peasants unsatisfied—failed to stop them. They became almost a regular feature of the rural life. And still the landlords continued their old policy of squeezing out of the peasants all they could. Still the officials continued to back the landlords against the peasants. And still the ruling class refused to take these regularly occurring disturbances as warnings of a coming storm. Had they not crushed numerous revolts in the past? Why should they worry about these new disturbances?

In this respect the landed nobility was not very different from that of France in the closing years of the Empire. A bitter pamphlet entitled *The Last Word of the Third Estate to the Nobility of France,* published one year before the Revolution said: "What have you done for so many advantages? You have taken the trouble to be born, nothing more." As a class, the Russian *pomiestchiki,* or landlords, had long been an anachronism, unable to contribute to the economic welfare of the country and usually unwilling to contribute much, if anything, toward the improvement of its social structure. This does not mean, of course, that none of the *pomiestchiki,* as individuals, had striven to bring about changes designed to serve the common good. Far from it. A great number of them proved progressive; and those took a decidedly active part in the struggle to better the lot of the common people, even though many later deserted the cause when frightened by the extent of the demands made by the people in the process of revolution that followed.

Personally I knew a number of *pomiestchiki,* who were genuinely good toward the peasants living around their estates. At least so I thought. For I have to confess that while in Caucasia I saw little at first hand of the life of the peasant. In other words, for me, the hopes, sufferings, and fears of that part of the people were not a matter of personal experience. What I learned from books remained more or less in the realm of the theoretical.

The economic condition of Russia at that time was not healthy, to say the least. Fabulously rich in natural resources, the country had been notorious for the poverty of its people and for its industrial backwardness. But after the emancipation of the serfs the national economy began to develop more rapidly with the impetus of the modern machine; and within a very short period Russia's position as an industrial country was markedly improved. Soon she began to lead in the production of oil and was developing her production in a number of other fields at a tempo considerably higher than that of all other countries. In the coal, pig iron, and steel industries she also made very good progress; and her financial system was officially regarded as functioning well, with a large gold reserve on hand. But the medal had its reverse side too. Much of the industrial boom, such as it was, had been the result of foreign investments. The gold reserve was swollen by external loans and the latter were not used in such a way as to guarantee the welfare of the nation. The external debt exceeded six billion rubles—a considerable burden for a budget of three billion and a half. Foreign capitalists, attracted by the unusual opportunities of getting rich quickly, were not interested in the cost to Russia and her people. Consequently, a series of crises arose which greatly handicapped progress.

At the end of the nineteenth and in the early years of the twentieth centuries there was feverish activity in railway construction. During the nineties, almost half a billion rubles were spent on the routes. Already Russia was the second country in the world, after the United States, in railroad mileage. Undoubtedly she needed very badly these new roads to serve and open up her enormous territory; but the way in which they were built (as I learned only much later) was far from rational. The government itself built some of the lines, encouraging private capital to build more, and then usually bought the roads, so constructed, at an unreasonably high price. To encourage the domestic production of pig iron and steel, the government made a practice of placing orders for rails with Russian firms at prices far above the cost of production. For example, I heard of one instance of a total of more than forty million *pouds* [1] of rails being ordered by the government at a price fifty per cent higher than the average cost of production. This amounted to a hold-up of the Treasury.

I happened to hear about this from my uncle, Novosielsky—a prominent figure in high financial circles and for a time Assistant Minister

[1] A *poud* was equal to thirty-six American pounds.

of Finance—who apparently had a slice in this rich "melon." In the past he had been credited with the "discovery" of Sergius Witte, that wizard of finance, when the latter was still an unimportant young man in the south. Now he was one of his advisers. Thus, I heard a great deal about the wonderful business in rails when visiting this uncle's home, while I was still in the cadet school. I heard about it also in the home of Professor Antonovich, then Assistant Minister of Finance. Antonovich was a provincial scholar who had come to St. Petersburg from Kiev, and was considered a "very ordinary man" who provided the "society" of the capital with many a good chance to sneer at his and his wife's manners and poor French. But to me these Antonovichs were real human beings, and their children became my chums. At that time, of course, I did not understand much of the conversation held by the older people, but I remember very well how excited they became when turning to the topic of railroads. The very word "rail" seemed to be pronounced with tenderness, and I could not fail to think of it with reverence.

Nor did I realize then that this crazy spending, advantageous to the higher strata, was harmful for the country as a whole. Taxes were steadily mounting, though already people had little to spare. Even when industry and mining were making a good showing—because of pathetically low wages and long working hours—agriculture was going from bad to worse. With their miserably small parcels of land, without synthetic fertilizers, and with no agricultural machinery, the peasants had a wretchedly low yield and often very poor harvests. But agriculture continued to be the backbone of Russia's national economy; some eighty per cent of the population being rural. The bulk of the export trade of the country constituted grain. The unusually severe and widespread famine that occurred in 1891 demonstrated clearly the weakness of the entire economic structure of the Empire; and, though the improved harvests that followed and the much better prices for grain which prevailed on the world markets for several years offered some relief, the whole agrarian situation was generally so bad that nothing short of a radical change could cure it.

Poor as they were, the peasants were taxed more heavily than the landlords.[2] The Czar's government, still relying on the landed nobility, was trying to support them through subsidies and other financial advantages. But in spite of this a clear majority demonstrated their inability to make good in agriculture. Along with the pauperization of the peasantry, there was also taking place a dispossession of the landed nobility. The latter considered their landholdings simply as the source of income to be recklessly spent in the large cities or abroad. A vivid example of this kind of landowner was given by Anton Chekhov in his well-known play *The Cherry Orchard* with the unforgettable Madame Ranievskaya.

Out of the ranks of the peasants who lost their meager parcels through foreclosure for nonpayment of their debts, a large army of unemployed was forming. By the beginning of the century there were some five million such peasants who had no longer anything to do in the villages and could not be absorbed either by the urban industries or by mining. They constituted the ranks of the *lumpen-proletariat* that was destined to play such an important, if not always glorious, role in the revolutionary years approaching.

If the industrial situation of the Empire was filled with ill omens, its international position was also far from reassuring. The expansionist policy of Russia had created animosity among those whose interests were challenged by the advancing colossus of the north. Great Britain for generations considered Muscovy as her dangerous rival in the Near East, Persia, and Turkey. London was suspicious lest the troops of the Czar, conquering the peoples of Middle Asia one after another, should descend on India and menace that pearl of the British monarch's crown. And more recently British interests in Eastern Asia had also been contested by the Russians. So, in an attempt to determine the spheres of their respective interests in China, London and St. Petersburg in 1899 came to an understanding with regard to the building of railroads in the Celestial Empire. But the presence of Russian troops on Chinese territory since the Boxer Rebellion of 1900 continued to disturb England, no less than Japan and China herself. In

[2] In 1899 the rate of the land tax was revised. For the landlords it remained twenty kopeks per *desiatina,* but the peasants were taxed thirty-four kopeks per *desiatina* instead of the nineteen they had paid since 1891.

spite of the international agreement about the evacuation of troops after the Boxer Rebellion, the Russian soldiers continued to remain in Manchuria. The pretext was that the Peking government could not guarantee order in the provinces adjacent to Russia, and that the latter was anxious to protect her interests, including a newly acquired concession for building a railroad across Manchuria.

About the same time, 1899-1900, the United States inaugurated the Open Door policy for China. Russia fully understood that the new restriction was partly designed as a check on her expansion. Japan, only recently out of seclusion, but already pursuing her road of imperialist conquest on the mainland of Asia, was worried by the plans of Russia in Manchuria and Korea. Consequently, Tokyo looked for outside sympathy and support. In 1902 she succeeded in signing a treaty of alliance with London. There was no doubt about its meaning to Russia. In the Far East she was facing serious trouble. The trouble actually broke out in 1904.

On the western frontier, likewise, Russia was far from secure. Germany, her friend while Bismarck was the Reich Chancellor, now became less inclined to co-operate with Muscovy. At the beginning of the twentieth century, Berlin had tried to get from St. Petersburg more favorable tariffs, and by this time there was a full-fledged customs war between the two countries. With the Ottoman Empire also there were certain difficulties. In 1903 a Russian consul was assassinated in Turkey. The Russian government sent its warships to the shores of Turkey and demanded execution of all those responsible for the act of violence. The Sublime Porte acceded to this demand, but the tension between these neighbors was aggravated.

Russia's interest in the Slavic nations of the Balkan Peninsula had always worried Turkey, and Great Britain never ceased fomenting their distrust of St. Petersburg. Russia's interest in Constantinople was unceasing. The charge that she planned to dominate all the Slavic peoples always had a certain plausibility—not that pan-Slavism, of which Lord Beaconsfield was so fond of talking with his friends from Berlin and Vienna, was ever a real menace, but it was a topic useful in creating suspicions against their rival, Russia. It certainly increased the number of her enemies and brought her no real friends.

The only friend St. Petersburg had in Europe of that time was republican France, which entered into a treaty of alliance with autocratic Russia as a measure against the growing menace of Germany. But, as the events soon proved, this alliance was of very limited value to Russia. Russia was already on the verge of a war in the Far East. And this war she had to wage alone.

CHAPTER V

WAR WITH JAPAN AND THE REVOLUTION OF 1905

(*Detached Observers*)

The Russo-Japanese War. Its beginning, development, and end. The Portsmouth Treaty. The Revolution of 1905. Bloody Sunday. Father Gapon. Role of the police. Evno Azeff. Mutiny in the Black Sea Fleet. General strike. The December insurrection. Pogroms. Attitude of the student officers.

EARLY IN FEBRUARY, 1904, Russia was at war with Japan. No troops stationed in Caucasia, however, were called to the Far Eastern front. Caucasia, being on the border of Turkey and Persia, had to keep its armed forces intact. Consequently, my plans for entering the War College were not affected by the outbreak of hostilities. In the spring I passed the preliminary examinations at Tiflis, which qualified me to appear at St. Petersburg for the main test. Incidentally this helped me to obtain permission from my superiors to marry, although I had not reached the minimum age set by the regulations. Immediately after the wedding we left for the north. By August I was in the College.

When the war broke out, people were told that it would be short and easy. We read in newspapers that Japan was "a small and poor island country. Its people—almost midgets—look like little monkeys. ...Only recently have they learned about modern Western methods of warfare....There is nothing to worry about....In a short time they will be defeated and punished for their insolence...."

After entering the College, however, I acquired a very different picture. Here we were aspirants for leadership in the Army and must learn not only the history of past wars but also the truth about the present. Already it was public knowledge that Japan had started the war without an official declaration. By staging a surprise attack on our squadrons at Port Arthur and in the Korean waters, she wanted, we were told, to undermine the Russian naval forces before an open contest would begin. This explanation sounded plausible. Considering the immensity of Russia, her inexhaustible resources in man power and raw materials, Japan, it seemed, was merely "playing safe." But all too soon we came to understand that this surprise assault had actually crippled our naval forces in the Far East, while the series of attacks on Port Arthur that followed practically paralyzed them. Thus the sea was freed of Russian warships; and the hitherto difficult and risky operation of conveying troops from the Japanese Islands to the continent of Asia could now be undertaken without let or hindrance. Little by little, we arrived at the realization that our adversary, contrary to what we had been told, was not backward and weak, but unexpectedly strong. The indemnity paid to Japan by China for her defeat ten years earlier, had been expended by the country of the Rising Sun in the building up of a large modern army and navy. And her alliance with Great Britain, not to mention the friendly attitude of the United States, whose bankers actually financed Japan in this war, gave Nippon's position additional security.

The Russian armed forces in the Far East were few in number at the outbreak of hostilities; and it was generally understood that in the early days of the war, before reinforcements could arrive from the west, they would have to retreat before the much larger forces of Japan. But very soon we learned, to our surprise and dismay, that in spite of the immensity of her resources Russia would be unable to cope with the problem. Siberia in those days was barely inhabited and was practically without industries of her own. Troops, ammunition, food, everything, had to be brought from the other side of the Ural Mountains. Furthermore, the sole railroad connecting European Russia with the front, the Trans-Siberian, was not even quite finished. The task of transporting great numbers of troops and enormous amounts of freight over the five or six thousand miles of an incompleted single-track railway, difficult in itself, was made even worse by the inefficiency and incompetence of the officials.

News soon arrived that a number of battles had been lost by our troops and that the retreat was continuing. Our professors at the War College preferred not to talk about these reverses, the excuse they gave being the scarcity of available details. But secrecy breeds suspicion; we grew more and more anxious. By the middle of August, 1904, however, considerable reinforcements reached the theater of war, and people were assured that before very long they would hear good news. And sure enough, by the end of the month we learned of a great battle near Liao-yang. It lasted for eight days, but ended ... in a new retreat. As I learned years later while translating into Russian the official Japanese history of the war, the battle of Liao-yang was actually won by the Russians, but our High Command was unaware of their victory. Unduly impressed by the Japanese attack on one of the flanks, they gave orders to curtail and evacuate the position. The Japanese, exhausted and short of ammunition, had themselves been making preparations for retreat; but they immediately grasped the new chance offered by the Russian mistake, and, starting an attack, turned the lost battle into a victory.

General Kuropatkin, the Commander in Chief, was, of course, blamed for this and every other disaster. But rumor persisted that he had been handicapped in his operations, first by the interference of the Viceroy, Admiral Alexeieff, who was ignorant in military matters, and secondly by intrigues at the Imperial Court, and in the War Office. It was public knowledge that the armies in the field were not properly supplied with ammunition. But, gossip asserted, ikons and printed prayers continued to arrive in quantity. They were generously shipped by the Czar and Czarina, as well as by certain pious merchants, who were making money out of the war.

The new year, 1905, was ushered in with black tidings. On January 2, Port Arthur, a fortress reputed to be invincible, capitulated after almost a year of gallant defense; and the Japanese troops hitherto occupied by the siege were now released for operations in the north. Thus, while by the middle of February the Russian Command had at its disposal about three hundred thousand men in the Far East, the Japanese had at least an equal number at the front. Another great battle, that of Mukden, ended after three weeks in a Russian retreat.

Our losses were estimated at one hundred and twenty thousand men, killed, wounded, and captured. The repetition of this story of disaster had its inevitable effect: the exasperation of the people mounted.

With the spring came even more alarming news of the tragic end of the squadron sent by the Czar from the Baltic Sea around Africa to the Pacific Ocean. It was common knowledge that our vessels were not only inferior to those of Japan, but practically worthless for a battle with a modern navy. Most of them found their grave around the island of Tsushima, where they were met by the entire Japanese fleet under the command of Admiral Togo.

I shall never forget the day that brought the tidings of this disaster. It was one of those beautiful mornings that one experiences only in northern countries, where spring does not come suddenly but approaches gently by stages, allowing one to watch the somewhat lazy awakening of Nature and admire its coming to full bloom under the caressing rays of the northern sun. The temperature was just pleasantly warm. The sun shone gloriously, and the young leaves on the trees, bathing in this rich sunshine, breathed freshness and health. The entire picture sang joyously of life, of creation, and of happiness.

We were on our way to visit my old aunt, who lived in the Taurida Palace, that was built by Catherine the Great for her favorite, Potiemkin. At present it belonged to the Imperial family, was divided into apartments, and occupied by a few pensioners of the Court. The following year it became the site of the State Duma and served for twelve years as the meeting place of the Russian Parliament.

The terrible news about the debacle at Tsushima arrived during lunch. An indescribable gloom fell upon all those present, and tears welled in many eyes. Words were useless; they could not honestly express the shock. We had, of course, relatives and friends on the ill-fated squadron, and most of them had, no doubt, perished. But their fate was definitely not the main concern. Something infinitely greater had been lost. Much more was doomed.

No wonder the Russian people were in despair and their resentment was mounting to the anger point. It was obvious that these undeserved humiliations were the result of a corrupt system of government, which was utterly unable either to prepare for the defense of the country's honor, or to resist the advance of a much smaller and poorer adversary. Our soldiers, certainly, could not be blamed. They showed themselves to be quite as valiant and fearless fighters as their ancestors. And the military history of Russia, that we were studying at the College, was full of heroic exploits and glorious victories. In 1707, for example, the Russian army, newly organized by Peter the Great, had defeated the Swedes under Charles XII, who was considered one of the best military leaders of that time. In 1760 they routed the German forces of Frederick the Great and occupied his capital, Berlin. Under Suvorov, the greatest of the Russian generals, they defeated French troops of Napoleon in Italy. In 1812 they showed Napoleon himself the way out of Russia, and in 1814 triumphantly entered his capital, Paris. An endless number of times did they defeat the Turks and other lesser states. If they suffered defeat in Crimea during 1854-5, when a coalition of England, France, and Sardinia attacked them while they were at war with Turkey, it was not for any lack of fighting capacity among the common soldiers. Their heroic conduct was testified to by many, among them Count Leo Tolstoy, who himself, as a young officer, had participated in the defense of Sebastopol. The cause of defeat was to be found then, as during the present war with Japan, simply in the corruption and incompetence of the government. As for the Emperor Nicholas II, he seemed to have little or no understanding of what was going on. It was his habit to think of everything in terms of God's wrath for sins committed by himself, the autocrat, or by his subjects.

Finally, in June, 1905, President Theodore Roosevelt came out with his proposal for starting negotiations for peace. This suggestion was opposed by many Russian military authorities, including the Minister of War, who pointed out that Japan was nearing complete exhaustion, while Russia had barely started on the concentration of large forces, and was well able to continue the war. But St. Petersburg decided to negotiate. Portsmouth, New Hampshire, was agreed upon as the place for the conference. On September 5, 1905, the peace treaty was signed. The war was over. By the terms of the treaty, Russia was forced to withdraw from the southern part of Manchuria and to make over to Japan the railway and everything that was built there with Russian money. She had to cede to Japan the southern half of Sakhalin Island, claimed by Nippon in the past. In short, Russia's position in the Far East was radically altered for the worse, and her further expansion in Asia was effectively checked.

Official circles, of course, proclaimed the Portsmouth Treaty as a victory for Russian diplomacy over that of Japan. It did not provide for an indemnity to be paid by the vanquished; and it is true that, generally speaking, it was very mild, if one takes into consideration the number of battles lost by the Russians. Nevertheless, the effect at home was that of a detonator for a coming explosion. The Russian people had disapproved of the provocative policy toward Japan, which was carried on by the government under pressure of certain courtiers and members of the Imperial family. Their greed had been responsible for the catastrophe. They had sought lucrative concessions in Korea and Manchuria. Their machinations had brought Russia to a clash with Japan. Even after the war had begun the Russian people never supported it wholeheartedly. And some, mostly among the radicals, even prayed for defeat, arguing that upon such an event a change in the intolerable domestic conditions would become imperative. Even the Cabinet Ministers of the Czar were opposed to the adventure, fearing its outcome, for they knew the state of affairs in the country and were not inclined to minimize the potentialities of Japan. Only one among them, the Minister of the Interior, von Plehve, advocated war, and he did so only as an alternative to revolution. But his calculations proved to be wrong. Russia had not only to fight and lose a war, but to live through a revolution. Von Plehve himself, however, did not live to see the latter. In July, 1904, he was assassinated by a young student, a member of the terrorist organization of the Social Revolutionary Party.

With the accumulation of misfortunes at the front, it seemed that the terrorist opposition was steadily growing bolder. The assassination of von Plehve was followed a few weeks later by that of the Grand Duke Sergius, uncle to the Czar. As the Governor General of the

Moscow district, he had been notorious for his ruthless and cruel treatment of radicals and for his persecution of the Jews. Years after those events, it became known that these and many other terroristic acts were planned by Evno Azeff, an *agent provocateur* who worked for the police and at the same time was active in the revolutionary circles. His close collaborator, Boris Savinkov, usually organized the details of the plots and supervised their execution. The young idealists who ardently desired to serve their nation were used as tools. They committed the deeds for which they were ready to sacrifice their own lives. They were ill advised, yes, but they were no cruel and bloodthirsty criminals. That was obvious to all, even to the police.

As a matter of fact, the Revolution had already started, and it began immediately after the capitulation of Port Arthur. Early in January, 1905, workers at the Putilov factory, then the largest in St. Petersburg, downed their tools and walked out, following the example of their comrades in Baku, where a few weeks earlier a large-scale strike had been successfully carried through. The police, with their elaborate organization of "stool pigeons," decided to take advantage of the situation. Their agent, Father Gapon, who was active in the labor movement, suggested that the strikers present a petition to the Czar. The idea was accepted. Furthermore, it was agreed upon that men, women, and children, with ikons and church banners, should march en masse to the Winter Palace and present the petition to the Czar himself.

On January 22 (the 9th according to the old-style calendar), thousands of people, old and young, started with humble reverence and solemn trepidation, on their way to the palace. They were filled with hope and trust in the Monarch. It was estimated that more than one hundred and forty thousand people were on strike and came out to the streets to take part in the procession or to watch it pass. But, instead of fatherly consideration of their grievances by the Czar, the marchers were met by military bullets. About one thousand were slain, with two thousand more wounded. This ghastly massacre was systematically planned and executed. As if uncertain of the loyalty of the garrison at St. Petersburg, those responsible for the preparations had even brought in troops from at least one other town. But the net effect of the slaughter was not to inculcate a salutary lesson but to rouse the people against the regime, as nothing ever had before. The wrathful indignation of the crowds beggared description. Gone for ever was the illusion of the Czar's benevolence. Gone was the hope of his fatherly interference on the side of the exploited. That day, called Bloody Sunday, was the real beginning of the Revolution of 1905.

In April of that year the revolutionary leaders met in London and in Geneva, the Bolshevik section, which then numbered some eight thousand five hundred, assembling in the English capital, while the Mensheviks met in Switzerland. Both groups considered the moment propitious for action, but they differed on the matter of leadership. The Bolsheviks asserted that proletarian predominance was necessary for the success of the uprising, while the fellow revolutionaries at Geneva regarded a leadership of liberal intelligentsia as essential. Both realized the importance of the stand which would be taken by the armed forces.

Two months later, about the time that St. Petersburg was getting ready to begin negotiations for peace on the front, a revolt broke out in the Black Sea Fleet; and one episode of this revolt, the mutiny on the armored cruiser *Potiemkin,* became famous all over the world on account of the daring conduct of its sailors. To suppress this mutiny other warships had been sent by order from St. Petersburg. But the sailors on those vessels refused to fire on the rebel ship. Short of food and fuel, the *Potiemkin* finally decided to leave Russian waters and sailed for Constanza, where she surrendered to the local Rumanian authorities. It is safely catalogued among the heroic chapters of Russian history today. But at the time of the *Potiemkin* mutiny, I, like the other officers of the War College, disapproved such acts of insubordination. We were for strict discipline and obedience under any circumstances. Particularly were we shocked by the fact that one of the leaders of another insurrection in the Black Sea Fleet was an officer, Lieutenant Schmidt. At the same time most of us realized that the causes of the revolt were valid. Whatever we may have thought of the conduct of the sailors and their leaders, we could not deny that they had demonstrated real courage, and courage has always been rated as the highest virtue by every military man.

Here, then, was a conflict and an important challenge to our powers of judgment. As officers of the Army, we were naturally interested in easing and ameliorating the conditions of our work. Such would be the attitude of any functionary. It was only natural for the majority to be exasperated by unforeseen complications interfering with routine; and while, as students, we were at present not directly affected, insubordination on general principles went against the grain. On the other hand, we were Russians, and we realized together with the majority of the people, that an intolerable condition had been created in the country by the regime. Together with the civilians, we hoped for reforms which would make our mother country strong and successful, respected by other nations, and wholly deserving of our love and devotion. It was not a question of revolution, but of long-overdue reforms. And while some of us could not always approve of the acts of those who fought for these reforms, there were few who could resist the temptation of according them at least a secret admiration.

By the end of summer, restlessness became widespread. Violence showed its ugly face. Under the pressure of events and at the instance of his advisers, the Czar decided to appease his people with a promise of a State Duma, or Parliament. His cousin, Kaiser Wilhelm of Germany, who was anxious about the fate of the Romanov dynasty, and hence about his own, also made an appeal to that effect. Now, according to the plan worked out by Bouliguine, the Minister of the Interior, the Duma was to be merely an advisory body formed of delegates from the people. But it was now too late for such a compromise. It was not enough to check the growing resentment of the nation. Leaders of even mildly liberal groups clamored for more radical changes. They demanded not a new bureaucratic machine, not a mere advisory appendix to the government, but a legislative organ with broad powers for the people's representatives. But the Czar stubbornly objected, and it was not until later that further developments forced his consent.

October was the climax of the Revolution. The nation was aflame. A cry went up for "Convocation of the Constituent Assembly, elected on the basis of universal, direct, secret, and equal vote." The working people and professionals proceeded to demonstrate their profound disapproval of the regime by means of a general strike. The stoppage was so general that it virtually paralyzed the whole country. No trains ran anywhere, no wires carried any private or official messages except the strike orders issued by the central committee. No factory, no shop was working; no stores were open, with the exception of a few dealing in food, and these only for one or two hours a day. No mail was delivered, except by a few young men from "high society" who tried in this way to break the strike. Many of the well-to-do were panic-stricken or hysterical. They cursed the "mobs," hurled threats at the "agitators," and expressed the hope that the government would act resolutely and find means to curb the revolt, protecting "all good subjects" and punishing the culprits. It was all very like what had taken place in other revolutions, in other lands, at other times.

No general strike later attempted in other countries was ever such a complete success as this in Russia. Neither the British general strike of 1926, nor that of 1938 in France, was permitted by the authorities to become so all-inclusive. Apparently the Russian lesson was well studied, and the respective governments knew what to avoid and what to do to prevent the results experienced by the Czar's government in 1905.

Realizing the gravity of the situation, two close advisers of the throne pleaded for the granting of a liberal constitution. One was the uncle of the Czar, Grand Duke Nicholas Nicolaievich, who later became better known as the Commander in Chief of the Russian Armies during the World War. The other was Sergius Witte, who had just returned home and been made a count in recognition of his services as the chief delegate of Russia at the Portsmouth Peace Conference. Nicholas II listened to their advice; frightened by the growing menace to his dynasty, he decided at last to make concessions. On October 30 (17th by the old style) he issued a manifesto, promulgating the "constitution" (though no such term was used) and guaranteeing inviolability of person, freedom of speech, press, assembly, and organization.

Nevertheless the Revolution did not end at once. Peasants continued their raids on the mansions of the landlords. Disturbances among various national minorities were reported from the outer borders of the country. Several armed insurrections occurred in scattered places; and one, which broke out at Moscow in December, looked serious. A part of the garrison seemed to be on the side of the people. But the majority of the armed forces were still loyal to the government. Troops were dispatched from St. Petersburg, and, after fighting at the barricades, succeeded in crushing the revolt.

Gradually the rebellion subsided. Numerous punitive expeditions were sent to all the parts of the country where disorders were occurring, and went through them leaving gallows and ruins in their wake. Generals Rennenkampf and Meller-Zakomielsky, both Germans from the Baltic Provinces, in particular displayed an unbelievable ferocity in restoring "order." Their names became synonymous for "hangman" and "murderer." Not less of a hero to the extreme reactionaries who were behind this orgy of bloodshed was Trepov, who, as Governor-General of St. Petersburg, issued an order "not to economize on bullets" when dealing with the "mob." Such was his name for the crowds of his less fortunate compatriots who suffered from the shortcomings of the regime and were demanding a change.

As one means of terrorizing people into submission and silence, the government applied the old method of persecuting national minorities. The Jews, of course, had always been traditional scapegoats for the Czarist regime; and all too frequently they were the victims of "pogroms," staged, with the knowledge and benevolent noninterference of the police, by the scum of the people. Led by ultrareactionary "patrioteers," these raids were sometimes even instigated by the authorities. Thus, the horrible Kishinev pogrom of 1903, celebrated throughout the world for its cruelty, was organized by von Plehve, then the Chief of the Department of Police in the Ministry of the Interior. And as a result the word "pogrom" has become part of the vocabulary of other nations, and a permanent blot on Russia's good name. However, we must never forget that the Russian people at large were not responsible for these outrages. Pogroms were not of their making. They never found approval among the population in general. And, terrible as they were, the Russian pogroms dim before the sadistic, all-embracing persecution of the Jews in Nazi Germany today. Again it would be wrong to accuse the German people at large for these atrocities.

In October, 1905, when the wave of revolution was at its crest, new Jewish pogroms were organized at Odessa and several other towns in the south. The orgy of Odessa, where several hundred were slain and thousands wounded, and Jewish property was destroyed and plundered, lasted for four days. In other places it was less bloody and prolonged than in Odessa, but not less horrifying for the population at large. But the purpose of the government was more or less achieved by this and other similar methods. People were terrorized, and their revolutionary ardor gradually disappeared. Disturbances continued in various towns, and especially in the villages, but at a rapidly decreasing tempo. By 1907 the country was outwardly "at peace."

How did we, the student officers of the War College, react to these events? Most of us were shocked by the outrages against the minorities and openly expressed our revulsion. But there were others who tried to absolve the government of any responsibility for the pogroms and even asserted that they were provoked by the Jews themselves. Were not the Jews leading the revolutionary outbursts? Were they not among the terrorists? This, by the way, if true in fact was false in emphasis. The Jews were not among the terrorists to a larger degree than other races. But that did not bother the gentlemen who took this line of argument and who were in general the same people who applauded the cruelty used in curbing the revolution. Nor were the Jewish people the only scapegoats. Armenians and other *inorodtzy* (aliens) were also targets of their wrath. There was never any difficulty about finding someone to hate. Moreover, the function of the common people, in the judgment of these gentry, was to obey, to work, and to pray. They had no right to make demands; the government knew best what to do and what not to do. Common people should not poke their noses into the affairs of the Empire. If they did, they must be punished. And mercy was a mistake. It was a sign of cowardice. It was out of place. Punitive expeditions were meant to terrorize, and terrorize they must.

To say that such was the attitude of the majority would be untrue. The majority were in sympathy with the people at large, even if they preferred not to express their views in public. In this connection I well remember the meetings we had in the College during the turbulent days of 1905. Again and again I heard indignant voices raised in condemnation of those responsible for the horrors and humiliation suffered by the nation. While the Revolution was on, a considerable number of us found occasion to exchange views, and there were plenty of officers who demonstrated that civic life was a matter of concern to them, even if they did not violate the regulations by taking direct part in political activities. Furthermore, their civic interest was not entirely without precedent. The Decembrists, who led the unsuccessful revolt in December, 1825, had been officers. Some of them served in the Imperial Guards, and several were born of the most aristocratic families. Prince Peter Kropotkin, the theoretician of anarchism, was an officer. So was Michael Bakunin, the fiery leader of the anarchists. And later on a number of officers figured prominently in the Revolution of 1917. One of them, Alexander A. Troyanovsky, became in 1933, the first Soviet Ambassador to the United States.

During the short-lived period of rejoicing and exultation that followed the October Manifesto, we heatedly discussed the meaning of the new era. Along with the freeing of the general press, a few liberal military organs made their appearance. This was one of the topics of our debates. There were those who bitterly objected to any attempt by officers to participate in political life through their own printed sheet. Certain articles that appeared in one of the new liberal publications were answered in the reactionary press by officers with conservative leanings. This was answered in turn by the liberals. Gradually the exchange developed to the point of hurling accusations, expressing suspicions, questioning good faith, and simply calling names.

One article in particular evoked protests from the conservatives, who demanded the name of the author. I do not recall what the article was about; but I remember very well that, when this matter was discussed at a meeting of the student officers, I was so enraged by the unreasonableness of the reactionaries that I asked for the floor, jumped on the desk that served as a platform for the speakers, and made an ardent appeal for tolerance, underlining the necessity of understanding and defending the right of everyone to have his own opinion. I objected to the attempt at eliciting the name of the author. In my opinion, this would lead us up the dangerous path of suspecting one another and indulging in spying, which, certainly, never contributed toward ennobling any person or group. I do not think it was a particularly good speech, but its sentiment was warmly applauded by the overwhelming majority of those present.

But, generally speaking, even if many among us demonstrated sympathy with the aspirations of the people, if many among us rejoiced when the Manifesto of the Czar announced the dawn of the new era, we were very vague about the problems involved and the principles implicated. The political ignorance of the officers, artificially preserved by the government's design, was abysmal.

CHAPTER VI

THE STATE DUMA AND THE RETURN OF REACTION

(*Hopes Betrayed*)

The State Duma. Growing interest in the press. Avalanche of speeches. The reaction of 1906-11. Stolypin's period. Retreat of the revolutionary intelligentsia. Away from political topics. The most privileged among the privileged: the General Staff. Audience of the Czar. Back to Caucasia. Again in St. Petersburg. Two years in command. Dramatics and spies. Sessions of the State Duma. Routine vs. young enthusiasm. To the Far East. Khabarovsk.

IN SPITE OF its final disintegration, the Revolution of 1905 had been far from fruitless. True, it is not to be compared with the French holocaust of 1789. It brought in its train no clean sweep of an old regime, no elevation of a new class to leadership, no fundamental change in the political system. But it did result in the granting of a quasi-democratic "Constitution" by a monarch frightened into a gesture of appeasement to his subjects; and in this it distinctly resembled the various revolutions that occurred in Central Europe in 1848. And in Russia, as there, it soon became obvious that the government was not sincere in playing at liberalism.

One result of the changes inaugurated by the October "Constitution" was that the newspapers became considerably bolder and more interesting. By reason of the clause relating to the freedom of the press, many topics hitherto under the ban could now be treated with at least a certain amount of independence. At the War College, as elsewhere, we began to read more avidly. We talked over the news and discussed public events with real feeling. The inevitable result was that as our sympathies diverged the drift of our political inclinations became more clearly discernible. But few, if any, of us dreamed of ever taking part in the political struggle. We were Army men, and it was "none of our business." If any one among us belonged to a political party, it remained his secret. Certainly I never heard of any instance of the kind.

When the First Duma was convoked, the newspapers were full of exciting material. Speeches of the delegates offered quite a thorough course in civics. They opened our eyes to the real meaning of much that we had previously but vaguely understood. For instance, it first became publicly known that there were some eighty thousand people held for political offenses in prisons and fortresses, or exiled to Siberia and elsewhere. The Duma called loudly for their release, though very few actually received their freedom. The Duma also asked for the establishment of responsibility of the Cabinet to Parliament. In an avalanche of speeches it advocated autonomy for Poland and Finland, liberal labor laws, and the abolition of capital punishment. For the first time there existed a forum for public discussion of matters of common interest, for airing grievances, and also, of course, for merely demonstrating vocal capacities. There were a number of outstanding orators among the delegates, for oratory, as might have been expected, played a considerable part in deciding the election results.

The electoral law was reasonably liberal, and a number of genuinely progressive people were included in the list of deputies of the First Duma. To be sure, a certain amount of verbosity was unavoidable, for a great number of delegates belonged to the doctrinaire type of intellectuals, so well epitomized in Russian literature by Turgenieff's Rudin. They admired their own eloquence and pled for the downtrodden so long as their own interests were not menaced. They advocated the Westernization of Russia, and demanded such liberal reforms as should raise her to the political level of countries more advanced. But few of the delegates were practical men of the world, and still fewer were fighters, willing to risk a real showdown. In short, the First Duma was not a revolutionary conclave, but a liberal club for discussion and the display of verbal fireworks. The word "parliament" derives from the French *parler,* "to speak." In spirit, if not in name, this was certainly a parliament.

For a while the government had no choice but to tolerate these representatives of the people, though it treated them with open contempt. Later, when the militant spirit of the country had subsided, the bureaucrats became bolder and intensified their campaign for the restoration of the "good old times." Suppressive measures, one after another, were introduced in various fields; and finally the time came for the taking of revenge upon the Duma. When the latter prepared to discuss agrarian reforms, advocating the confiscation of certain lands and their distribution among the needy peasants, the Czar decided to put a stop to this "nuisance." On June 8, seventy-two days after the opening of the parliament, troops were sent to surround the Taurida Palace, where the Duma was in session, and its delegates were curtly informed of a decree sending them home. We learned about this dissolution, only when it was already an accomplished fact, from the announcement posted in the streets.

After this unceremonious ending of their deliberations, a large group of delegates, members of the Constitutional Democratic Party (the Cadets, or the KD's) gathered for a political demonstration at Viborg, a near-by town in Finland. They issued a proclamation advising the people to refuse paying taxes or submitting to military service, since it was unconstitutional for the government either to levy taxes or to conscript soldiers and sailors without the consent of the Duma. These "KD's" were mainly members of the various professions, supplemented by a few progressive landlords, and their leader was Professor Miliukov, who had played an outstanding role in the Revolution of 1905 and was destined to play a still greater one in the February Revolution of 1917. The signers of the Viborg Manifesto were sentenced to three months' imprisonment. This seemed to be the total effect of their demonstration.

The Second Duma was convoked and dissolved in the same manner. Its composition was more radical than that of the First, partly because the population had become better acquainted with the process of election, partly because indignation at the fate of the First Duma was widespread and people wanted to show their displeasure by voting for more progressive elements. Besides, the radical groups that had boycotted the First Duma, decided to seek nomination in the Second.

So, in spite of the efforts of the government to control the elections, more than one third of the total number of delegates came from the Left—namely the "Trudoviks" (Laborites), the SD's, and the SR's. In such company the old-time liberals seemed very tame and accommodating. Nevertheless, after three months the Duma was dissolved, and a number of radical deputies were arrested. Now the government did not want to take the risk of having to deal with any further radical representation, and so it decided to change the electoral law itself. Contrary to the "Constitution," which required that no change could be incorporated in it in any way but through the vote of the Parliament itself, the Czar simply issued his ukase in the form of a "law" providing for a larger representation of the propertied groups, especially of the landlords. The agrarian question was paramount to the privileged classes.

By this time the country was again well under the heel of the dreaded *Okhranka* (or Secret Service) and the gendarmerie. Many recent converts to radicalism from the intelligentsia now turned their backs on the revolution. Partly they were terrorized by the ruthlessness of the government; partly they claimed to be disgusted with the tepid revolutionary ardor of the working class. A number of such "disappointed" radicals of yesterday published an antirevolution symposium under the name *Viekhi,* or "Guideposts," which appealed to the populace to exercise moderation in its demands. Actually the half-heartedness among the workers was due to the fact that labor was still poorly organized and disunited. But the courage and readiness for self-sacrifice of the workers was demonstrated over and over again, not only in Moscow, but at Rostov-on-the-Don, and in countless other industrial towns.

Meanwhile the Monarchy received a respite. It could use this breathing spell to appease the population by gradually introducing necessary changes. Or it could consolidate the position of the old order. Actually it did neither. It wanted to preserve the old order but had nothing constructive to offer. So the reaction simply tried to intimidate the country into the acceptance of despotic rule as the most desirable for Russia, which had seen many days of glory under the Autocracy.

Extreme "Rights" received a chance to demonstrate their talents to the limit. And new French loans, attracted through the quasi-constitutional reforms, actually financed the reaction.

The deliberations of the Third Duma were consequently less important than the demarches of the new government. Now the new Duma was composed mostly of reactionaries who knew "how to behave"; and for a while Russia was under the almost absolute rule of Peter Stolypin, the omnipotent Prime Minister, who was reputed to be a liberal, but whose slogan was "Appeasement first—reforms afterward." His innovation in the field of agrarian problems was the idea of decentralizing the peasantry through resettlement. The old system of villages was considered by some students as tending toward socialism. Under it the "Mir," or land communes, were bound together not only by labor on the same fields, which were periodically redistributed among them, but also by collective responsibility for taxes. It was argued that such close affinity of interests might develop collective-mindedness beyond the bounds acceptable to the regime. That, in Stolypin's opinion, was a danger which ought to be eliminated. So he set about to encourage the disintegration of the villages, and to substitute a system of *khutora,* or separate homesteads. Various inducements were offered by the government to those who would leave their villages and settle apart. Comparatively few fish, however, rose to this bait; for while some of the more enterprising peasants perceived advantages in the idea, the rank and file had neither the money to pay for new lots nor the desire to move and abandon their homes, poor as they were. Most of the land communes were not favorably inclined toward the withdrawal of any parcels out of their holdings. Besides, the majority had learned through experience that the bureaucrats could hardly be classed as friends and so were in no hurry to follow their advice.

Stolypin and his program were the topics of the hour. The "very respectable" newspaper *Novoye Vriemia* waxed ecstatic in approval. It was published by a former liberal, Souvorin, who gradually became a most obliging servant of the regime, and was long regarded as the mouthpiece of reaction and the journalistic bible of the "law-abiding" subjects of His Majesty. The more extreme organs of the Right were read chiefly by the ultrareactionaries. Of the more liberal papers, the chief were *Rietch* (Discourse), published in St. Petersburg by the KD's under the editorship of Professor Miliukov; and *Russkyie Viedomosty* (The Russian News), issued at Moscow with the participation of a number of progressive professors. Their editors and writers were not so sure about the plans of Stolypin. Indeed, they seemed united in believing that the terror practiced by his government was horrible enough to justify nicknaming him "the hangman." They called the noose of the gallows "Stolypin's necktie." During the five years of Stolypin's dictatorship, some five thousand people were condemned to death, and of them three thousand five hundred were actually executed. But, in September, 1911, Stolypin himself was assassinated while attending a gala performance at the Kiev Opera House. There is some reason to believe that the Police Department was involved.

As the result of Stolypin's terrorism and other causes, the liberal papers and magazines gradually either ceased publication or toned down their attacks on the government. Once again, as in the long era of reaction known as Pobiedonostzeff's period (1881-1905), journalists were forced to resort to allegory and the language of Aesop, in order to smuggle in things that otherwise would be expurgated by the censors. In the field of literature and art there was a noticeable infiltration of decadence. A definite social purpose was increasingly eschewed, and the "Art for Art's sake" theory became predominant. Writers and artists, in increasing numbers, tended to avoid direct or indirect criticism of contemporary conditions, to closet themselves in the ivory towers of their own frequently morbid minds. Realism yielded place to the sheer aestheticism of Balmont, Hippius, and Igor Severianin, the mysticism of Andreieff, the imaginative or symbolic poetry and fiction of Block, Briussoff, and Merejkovsky. Melancholy and despair characterized the trend of that period, which was also marked by an exaggerated interest in sexual problems, best illustrated by Arzibasheff's novel, *Sanin*. Leo Tolstoy in those days was absorbed by philosophy and theology. Chekhov was dead. Only Maxim Gorky, the Stormy Petrel, the rebellious, daring optimist, continued to appeal for action, to speak out against the black conditions of the time.

In this atmosphere of decadence and reaction it is not surprising that our heated discussions were discontinued and that our interest in politics waned to the vanishing point. There were other things to do. Books and periodicals had little to offer that would tend to stimulate debate. And the revolutionists had been discredited by clever propaganda which not only held them up as self-seeking egoists and demagogues but twisted their "expropriations" for replenishing the meager funds at their disposal into an appearance of dishonesty. So to us it seemed that there was little inducement to continue an interest in the affairs of a class not our own—which, of course, was just the effect the manipulators of public opinion intended. Without particularly potent stimuli before their eyes people are apt to forget about the grievances of another class and keep aloof from its struggle for the betterment of its lot.

This is likely to be particularly true of officers in the Army, who are bound by oath to remain loyal to the throne, an oath which might quite easily be interpreted as covering loyalty to the government, and to their own class, which was behind the government. In any case, as long as we remained on active service, we were not supposed to take any direct part in the political life of the country. Most of us failed to realize that by this regulation we were made *de facto* defenders of the existing system, and hence that we were definitely partisan in the political sense.

And so we soon calmed down, along with the rest of the country, and continued our studies without bothering about "civilian" affairs. In my first two years at the War College I had enjoyed plenty of leisure, in spite of the enormously large programs, for I somehow passed my examinations without any extra effort. The third year required more work. In this last year there were no classes, but one had to prepare two theses and one final major problem on strategy, tactics, and administrative details. My first thesis concerned the Russo-Polish relations, and the war that ended in the partition of Poland. My professor-opponents were General M. Alexeieff, the future Chief of Staff of the Emperor during the World War, and General A. Mishlaievsky, who was soon to become the Chief of our General Staff. My second thesis was on the use of mounted artillery with the cavalry masses, and my opponents again were two outstanding officers destined to play important roles during the World War—Colonels N. Danilov and G. Elchaninoff. For both theses I received the highest marks, and the second was recommended and accepted for publication. It was a new experience for me to find myself in print, and I was childishly delighted. The major problem was solved very well, too, with the result that I was graduated third in a class of some eighty men.

Graduation from the War College of the General Staff opened boundless opportunities. Officers of the General Staff in Russia were the most privileged among the privileged. There were virtually no posts beyond the reach of members of that favored caste. They were found not only in all the highest posts of the Army, but as governors of provinces, chiefs in various Ministries, and as diplomats and what not. It was said, jokingly of course, that officers of the General Staff could even become archbishops. For my part, I had no particular desire to become an archbishop, a governor, or even a general of the Army. Those were not my ambitions. But, for good or ill, I was carried away from my true line of interest on the wave of easy success. Not until long afterward did I notice the extent of this deviation.

As was customary, the Czar honored the graduating class with an audience. A special train took us to Tsarskoye Sielo, a small town some twenty miles from St. Petersburg, where the Imperial family had lived since Bloody Sunday. Imperial coaches, with servants in pompous red liveries, met us at the station and brought us to the gorgeous palace built by Catherine the Great. We were lined up in a large, beautifully decorated hall, awaiting the Emperor's arrival. The Czar came out smiling and at once started down the line shaking hands with every officer. But at the very second he reached me a terrible thunderstorm broke out. It was so sudden and nerve-shaking that His Majesty shuddered slightly, but immediately regained his composure, smiled again, shook my hand after I reported my name and the name of my regiment, and passed on down the line. Later, while on the way to luncheon in the huge adjacent hall, a classmate, Captain Petin, laughingly inquired if it had really been a thunderstorm, or a bomb in my pocket, that had exploded so noisily as the Emperor approached. We were good friends and had much in common. He knew of my mood during the days of the Revolution of 1905, and knew that I disapproved of political terrorism. Soon after the Revolution of 1917, he himself became the Chief of Staff of a large unit to which Stalin was political commissar.

For the summer I returned to Caucasia for field work, but this time to teach other officers, and during maneuvers to act as a staff officer. But for my two years' experience in command, which was required before becoming a regular staff officer, I went back to St. Petersburg. These two years were, in my estimation, the most fruitful I had in the Army, for they gave me an opportunity of learning more about military life and brought me into closer contact with the rank and file, with whom I established very cordial relations. Being in command of a company, I had its entire life in my hands; I was charged not only with the training of my men, but with the care of their welfare in every respect. I had an opportunity now to do things according to my own ideas.

First of all, I made a point of developing a real interest in all my subordinates and tried to know as much about each of them as possible. Soon we became real friends, for I knew about their families, their home troubles, their interests, and their plans for the future. And I have, as a consequence, some very warm and dear memories. Furthermore, realizing the importance to them of literacy, for illiteracy was widespread in the Russia of those days, I resolved with the help of other officers to teach them the three R's. This was not as difficult as might be imagined, for they earnestly wanted to learn and there was not a single soldier in my company who did not read and write before leaving the service. In addition, I arranged lectures, using slides which were available without charge from the Museum of Natural History. I helped them to arrange shows, concerts, and even dances to which outsiders were invited. Once, I remember, I suggested to my soldiers that they collect from the barrack's yard the Christmas trees which had been thrown out by the officers' families. With them they arranged an attractive winter garden in the halls, and a dance was held the same evening. Contrary to the warnings given by other officers that such a fantastic innovation might end in a scandal, there was perfect order. Everybody apparently enjoyed it, and not a single case of drunkenness was reported. To the American reader it may seem strange that anything so natural could evoke criticism. But many other strange things occurred then in Russia.

On one occasion I had an amusing conversation with the Colonel. He was a cultured man, open-minded and reasonable. His attitude toward me was most friendly. He considered my company the best in the regiment, and said so again and again in his Orders of the Day. In other words, he approved of me as an officer and as commander. On this occasion I suggested that it would be a good thing if the Army would make a point of teaching every soldier to read and write, as a recompense for the time lost through compulsory military service. He laughed and said that I was going too far. "The Army is not a university," was his terse summing up.

I mention these matters in order to make more comprehensible what happened to me later. Once I was tipped off by a friend of the family that I was suspected of revolutionary tendencies, and that a spy had been assigned to my company to watch me and report to the authorities. It was a welcome warning; not because I had anything to hide, but because detectives are apt to use their imagination too liberally when they fail to find what they are expected to discover. It was easy enough to identify the spy, too. He was not a regular private, but a so-called "volunteer" who was able to enlist for a shorter term because of his educational qualifications. I never gave him the slightest idea that I knew who he was; but I am sure that he did not report much, if anything, that was irregular, aside from the really friendly relations which prevailed in my company between the officers and the rank and file, the theatrical performances we continued to arrange, and, possibly, my regular and strict inspections of meat and other products for the soldiers.

Why did they send the spy? It is difficult to say definitely, but it was quite possible that among the officers and soldiers of the regiment there were agents of the secret service, who, considering my zeal unusual and my relations with the soldiers unduly friendly, suspected some political motive. Suspicion leads to gossip; gossip may have resulted in measures of precaution. The police and their secret service were on the alert, especially around St. Petersburg and the residence of the Czar. And other things besides my conduct in the regiment may have worried the watchdogs. They may have disapproved of my interest in the State Duma, whose sessions I used occasionally to visit. They did not know, of course, that there was a very simple explanation for this; that I had a friend on the staff of the metropolitan newspapers, who used frequently to get me passes to the sessions. But it was unusual for an officer to take any interest whatever in such matters. In other words, visiting Parliament was enough of an irregularity to justify not only suspicion, but even the assignment of a special spy to watch me.

During the sessions of the First Duma I was so impressed by some of the speeches delivered there by the deputies that for a time I cherished the earnest hope of one day being chosen as a people's representative myself. Naïvely I believed that election to the Duma was evidence of popular approval and respect. I wanted to deserve this approval.

My relations with the other officers of the regiment were most cordial and pleasant. Even my elders, who for a short while frowned on my youthful zeal, treated me with genuine friendliness. And this, I think, represented a very real testimonial to their caliber as gentlemen and human beings. For there was a chasm of long-range interest, as well as of age, to separate us. I was to be on the job for a maximum of two years, but this was their life's work. My unorthodox methods tended to make their own routine efforts seem inadequate. They had no urge to enter into competition with my young enthusiasm. Monotony, the lack of opportunity for mental progress, and the convenience of routine conditioned their attitude. They neither liked nor saw the need for change.

The two years seemed to pass quite rapidly, for my time was fully occupied, and I had little leisure for strictly personal pursuits. Hence, I did not read much in that period, aside from military literature, on which I had to be well posted, first of all in order to keep up to date, and secondly because it was part of my duty to lecture before the officers' clubs. Late in the fall of 1909, my term came to an end. I left the regiment, was put on the list of the General Staff, promoted to the next rank, and assigned for service at Khabarovsk, the headquarters of the Far Eastern District. This was by my own choice, for I wanted to become acquainted with a region where only recently two wars had been fought, and where a war of revenge seemed to be impending. This region was to be the field of my work and study for over a quarter of a century.

It took us eighteen days to travel over the Trans-Siberian Railway with no long stops en route. All along the line one was impressed by the immensity of Siberia, and by her obvious, but practically untouched, wealth. This was a country of abundance. Living there was unbelievably cheap, as indicated by prices one had to pay while traveling by train. At most of the stops there was a large choice of food offered by the peasants from the near-by villages, in competition with station restaurants. For one half of a large, fat, roasted goose you were charged only forty kopeks, or about twenty cents in American money. As for the landscape, it was one of boundless plains, large beautiful mountains, and endless forests. Some of the Siberian rivers are among the longest in the world, while Baikal Lake is reputed to be the deepest of all inland waters on our planet. But the very scale of the landscape produced an irresistible impression of monotony. If there were steppes, there seemed to be no end of them; if mountains followed, one felt that there could never be anything but mountains in this vast land. The train seemed veritably to crawl across the snow-covered panorama... when only twenty miles from our destination, we were marooned by a snowstorm for a whole day.

Next morning, however, we were in Khabarovsk. We knew, of course, that the winters in this part of Asia are very cold, but we were not prepared for a Fahrenheit reading of about sixty degrees below zero. But, cold as it was, it was very pleasant. The air was dry and invigorating; the dazzling sun drew forth real joy in living. And this was no ephemeral exhilaration. The Far East, still a pioneer's land, was full of interest, and of peculiar, savage beauty. It seemed to offer unlimited opportunities for everyone. It was up to us to use these opportunities in a proper way.

Khabarovsk was not only the site of the headquarters of the military district to which I was assigned but the capital city of the Russian Far East. It was also the seat of the Governor General of a vast region on the easternmost end of the Empire, facing the Pacific Ocean. A picturesque town on the hills beside the mighty Amur River, it was built in 1858, the year when St. Petersburg obtained, through treaties with China, a formal recognition of Russia's right to the Amur region. Its very name recalled a romantic epoch rich in fascinating exploits, in the glamour and wonder of a fairy tale. Khabarov, who reached the mouth of the Amur two hundred years before the town bearing his name was founded, was one of those Cossack adventurers whose feats of exploration throughout the north of Asia read like legends, and who were pioneers in adding this vast terrain to the Empire of the Czars.

This eastward expansion in Asia began in the second half of the sixteenth century, after Russia had succeeded in casting off the Mongolian yoke, under which she had suffered for more than two hundred years. In 1555 one of the Tartar Khans, Ediger, sent envoys to Moscow to entreat the Czar to take Sibir, or Siberia, under his protection. From then on events proceeded apace.

In its early stages this expansion was left mostly to private initiative. The immense territory of Siberia, rich in big game, was slowly penetrated by hunters, trappers, and other adventurous individuals. Real conquest did not begin, however, until 1558, when Czar Ivan the Terrible accorded the rich merchants Stroganoff a concession to develop and exploit a region in the Urals on the threshold of Asia. Besides the various trading privileges, the Czar conferred on the Stroganoffs the right to administer justice and levy troops for the purpose of protecting the country from outside encroachments. The next important step occurred in 1581, when Yermak, the military leader of the Stroganoffs, descended eastward from the Urals with a few hundred Cossacks and occupied Sibir, the capital of the local Tartars. Moscow's foreign policy at that time was concentrated on her western border. After the elimination of danger from the Tartars, Moscow had no great interest in a further advance in Asia. Nevertheless, the Czar did not refuse to accept this unexpected addition to his domain and consented to incorporate Siberia into his Empire.

In its first stage, the Russian colonial advance into Siberia followed the rivers. Within a few years the Cossacks had reached the Obi River. By 1628 they had crossed the Yenissei, and ten years later they established themselves in the basin of the Lena. At approximately the same time they reached the Arctic Ocean, and by 1648 they were on the Pacific. Thus, in less than sixty years the whole continent had been traversed from end to end. It was an unparalleled achievement, for the advance of the American settlers from the Atlantic to the Pacific, a much shorter distance, occupied nearly two centuries. This might be explained by the fact that, while the American colonists had to fight the Indians, the Russian penetration of actually unclaimed country met with little serious resistance.

Especially amazing were the discovery and gradual occupation of the Amur region. A small group of brave, adventurous men, fascinated by vague stories heard from the natives about faraway lands lying along an unknown river, conquered the wilderness, step by step, and advanced toward the Pacific. Undergoing incredible hardships, hunger, and violent cold, they reached at last the Sea of Okhotsk, and finally stood on the shores of another sea, further to the northeast, which later took the name of Bering, a Dane who led a Russian expedition to this part of the world at the time of Peter the Great.

Acquired in this fantastic manner by pioneers acting on their own initiative, the enormous virgin territory remained relatively neglected by the central government for centuries. Even at the time of my arrival there it was so sparsely colonized that there were only some fifty inhabitants to every hundred square miles. Like the rest of northern Asia it was chiefly used or, should we say, misused as a place of exile for offenders against the law. A considerable number of political exiles died there. But some of these prisoners decided to settle there after the end of their terms.

Aside from its gold fields, the Russian Far East offered little to attract investors. There was no large accumulation of private capital in Russia at that time. It was not large enough for an extensive development of industry and mining even in the European parts of the Empire. The more considerable investments in both of these fields were made by foreigners. But after the two wars fought during the opening years of the twentieth century in the neighborhood of eastern Siberia there was more interest in this far-distant colony. St. Petersburg dispatched a better kind of functionary for administration purposes, revised and enlarged the program of colonization, and appropriated more money for new construction and general development.

Nevertheless, eastern Siberia remained essentially a colony, with a life of its own. People even used to say "over in Russia," when speaking of the European homeland. The remoteness of the area from the capital and its bureaucracy necessitated a relative independence and greater local initiative. But economically the Amur region was far from self-sustaining. Practically everything had to be imported, partly from home, mostly from other countries. Railway freight rates from Russia beyond the Urals were higher than those from the near-by foreign lands, and much higher than seagoing freight. There was an abundant supply of local game and fish, plenty of wood and lumber, but few vegetables outside of those cultivated by the not-so-numerous Korean truck farmers. Meat was brought from Australia, and wheat from Manchuria or from western Siberia. Fruits came from Japan, or perhaps the United States. Factory goods were brought from Russia and abroad. Hardly anything was manufactured locally.

A majority of the rural population were Cossacks, who as "old-timers" controlled the best lands. The newer settlers, few in number, were mainly peasants who had been induced by the government to migrate to this remote region through the promise of somewhat larger acreage and modest subsidy for pioneering. As for the city dwellers, they were mostly either newcomers or transients, a considerable per centage being functionaries of the various services. Most of the latter looked upon their presence in the Far East with much the same point of view as that of British officials in India. Salaries were on a higher basis than in other parts of the Empire, and permitted a better standard of living. The service itself was counted with a certain allowance for the years spent there. Furloughs were longer than elsewhere, since it took so long to reach one's home in Europe. And comparatively few officials remained in the Far East for more than a short time. Especially was this true of the officers of the General Staff, who came and went with great frequency.

CHAPTER VII

IN JAPAN

(*Between the Acts*)

Tsuruga. On the train: people, their dress, food, and customs. Our living quarters. Japanese and Westerners. The language. Improvement in the Russo-Japanese relations. The advice of an American engineer. Conditions in Japan. New complications in the Far East. Back to Khabarovsk.

AFTER LESS THAN four months at Khabarovsk, I was offered a chance to spend two years in Japan as language officer. I accepted this appointment without the slightest hesitation. In a few days my little family was ready to start. Early in the spring we sailed from Vladivostok for Tsuruga on a boat of the Russian Volunteer Fleet.

Our first impression of Japan was enchanting. The contrast with the severe, almost wild, landscape of the Russian Far East was striking. Tsuruga, an important commercial harbor on the western coast of the main island of Hondo, was picturesque and colorful. The encircling soft hills were covered with rich vegetation and were bathed in glorious sunshine. Small houses with wooden frames and sliding paper walls, which formed doors and windows, added to the feeling of charm. Everything was small, neat, clean, and showed an artistic touch. This first impression remained almost unchanged, even after many years spent by us in Japan.

Immediately after we landed, we were confronted with a local institution which our Western prejudices and humanitarian instincts found it difficult to accept at once. To reach the railway station we were offered the services of the jinrikisha, or riksha, as they are called by the foreigners. We balked at the very thought of being pulled by human beings playing horses, and decided to walk. Probably it was a funny picture for the natives to see us march, father, mother, and daughter carried by a nurse, with my orderly and the baggage behind.

I may add that this "idiosyncrasy" of ours soon disappeared, for this was and still is the normal method of transportation in Japan. Indeed, the same evening, at Yokohama, we were orientalized enough not to object. Behind the interpreter who was sent to meet us, we were pulled to our hotel, as everybody is in Nippon.

On the train from Tsuruga to Yokohama we had stared at our fellow passengers even more unceremoniously than they stared at us. They had seen foreigners before. But we were in a country entirely new to us and were observing a people whose ways were completely unfamiliar. Different in their looks, their dress, and their manners, and speaking a language of which we did not know a word, they seemed alien indeed. It seemed impossible that we should ever learn to know and understand these people who had been our adversaries in a war only a few years back. Yet, after all, were they really our past and future enemies, these people and their children in the train? Surely not, we told ourselves. They were no more responsible for the policies of the government than we for those of ours. In the war the rank and file of them had borne the reputation of honorable fighters, valorous and filled with ardent patriotism, doing nothing to cast discredit on their race and nation. Thus we reflected; and so reflecting came to the realization that it ought not after all to be so difficult to find something in common with them, even to become their friends.

And so we watched them in the crowded train, looking for that thing in common. We observed what they wore and did and took delight in.

The easiest thing was to get used to their garb. Men, women, and children were dressed in the familiar kimono of cotton or silk, differing only in the design and color of the fabrics used and in the accessories. The men had simple belts of silk or other material, but for the ladies the belt (called *obi,* as we learned later) was obviously the most important part of their attire, and was elaborately arranged on the back to form a butterfly or some other similar effect. The children's kimonos were of bright, cheerful colors. Instead of shoes, practically everyone had straw sandals, called *zori,* fitted with leather soles, or wooden clogs. Sitting on the benches, arranged lengthwise down the car, they left their footgear on the floor and remained in their *tabi,* a kind of sock reaching only to the ankle and having a separate compartment for the big toe. Very few men, and hardly any women, wore European dress or shoes. As for the headgear, most of the men had hats or caps, the women either scarfs or nothing.

Next we observed their eating habits. Special lunch boxes, called *bento,* were sold at the stations. Two or three in number, these boxes were placed one over the other and contained tiny pieces of fish, chicken, omelette, vegetables, mushrooms, and the inevitable rice. The chopsticks, used instead of forks and knives, were in paper bags, attached to the boxes, and a toothpick served as fastener for the complete package. Tea in small teapots, with a cup on top of each pot, was sold for a penny or so.

Besides the voices of the vendors of food, beverages, cigarettes, and newspapers, and the talking and laughing of the crowd, a peculiar clacking noise went up at all the stations. This was produced by the wooden clogs, or *geta,* as they are called. The general impression we gathered from that crowd was one of cleanliness, a marked but very studied courtesy, and smiles, and smiles, and smiles.

In the evening we reached Yokohama, then the largest foreign settlement in Japan; and to tell the truth we were genuinely relieved to find ourselves alone in our comfortable rooms in a hotel which catered to foreigners in their own Occidental style. We were tired not only by the trip but by the strangeness of the surroundings and the strain of trying to comprehend a little of their nature and meaning. This feeling of being completely out of the picture did not, however, last long. A few days spent in Yokohama, where foreigners had learned to adjust the problem of housekeeping to their own Western tastes, and a few trips to Tokyo to get acquainted with our diplomatic representatives, served merely as a short intermediary period before our real induction into Japanese ways. For we never allowed ourselves to forget that we had come to Japan to learn to know the Japanese. Therefore, following the advice of General Samoyloff, the Military Attaché at our Embassy, we decided to settle away from the foreigners, in Sidzuoka. This town of more than one hundred thousand inhabitants was the center of Japan's tea industry, and was located between Kobe and Yokohama, the two largest foreign settlements. It was said to be the place where the purest Japanese was spoken.

It was no easy matter, of course, to tear ourselves from people with whom we could converse and settle amid those by whom we could not be understood. Fortunately we were met at the station in Sidzuoka by the former teacher of another language officer, and with his help we rented a house belonging to the Rinzai-ji, a Buddhist temple on the outskirts of the town.

Like most Buddhist temples, this place of worship was located in very picturesque surroundings. Standing at the foot of a high wooded hill, it was almost hidden in a garden full of flowers, bushes, and trees fantastically trimmed to resemble boats, birds, and what not. Our house, a two-storied building of purely Japanese architecture, with sliding walls of wood and paper, was connected with the temple by a stairway. On the other side of the temple were buildings occupied by the priests and their disciples.

The floors in all the rooms were covered by heavy straw mats, as in all Japanese homes. This meant that we had to take off our shoes when entering the house and to go about in socks and stockings. Our furniture was brought from Russia and it was no small problem to protect the delicate flooring from damage by our Western beds and other heavy objects. But boards under each piece of furniture did the trick. The bathroom, very small in its dimensions, contained a wooden tub shaped like a huge barrel; and into this hot water had to be poured by hand. Before long we learned that it is customary in Japan for the same bathwater to be used by the entire family, including the servants, one after another. There was but one stipulation: everyone must soap and rinse himself before entering the tub.

As soon as we were settled, I asked the interpreter to provide me with teachers. The next day I had my first lesson in Japanese. To acquire a working knowledge of the spoken language proved less difficult than might have been expected; but to become familar with its complexities, such as the use of one vocabulary for addressing superiors, another for equals, and a third for the servants, was a different matter.

Most of our diplomats at Tokyo told me that the written language was too difficult to learn, and that it would be enough if I mastered spoken Japanese. But I was convinced that this was not the proper method of study, and I resolved to learn the ideograms as well. This was a formidable task; to read even ordinary articles in the daily press one must learn to differentiate between not less than three thousand of these puzzling little pictures, each the graphic image of a definite idea. But the more difficult the task the more fun there is in achieving it. I started at once to copy my ideograms on small cards, and to keep them in my pocket in order to look at them as often as possible until the images of the newly recorded signs were stamped on my memory. This method, used by practically everyone who has ever studied written Japanese or Chinese, proved very effective.

The surroundings were most conducive to the quickest possible mastering of the language. There were, for a time, no foreigners near. My family did not interfere with my work. And my two instructors, though not experienced as teachers, were very obliging and did everything possible to make my task easier. Several months later I added yet a third teacher. Now I was working fourteen hours per day and repeating Japanese words even when asleep.

In due course we were discovered by other foreigners living in Sidzuoka and became less isolated. The French nuns of the local Convent of the Sacret Heart made welcome companions for my wife, and there were a few priests with whom I became friendly. Having resided in Japan for many years, and constantly studying, they were veritable mines of knowledge about things Japanese. There were also several American and English missionaries of various denominations, and finally a French naval officer who had also heard of the purity of the local language and decided to settle in Sidzuoka for his studies. With him we made a number of trips, traveling all over the country by bicycle and rail, stopping at Japanese hotels, living in the Japanese way, and generally coming into contact with the people. At Sidzuoka, meanwhile, we were gradually acquiring friends among the Japanese. The chief of the brigade stationed in that town was a general who had just returned from Russia, where he had served as Military Attaché to the Embassy at St. Petersburg. He called on us, and his visit led to my making the acquaintance of several other officers, one of whom had the rather strange idea of paying his respects at seven o'clock in the morning. The relatives of my teachers were another group with whom we exchanged visits.

With the coming of winter it seemed better to move from our enchanting temple, for the house was too much in accordance with purely Japanese ideas of what constitutes a shelter. It would hardly provide a comfortably warm abode for our little daughter during the colder days of the year. Fortunately, one Englishman connected with the local tea business was planning to sail for his home country, and his house was for rent. So, we moved into town. The new house was much better equipped for a life in the Western fashion, and by adding glass screens and a few oil stoves, we were enabled to spend the winter in Occidental comfort.

It was at about this time that I received word that I had been assigned to a post in St. Petersburg. This was none of my seeking, but a consequence of my scholastic standing while in College. So, as I was not inclined to abandon a work that interested me and was still very far from completion, I asked to be allowed to stay in Japan. The permission was granted. There were always more people anxious for appointments at the capital than there were vacancies. It was rare, indeed, for anyone to refuse these coveted commissions.

As my vocabulary grew, our Japanese circle widened. A physician who lived in a gorgeous house across the street and whose wife spoke English and a little French became friendly. The headmaster of the high school, who occupied a small house next door and lived in the modest way characteristic of most Japanese, except a few high officials and the very rich, also showed an interest in us, and we exchanged visits.

Our removal to the neighborhood of a foreign colony brought us the acquaintance of a number of missionaries of various denominations. They were good, pleasant folk, but sad victims of professional jealousy, and we soon learned that it was unwise to entertain more than one at a time. Each was looking for more converts, and each proclaimed his own to be the only true church. And in this connection I note, by the way, that the Japanese converts were apt to remain affiliated for rather a short time. Not that in the embracing of a new faith they were not sincere. But the question of faith was incidental, their primary object in joining the church being to learn English, which was very valuable in business. As their knowledge of English increased, their interest in Christianity was apt to wane.

By this I do not mean to imply that the teachings of Jesus were contrary to their liking. The point is simply that very few Japanese ever take any profound interest in religion, in the Western sense, in spite of the impressive number of shrines and temples in their country. Their attitude toward faith is different from any known to us. Their great, nationally revered shrines are not so much temples as monuments to heroes of the past, designed to remind the living of their patriotic duty. The oldest and the only genetically Japanese faith is Shinto, which is more a cult of loyalty and patriotism than a religion.

A number of my Japanese friends insisted that I go to Kunozan, a few miles from Sidzuoka, to see the tomb of Ieyasu Tokugawa, a famous statesman, who founded the dynasty of the Tokugawa Shoguns. These Shoguns were military dictators who actually ruled Japan for more than two hundred and sixty years, while the emperors were relegated to a titular position and were expected to devote their lives to the gods. I made the pilgrimage, and found it worth the trouble. The temple, situated at the top of a high hill, was really impressive. But the story told by the guides about it being the burial place of the great Ieyasu was wholly false. I learned later that Ieyasu's remains had long since been moved to Nikko. This disregard of facts, so common among professional guides, reminded me of the endless number of "castles of the Czaritsa Tamara," that one is shown in Caucasia.

In the spring the headmaster invited me to the commencement ceremonies at his high school. Part of the program was in French, which

I knew quite well, part in English, of which I then knew very little, the rest in Japanese, most of which I could now understand. One of the orators reminded the boys that some day they might be asked to defend their country against the Russians, who might seek revenge for the defeat suffered in the war of 1904-5. Then they would have to demonstrate the *yamato-damashi,* the real spirit of the ancient heroes of their land. I was duly impressed—by the naïveté and gaucheness of the school officials. In my later years in Japan I found these characteristics rather typical of her petty officials. Provincial in the extreme, insular in their political ideas, they are usually very modest and courteous. But, when discussing the fighting capacities of their men, they become boastful to a point where it becomes difficult for the listener not to smile. Usually they mean well, but they lack the imagination to put themselves in the place of the foreigner. However, I am sure that I also gave them plenty of reason to smile at my errors in etiquette and lack of knowledge of their conventions.

At the end of my first year of study I had to return to Khabarovsk for a short time in connection with the renewal of my assignment. In less than a month we were back in Japan, where we again spent the summer in Sidzuoka amid the familiar surroundings and among old friends. In the fall we decided to move to Yokohama or Tokyo, for I was expected to visit various military establishments in and round those cities. There was no longer any particular reason to refrain from meeting foreigners, as the foundation of my Japanese was solidly laid. Moreover, I could easily find excellent teachers in a city where so many foreigners lived and created a demand for their instruction.

While staying in Yokohama, and later on at Tokyo, we were able to visit a number of the various flower displays for which Japan is famous. Early in the year comes the plum blossom. March and April bring the flowering of the peach, and the first half of April the celebrated cherry blossom. Then follow one after another the peonies, the graceful wistaria, the multicolored azaleas, irises in the summer, the exotic lotus through August, and the chrysanthemums in endless variety during the late fall.

A garden party at one of the suburban Imperial palaces offered us the most gorgeous display of chrysanthemums. They were in all colors, shapes, and sizes imaginable; and there were some wonders of horticulture, such as the presence of different-colored flowers on the same bush, or hundreds of blossoms on a single stem. Unfortunately, our delight in seeing this marvelous and beautiful exhibit was somewhat modified by the extreme ceremoniousness of the affair. Prince Alberts and silk hats were *de rigeur* and none of the formality that goes with such attire was absent. The vanity of human beings seems especially absurd amid the simplicity and beauty of nature.

Before the end of my second year in Japan, I was at least able to read the newspapers, with some assistance from my teachers. So I decided to try my hand at translating a book on the military tactics of the Japanese Army in the light of experience gained in the war with Russia. It was a bold undertaking, indeed. But word by word, with the constant assistance of my teachers, the translation was at last completed. Our Military Attaché sent it to St. Petersburg with his recommendation for publication. When I learned that the Headquarters of the General Staff had accepted it, I asked that the book be prefaced with an explanation that my role in the translation had been very minor, indeed.

While studying the ideograms, I used the splendid Japanese-Russian dictionary of Pozdneiev, the former Professor and Director of the Institute of Oriental Languages at Vladivostok. But, while translating my first book, I found that Pozdneiev was inadequate with regard to military terms. Therefore my next plan was to fill this gap. I started at once working on a military dictionary, using as a basis similar works in other languages. Eventually my manuscript contained several thousand words, but, owing to the pressure of other work, I had to abandon it, before completion. On leaving Japan in 1918, I left the manuscript to my successor, but unfortunately it never found its way to the press. In the turbulent days that followed, it was no doubt either lost or left in the hands of persons unable to communicate with officials in Russia after she became the U.S.S.R.

I was allowed to inspect a number of regiments and various military organizations during the second year. Once, while attending maneuvers near Tokyo, I was introduced to Prince Kanin, then in command of the Division of Imperial Guard, and later the Chief of the General Staff at Nippon. He impressed me as a very able officer and a very pleasant gentleman. Much later, when on the staff of our Embassy, I met him again, this time not as a military officer but as the President of the Japanese-Russian Society, of which he made me an honorary Councillor.

The Russo-Japanese relations, though never especially cordial, by this time had been greatly improved. There was a definite trend toward finding a basis for co-operation. Nineteen hundred and seven had witnessed the signature of two conventions, one open and the other secret, delimiting the interests of the two countries in Manchuria. In 1910 two more conventions were added, strengthening the rapprochement. This time the former adversaries were drawn closer by their determination to resist the attempted penetration of Manchuria by certain American groups, headed by Edward H. Harriman and financed by a number of banks. The so-called Knox plan for neutralization of the railways there was the vital factor. Six years later, namely in 1916, Japan and Russia became allies, obligated to help each other in case of any encroachment on their spheres of interest by a third party.

It was in 1910 that Japan completed her annexation of Korea. The official declaration maintained that the failure of measures designed to restore order in that country had compelled Japan, in the interests of peace and tranquillity in Asia, to incorporate Korea into the Mikado's Empire. This same technique, with a few modifications, was applied to Manchuria in 1931. The end of "independent" Korea was not unexpected by St. Petersburg and did not affect relations with Tokyo. The two capitals were still determined to improve their mutual relations, and they continued working toward this end.

But, in spite of improvement in official relations, no foreigner ever found himself quite at ease in Japan. This was true even of numerous missionaries who devoted their lives to the service of the

Japanese. Even the venerated Archbishop Nicholas of the Russian Orthodox Church in Japan, who lived there over fifty years and died at Tokyo, never felt entirely at home. Spying is almost a national sport in Nippon. Agents of the police, uniformed, in plain clothes, or simply amateurs, constantly watch the foreigner's every movement. As a Russian officer of the General Staff, I could scarcely hope to escape this surveillance. While traveling through Japan as language officer, as well as on my numerous later visits, including a sojourn at the Embassy, I certainly had a full taste of this espionage. Usually it was amateurish and even laughable. But it could be most annoying.

Arriving one day at a small town near Kagoshima, in the south of Kiushiu Island, I had a rather amusing experience which was later repeated in other places with practically no important variations. After a tiresome trip on a small horse-driven omnibus, I was enjoying my rest on the floor, covered with blankets, *futon,* in true Japanese style. Suddenly I was awakened by the rattle of the sliding partitions and looked up into the smiling face of a policeman with his hand lantern turned on me. He wanted to know, as policemen in Japan always do, my name, the names of my parents and grandparents, their past and present abodes, and other similarly compromising information. But above all he wanted to know my business in their neighborhood? I answered everything with patience, for I had learned long before that there was no use trying to cut short the interminable catechism. They are persistent to an incredible degree, rarely impolite according to the code of etiquette, and meticulous in the performance of their duty.

My answers seemed to satisfy the inquisitor, and he disappeared with bows and smiles. I lay down again, certain that I would not be disturbed again that evening. But in the middle of the night the visit was repeated. The overzealous minion of the law had come to ascertain if I was still there. No one could tell what a foreigner might do!

On this same trip through Kiushiu Island I had a wholesome reminder of the problems of my mother country. I was on my way from Kumamoto to Kagoshima by night train and sat in the dining car at the same table with a pleasant-looking, clean-shaven, middle-aged gentleman. We started talking, and he soon discovered that I was a Russian. Thereupon my table companion offered me all kinds of advice as to how Russia should be governed; and he inveighed against her tyrannical regime and the inequality of her classes, of which he simply could not approve. The gentleman explained that he was an American engineer; and, though I was not convinced that his manners were perfect, I thought that he was a simple, straightforward fellow, very much in accordance with what I expected an American to be. I must confess that my knowledge was limited. I had added very little to my reading of Fenimore Cooper and Mark Twain; and in the few theatrical performances that I had seen at various times, the Yankees were usually treated as comic relief. On the other hand, I had heard enough about the great transatlantic republic, where people were equal, where justice was the same for all, where there was no poverty, and where everyone had enough to eat and to live decently; and I wondered whether my table companion was justified in his critical attitude toward Russia by the achievement in his own country. So this casual conversation had the double effect of making me want to see the United States of America and redirecting my mind to the political, social, and economic evils of my country. Throughout most of the time I had spent in Japan my thoughts had been so completely centered on my study that I had almost ceased thinking of anything but learning the Japanese language and acquiring knowledge about Japan and her people. If ever my thoughts turned to the hardships experienced by my countrymen, I quickly called them back to other things. I rationalized this attitude of detachment by telling myself that my work at that time was more important than futile lamentations. My duty was to acquire knowledge for the service of my mother country, and I had to continue the work to its completion.

Besides, what I saw in Japan was little better than what I knew of my own country. The poverty of the peasants, working very hard in their midget rice fields or on tea plantations and living in shacks that hardly deserved the name of houses, was simply appalling. Shocking, too, were the living conditions of the industrial workers; though

I had not yet seen enough of their working conditions to form a judgment. I had heard that they were extremely bad. The inequality of classes was obvious, and the arrogance of the well-to-do toward the rest of the people was no less marked than in Russia. The methods of the police, if overtly more polite, were actually fully as brutal, as evidenced by the case of Kotoku, the labor leader and anarchist, and the merciless persecution of the Radicals. The terror inaugurated by the Japanese administration in Korea under Count Terauchi recalled the methods familiar to Russia. Generally speaking, Utopia was not to be found in Nippon. Her administrative machine worked much more efficiently than that of Russia; but political, economic, and social evils in the two countries were basically the same, though in Japan they had not developed to the point reached in Russia. Riding on the crest of the still-fresh memory of two successful wars, the government of Japan had great advantages over the rapidly decaying regime of the Czars.

In December, 1911, the people of Japan were excited by the news that revolution had broken out in China. Dr. Sun Yat-sen, who had many friends in Japan, had returned to Shanghai from abroad and had been proclaimed the first Provisional President of the Chinese Republic. The following January the infant Emperor "abdicated," and soon afterward Yuan Shih-kai was elected Provisional President, Dr. Sun resigning voluntarily in Yuan's favor. At this, a sigh of relief went up in the official circles of Japan, for republican ideas were not to their liking. Worship of the Emperor was the basis of their political philosophy. So, as Yuan Shih-kai did not seem to be a proponent of democracy, hopes were placed in his ascent to power. Intrigues were intensified by various interested parties, with Japan, apparently, in their lead. It was more important to her than to any other Power that national interests in the Celestial Empire should not suffer from a popular upheaval.

Actually the Revolution of 1911 did not strengthen China. Her internal dissents were further aggravated, and Japan knew how to turn this situation to her own advantage. She was right in applauding the election of Yuan, for he was an intriguer of the first magnitude. Later, it became known that he had planned to elevate himself to the vacant throne of China and had thereby become a front for Japanese schemers, who watched him closely and knew how to exploit his weaknesses. To stiffen her grip on the young republic, Japan used still another method. Knowing only too well how badly Peking was in need of money, Tokyo generously offered her assistance. She financed the construction of a number of railways by the Chinese in Manchuria—only to foreclose when the latter failed to pay back the loans. In her ardent desire to help, Japan went far beyond the actual requests of China and forced on her the so-called Nishihara loans to the amount of one hundred million dollars in gold. A considerable part of this money disappeared in the bottomless pockets of various warlords and other grafters of the old order. Three years after the Chinese Revolution, Japan took advantage of the involvement of the other Powers in the World War to present the infamous Twenty One Demands, which, if accepted, would make China practically her vassal.

Nineteen hundred and twelve was a troubled year for Japan, both at home and on the continent of Asia. In her newly acquired colony, Korea, things were not going smoothly either. In January, an attempt on the life of Terauchi was discovered. Rumors persisted that it was staged by the Japanese authorities themselves. But, be that as it may, the terror became still more widespread. In the summer of the same year the Emperor Mutsuhito, or Meiji Tenno, as he was more commonly called, died. His heir, Yoshihito, was not a promising successor. He was a sick man and was said to possess neither a keen mind nor any great talents.

By this time I was already back in Khabarovsk, having completed my two years' commission by passing the examinations at the Institute of Oriental Languages at Vladivostok. After the examination, Professor Spalvin, the best Russian authority on Japanese, complimented me on having demonstrated that in two years of hard work in Japan itself one could learn the language well enough not only to speak it fluently, but also to read and write. The highly flattering opinion of Professor Spalvin was published in the Order of the Day of the Military District Headquarters, and it was my best reward for the two years of really strenuous work.

The Institute of Oriental Languages at Vladivostok was founded to meet the need for preparing specialists on the neighboring eastern Asiatic countries. The students were both civilians and officers; as the name of the Institute implies, the teaching of languages was its most important, though by no means its exclusive, concern. The history, economic geography, jurisprudence, religion, philosophy, and art of China and Japan, and, to a lesser extent, of Korea and Mongolia, were also studied. The curricula being so extensive, the students had difficulty in mastering the languages to the point of speaking them fluently. Furthermore, out of four years at the Institute they were allowed to spend only about three months each summer in the countries of their special study—a quite inadequate period. The consequence was that, though they always had a good general background and usually quite a satisfactory theoretical knowledge of the language, few among the alumni of the Institute were good interpreters.

So, partly as a result of my success, it was decided to try another method. Each year a group of officers was attached to the Institute for eight months to acquire a rudimentary acquaintance with the language they intended to study abroad. Then, after an examination, they were sent for two years to the countries of their choice, to study the language "on the spot." I had to supervise the work of these officers for two years and took part in examining them before and after their stay abroad. The results were definitely satisfactory and in the main better for our needs. The full-time alumni of the Institute, being much better educated and capable of occupying responsible positions in the Far East, where solid knowledge of things Asiatic was important, were not anxious to become mere interpreters, even if they qualified as such. Naturally, those who stayed abroad after graduation mastered the languages and were then superior to the "erzatz" which we produced by a more simplified method out of a less specifically educated personnel.

Back at Headquarters, I was expected to use my newly acquired knowledge, and was therefore appointed Assistant Chief of the so-called Division of Military Statistics, or Intelligence. In the absence of its chief the full work fell on my shoulders. This included getting out a weekly magazine called *China and Japan,* which was a sort of digest of the newspapers, in six languages and in various countries, dealing with the Orient. Each of the ten officers on its staff was a linguist, and each was responsible for a number of papers in two or three languages. My duty was that of chief editor. This was for me the beginning of a long association with literary work concerning the Far East.

CHAPTER VIII

RUSSIA AND THE FAR EAST

(*Chauvinism and Patriotism*)

Journalism without romance. Intelligence service as an adventure. Dangerous collaborators. I offer my resignation, but am asked to remain. Traveling in China, Manchuria, Korea, and Japan. Pamphlets. Rivalry between the military and civilian authorities. The Chinese coolies. The Korean farmers. The Japanese "barbers." The Russian interests in the Far East. The tiger hunters. Affaire Beilis. Minister of War Sukhomlinov's visit. Translating the Japanese History of War. Trip to western Europe. Back to Khabarovsk. In Japan. War is declared. Volunteering for the front. On the way to the front.

MY EDITORSHIP OF the weekly *China and Japan* was a tedious affair. It was journalism without romance. Being simply a digest of clippings from various newspapers, it offered no scope for creative work. There were no editorials to be written, no comments to be added. It was simply one of the methods of recording events in, and information about, Russia's neighbors in Eastern Asia.

The intelligence service is pictured in fiction as a mélange of slinking adventuresses in black velvet stealing documents from men captivated by their feminine charms, dangers lurking in every corner, secret meetings in the dark, messages slipped under tables, daggers, pistols, and endless complicated stratagems. Actually it is apt to be a fairly routine matter of amassing information, and we had had several quite above-board ways of doing this. One was to send the members of our staff on periodic personal visits to the countries in which their interests lay. I myself made numberless short or long trips to various parts of the Far East for this purpose.

One such trip, covering about two months, took me through China, Manchuria, Korea, and Japan. I started from Khabarovsk in December, 1912, and returned late in February, 1913. And true to the traditions of melodrama the agents of the Japanese secret service were on the alert. They followed me from Tsuruga to Tokyo, and south to Nagasaki. I met them again when crossing from China to Korea, and their touching interest in me continued right up to the Russian border. So the trip did have its funny side, for in point of fact it had been educational rather than otherwise; and I had, moreover, long ago made up my mind that there were so many sources of information open for public study to be exhausted first, that it would be ridiculous to plunge into a fantasy of conspiracy. In short, the chief element of adventure in intelligence work to me has always been that it takes a certain amount of ingenuity to find material of interest. As for the nature of my "espionage" on this trip, it may be judged by the fact that the high lights of my report were a description of the means of communication in Korea and a discussion of the status of the railways in China. Both these dissertations were published in pamphlet form, introducing me in yet another capacity to the then very limited circle of Russians who were writing on Far Eastern topics.

Soon after my return to Khabarovsk I was made Chief of the Division of Military Statistics, my predecessor having been promoted to a higher post. Now in addition to our service, which was devoted to collecting information about neighboring countries, there was a division whose activities were directed toward preventing other nations from learning too much about our military and other arrangements. The head of this division was an officer of the gendarmerie. One day I received from him a communication in which he requested any information available about a certain officer in Vladivostok. I wrote in reply that "nothing is known in my division about the person in question, for the simple reason that it is not its function to watch the officers of our Army," and returned the communication to the sender.

Next day, to my astonishment, I was summoned by the Chief of Staff and, in the presence of the General in charge of all the officers of the General Staff in the Far East, was asked to explain the meaning of this written comment. The Chief of Staff, before coming to Khabarovsk had been in the corps of the gendarmerie and was, apparently, piqued by the supposed implication that the role of the gendarmerie was to spy on officers. I replied that I did not see how it was justifiable for officers to spy on one another. The General then produced the text of the oath and asked if in my opinion there was no justification in it for ascertaining any danger to the regime in whatever place and circumstances? My answer was that I remembered the oath very well, and this was exactly why I thought that officers of the Army, who are bound by the oath, should be above suspicion. I was wrong, of course, but so deep was my conviction that we officers could not be anything but loyal that I was disgusted by the interference of the gendarmes.

Seeing that I was furious and, apparently, to appease me, the Chief asked if I had heard the story about the formation of the corps of gendarmes? Czar Nicholas I, when creating this new instrument for the protection of the regime, had dramatically handed to its first chief, Count Benkendorf, a clean handkerchief, with the words: "Here is the idea of your duty; you have to dry the tears of those who suffer, protect the innocent, and expose the schemers against the welfare of the country."

Such was the story. Actually, the gendarmes were anything but protectors of the innocent and friends of the suffering. They represented the worst in the regime, were generally hated by the people, and were not received in the "best society." Even in the officers' clubs, they were not always welcome. But there was no use debating the question with my Chief, even if one forgot discipline; so we parted. He was satisfied that he had reprimanded me and had given me a lecture on the virtues of his beloved gendarmes. I was determined to resign.

Immediately after returning to my office, I addressed a petition, according to the rules, to His Majesty, asking for permission to leave the service, and sent it to my superior. But he summoned me to his office and assured me in most friendly terms that I should not take the matter so seriously. It was obviously a misunderstanding. I was considered one of the best officers, a valuable asset to the General Staff, and therefore to my country. Would I not reconsider? So I withdrew the petition and remained at my work. But my opinion of the gendarmes was not improved by this experience.

It was not a healthy state of affairs, of course, that the component parts of the administrative machinery of Russia should not be willing to co-operate. But this malady was widespread. Sometimes it was the result of rivalry between various departments, sometimes between the civilian and military elements. And sometimes it was such as to produce a smile. Among the numerous holidays there were a large number devoted to the glorification of the Imperial family. The birthdays and saints' days of the Czar and Czarina, the heir apparent and the Dowager Empress, the anniversary of the coronation and that of the ascension to the throne, were all celebrated by special church services and military parades. I remember well how particular Governor General Gondatti and the Commander of the Military District, General Letchitzky, were about their place in the church on such occasions. Neither one would tolerate seeing the other step even an inch ahead of him. But there were less amusing and more harmful examples of these conflicts over precedence, for these two very intelligent and otherwise reasonable representatives of bureaucracy were sometimes almost at loggerheads over issues of policies. One particular case of that kind, I remember, was the issue of the Chinese coolies.

The Chinese coolies were the recognized source of cheap labor, but at that time it was considered desirable to stimulate the Russian migration to these regions and curb the influx of foreign elements. Unfortunately, the Russian colonists were slow in coming to the Far East, as the government subsidies were inadequate and hardships of pioneering in this rigorous climate and virgin land were uninviting. But the Chinese coolies from Manchuria were willing to come even for a short time and work for very little. The numerous Koreans settled on Russian territory were less unwelcome; most of them were truck farmers, and they were allowed to stay. Japanese were less numerous, but too many of them were "barbers" or "watchmakers," who were suspected—in most cases wrongly—of being agents, if not officers, of the Japanese General Staff. Hence the military authorities wanted as few Japanese residents as possible. They had no objections to the others, though some disapproved of encouraging immigration by the Chinese.

Russia's main interest in the Far East at that epoch was to keep her possessions intact. Though relations with Japan had improved, the annexation of Korea had made Nippon a next-door neighbor, and Russia was somewhat nervous about possible encroachments. In regard to China, our policy at that time was concentrated on north Manchuria, where the Chinese Eastern Railway continued to be nominally a joint possession, though actually under the control of Russia. Harbin was for all practical purposes a Russian city.

Further to the west the Russians were active in Mongolia, whose independence from China they recognized in 1911. The ties with Mongolia were strengthened by a series of treaties, and there were military instructors and political advisers at Urga, the capital. Unfortunately, this was not all. Behind the screen of official amity were several concessions, such as "Mongolor," for prospecting of gold, which had been acquired by Russian capitalists. In reality these concessions had hardly been exploited beyond the phase of inviting investment and of making extravagant promises to prospective shareholders. But those concessionaries were sharks looking for more prey, whatever the consequences to their mother country. At the same time they were the most aggressive chauvinists, advocating more audacity in dealing with Orientals; for otherwise, they said, the Orientals would consider us weak and make trouble.

But, generally speaking, the time of reckless chauvinism in the Far East had ended with the unfortunate war against Japan. A more sober attitude, dictated by truer patriotism, prevailed. Japan's real worth had been learned, and a repetition of silly adventures was sought neither by St. Petersburg, the press, nor the people. The atmosphere was incomparably healthier than in the prewar era.

The problems worked out in Far Eastern maneuvers and military games never included plans of aggression. They were strictly limited to the tactics of defense. And there was much work to be done in the Far East in this connection, for we ourselves knew little about our own territory. Indeed, a considerable part remained unexplored. One of the duties of the General Staff consisted, therefore, of exploring little-known portions of Siberia, and making maps and descriptions.

During one of these exploring trips in the northeast I happened to pass a night in a small town called Anutchino, in the house of a famous tiger hunter. He was one of a family of four brothers, all famous for their ability to catch tigers alive. A party of hunters used to surround a young tiger; and, when quite close to him, would unleash the hounds and rush him. One man, his arm bound in heavy toweling, then attempted to thrust his arm into the tiger's mouth. The fangs would not cut through the heavy wrappings, so the tiger would try again. Thus, the animal's attention is diverted to this one man. In the meantime the other hunters would close up and rope him. This method of catching wild animals was so unusual that, relating it many years later to some American friends, I realized, to my embarrassment, that they did not and would not believe it. Yet the story originally told me by local peasants has been confirmed time and again in the press, and not so long ago a Soviet film on the Far East recorded such a hunt on the screen.

At the end of this particular expedition, when passing through Spasskoye, the town where the first Far Eastern airdrome was built at that time by the Russians, I had one of my "narrow escapes." On my visit to the airdrome I was invited by one of the pilots to take a flight with him. I gladly accepted the invitation. After we landed, another staff officer asked the aviator to take him up too. The pilot and his second guest entered the cabin. The mechanic began turning the starter. But the motor refused to work. After several futile attempts, the pilot got out of his seat to investigate. The inspection showed that there was not a drop of oil left in the engine. In other words, had we stayed in the air a minute longer than we did, probably we and the plane would have been burned.

Officers of the General Staff, as a rule, took their duties rather seriously, and many were excellent workers. Yet our life in Khabarovsk was far from monotonous. There were countless social affairs: parties and balls, concerts, and plays staged by amateurs—for good companies of professional artists came to the Far East rarely. But there was no place for political discussions or for activities even remotely resembling politics.

Even so, we were perturbed for a while by a sensational trial which was going on in Kiev. This was the "affaire Beilis," one more case in which a Jew was accused of committing a murder for ritual purposes. It was perfectly clear to me that the whole business was just an attempt to excite the hatred of one part of the population against the other. There was no evidence, but only a very clumsily concocted fabric of lies, with policemen and a former prostitute as witnesses. But learned professors of theology were called as experts, and there was a compaign in the reactionary press to condemn Beilis at any cost. People were stirred up to a high pitch, pro and contra Beilis. I had several clashes with my colleagues, and a number of heated discussions, for I became quite convinced that the trial was a flagrant travesty of justice. However, soon our nerves returned to normal. The affair disappeared from the newspapers and was forgotten.

Excitement of a different kind was produced by the visit to the Far East of General Sukhomlinov, the Minister of War. He was a peculiar personality, an intelligent and able man, who at sixty-five continued to act like an irresponsible young cavalry officer. In later years, during the World War, he became involved in a series of scandals and was even accused of treason. Arrested by the Czar's regime, he was transferred to the fortress of Peter and Paul after the Revolution, but was finally released and allowed to leave the country. He was the man who boasted before the cannons started roaring that Russia was ready for an armed contest with Germany.

The story that went around at the time was that Sukhomlinov's arrival in Khabarovsk was just a stage on a money-making journey. It was said that the Minister was constantly traveling to increase his income, for which his wife always had some good use. Traveling expenses were calculated on the basis of so many horses per mile, and, in the case of a General and a Minister of War, naturally amounted to a fabulous sum. It was worth His Excellency's trouble to go as far as possible, and there was no longer distance to cover than the trip to the Far East and back. Nevertheless, I still cannot help thinking the visit had something to do with the general preparation for the conflict that was soon expected to break out in Europe. It was necessary to check on the eastern border of the Empire lest anything unforseen should happen to spoil the plans.

Since the Russo-Japanese War, the international line-up in the Orient had changed drastically. There was now no likelihood of any impending clash at this end of the Empire. Russia's advance in the Far East having been checked by Japanese arms with American financial backing, Great Britain had changed her policy toward the "bear that walks like a man." Now she temporarily needed Russia on her side in the coming contest with Germany. In 1907 a convention had been signed by London and St. Petersburg, and rapprochement begun. The Franco-Russian Entente, which in 1891-94 brought Paris and St. Petersburg together, was strengthened by a similar, though not identical, understanding with London, preparing the way for the World War.

So the strong probability was that Sukhomlinov was making a final inspection tour before reporting to the throne. But we were not told anything of the kind, and I have to confess that I had no idea at the time that war was impending. All we heard from the Minister was the necessity for speeding up work on the Vladivostok fortifications, and his satisfaction with the state of affairs in the Far East in general. True to his style, he vanished from our ken as quickly as he came. Soon we forgot all about his meteoric visit.

In point of fact I saw little or nothing of our preparations for war. I received a new appointment that took me completely away from the theater of events. I was asked if I would not be interested in supervising a projected translation of the history of the Russo-Japanese War, published by the General Staff of Japan. I accepted the call and was soon on my way to St. Petersburg in connection with this tremendous undertaking. There were ten enormous volumes to this monumental work, and ten more volumes of appendices.

Early in December, 1913, therefore, I was again in the northern Palmyra, as one Russian poet has called our beautiful capital. My arrival coincided with promotion to the rank of lieutenant colonel.

In a few days I was summoned to a conference on the subject of the history and almost lost my chance of getting this very interesting job, through a risky remark reflecting on a statement uttered by the presiding general. Being very impatient by nature, I was tired by the long and seemingly useless discussion of details and impatiently asked the committee if they considered it at all useful to know the Japanese language when undertaking a translation. Fortunately, this was taken as a witticism, and the job was mine. As a matter of fact, there were only two other possible candidates. One was Samoyloff, our Military Attaché at Tokyo, whose command of spoken Japanese was above anything I could claim. But he did not know the written language, and, besides, could not be spared for this rather minor work. He was the best Military Attaché a country could desire and remained in Japan up to his death in 1916. The other candidate was an officer of the General Staff who had the same experience of Japan as myself. But he did not know enough ideograms even to undertake editing the translation made by others.

It was one thing to be approved for the appointment and quite another to get the appointment officially announced and the necessary appropriations passed and assigned. Christmas, a three-days' holiday in Russia, was at hand, and with the coming of New Year festivities no results could be expected before the end of January. Efficiency was not among the virtues of the Russian bureaucrats. So, instead of staying in St. Petersburg and waiting for the slow machine to start working, I decided to make a flying trip to western Europe. In a day or two I obtained the necessary permission and the passport, without which no Russian was ever allowed to leave the country.

Through the December snows I traveled to Abo, the westernmost harbor of Finland, took a night boat, and in the morning was at Stockholm, warm and smiling in beautiful sunshine. I then made my way through Oslo, still called Christiania, down to busy Hamburg, and through Belgium to Paris, the always alluring City of Light, old in history, yet incomparably young and gay. I was on a pleasure trip and did my best to enjoy myself. Unfortunately, the time at my disposal was short, and within a few days I was on my way back through Berlin and Warsaw. Upon arrival at St. Petersburg, to my pleasant surprise, the formalities were quickly arranged; and soon I was on the express train, with my family, hurrying back to the Far East. This time there was no interference from snow storms, and we arrived at Khabarovsk in some ten days.

The headquarters of my organization had to be in Khabarovsk because I needed a number of translators who were stationed there and could not be transferred far from the field of their special work. Another reason was that the Far Eastern affairs were of more direct concern to the Far Eastern Military District. Finally, it was considered desirable to have the organization close to Japan, for it was obvious that various questions would arise which could only be cleared up in Tokyo.

My staff consisted of six officers who were specialists in the Japanese language and two specialists in Chinese, for the maps of the Manchurian theater of war used Chinese names, and we needed Sinologues to transcribe them into the Russian. The entire arrangement was most advantageous to me. My authority was practically unlimited. I was allowed one trip per year to St. Petersburg, and as many as needed to Japan, with all expenses paid, besides a very generous salary and additional pay for the duration of this particular appointment.

The work itself was very interesting, and I was soon in it heart and soul. There was absolutely no time for anything else. I refused to attend any social functions, and I did not read anything for pleasure. I was working all day and a good part of the night. The results were encouraging. The translation went quite rapidly. In March I decided to go to Japan to check up on certain points. We stayed there for about a month. Early in the spring the first volume, over one thousand pages in octavo, was printed. But, when it came out, we discovered to our horror that a bad typographical error had been allowed to remain. The beginning of the war was dated 1905 instead of 1904. The Chief of Staff ordered a new sheet printed, and the entire work rebound and reissued. Expense was no consideration: "This was an official publication and must be perfect."

When the second volume was ready for the press, I made another visit to Japan. This was late in July, 1914. One night I was awakened by knocks at my door. Correspondents from metropolitan papers had come to interview me. What, they asked, was my opinion about Russia's chances in the war just declared by Austria? It was as big a shock and surprise to me as if they had announced that my hotel was on fire. I mentioned a few generalities to be considered in the situation, but was careful not to make any sweeping statements and to explain that I had been away from my country for a considerable time and lacked adequate information. The next morning I was on the front page, and the statements ascribed to me were so unlike what I had actually said, and so silly, that I had to ask our Embassy to intervene and demand a refutation. The refutation duly appeared, needless to say, in the smallest possible type and in the most inconspicuous place.

The same day I started homeward, but to reach Khabarovsk proved no simple matter. The Russian boats plying between Tsuruga and Vladivostok were not running, for German and Austrian warships were reported in the neighborhood; and I did not learn about it until I had already reached Tsuruga. Immediately I took another train for Shimonoseki, whence it was easy to reach Korea. There were daily boats for Fusan. But in Fusan I found that my money was no longer good. I was unable to change my rubles into the local currency. Fortunately the Russian Consul was home and proved more helpful and accommodating than the Japanese money-changers at the pier or the station.

So I reached Khabarovsk at last, after much delay, but without further inconvenience. At home I found my wife recuperating from pleurisy, an illness about which nothing had been written to me while I was in Japan. At the Headquarters I obtained a more authoritative account of the war situation than the newspapers could provide and immediately asked to be sent to the front. However, it was about three weeks before I was allowed to leave for Petrograd, as the Czar had just rechristened the capital. German names had suddenly become unfashionable—even for cities.

On my arrival in Petrograd, I was attached to the Headquarters of the General Staff and put on the list of candidates to be sent to the front when a vacancy should occur. Meanwhile I was assigned to deciphering the most secret of the dispatches coming from the front and from the foreign governments. It was not exciting work, but informative. Unfortunately, by that time the tidings of brilliant Russian successes, that marked the opening of the war, had given place to news less encouraging. Our French allies were retreating, and the Germans were steadily advancing through Belgium straight on Paris. Our own troops, mobilized in an unexpectedly short time and generally without much friction in the execution of the plan, were now becoming entangled in red tape and bureaucratic inefficiency. Some regiments lacked vital equipment, others were calling for trains to transport units somehow left behind. Some demanded explanations for instructions issued and then altered or modified. The Headquarters of the General Staff offered a sad picture; most of the personnel was away, at the front, for practically all were attached to the Headquarters of the Supreme Commander. Those who remained in Petrograd were few and overburdened with work which was poorly organized. I was anxious to get away from this distressing spot, and my turn came after the Tannenberg tragedy.

CHAPTER IX

THE WORLD WAR

(*Universal Cataclysm*)

The whats and whys of the World War. Rapid mobilization. Russian cavalry occupies East Prussia. S.O.S. from France. The sacrifice at Tannenberg. Successes on the Austrian front. Bedlam called Army Headquarters. Our Tenth Army again occupies part of East Prussia. Marggrabowa. A soldier with woman's shoes. Pianos are made of wood. My new assistants. A lucky visit to the trenches. Bad news: no guns, no ammunition. Conscripts with no rifles.

MANY AUTHORITIES HAD predicted a European war long before its actual outbreak. They said it was inevitable because the conflict of interests of various countries under the existing system seemed to exclude a peaceful settlement. Indeed, the economic rivalry of the parties interested in obtaining control over markets and raw materials had long ago prepared the way by bringing about the formation of two opposed groups of countries: the Triple Alliance and the Triple Entente. In 1891, Germany, Austria-Hungary, and Italy had renewed their Alliance, which would have expired the following year, to counterbalance the rapprochement between Russia and France. The renewal of the Triple Alliance served in its turn to bring Great Britain into line with France and Russia to form the Triple Entente.

The two main centers of rivalry were the Balkan Peninsula, which held a key to the so-called Eastern Question, and Alsace-Lorraine and the Saar basin, with their rich ores. Colonial aspirations and rivalry in sea power were contributory factors. But the immediate chain of events which led up to the universal conflict originated in southeastern Europe. The annexation by Austria of Bosnia and Herzogovina in 1908, in which the Russian Minister of Foreign Affairs, Izvolsky, was outwitted by the Austrian, Aehrenthal, led to the Balkan Wars of 1911-13. These served as a sort of a rehearsal and preliminary check-up of forces. The following year the World War was on.

Who was responsible for setting fire to the European powder keg is immaterial to this narrative. There is no doubt that the war was in preparation for years, and that none of the Powers had remained aloof. If the actual outbreak of war took me by surprise, on account of my absorption in literary work, the idea of war was certainly no bolt from the blue.

The excuse for starting Armageddon was found in the assassination at Serajevo, on June 28, of the Archduke Franz Ferdinand of Austria by a young Serbian student. On July 23, Austria served an ultimatum on Serbia imposing humiliating demands. Serbia refused to accede, knowing that Russia and France were behind her; and the efforts of other Powers, Germany and Great Britain in particular, to pour oil on the troubled waters were as unsuccessful as they were half-hearted. Austria ordered a partial mobilization and declared war on Serbia on July 28. Russia retaliated; and on July 30-31, the Czar ordered a general mobilization. If he later made an attempt to countermand it, as was asserted, his reconsideration came too late. Belgium mobilized on July 31, Germany and France the next day, and on August 4, England followed suit.

On August 1, Germany declared war on Russia; two days later on France, and the next day on Belgium, which was neutralized and supposedly immune. When Germany asked Belgium to let the Kaiser's troops march through her territory and the latter refused, the Germans crossed through Belgium anyhow, to the echo of the now famous remark about scraps of paper. This was the signal for Great Britain to enter the war, too, in spite of her efforts to remain aloof as long as possible. Contrary to the assertion repeated by a number of students that Germany was not sure what England would do in case of war involving France, it seems definitely established that the General Staff of Germany, or von Moltke, at any rate, had long entertained no illusions about England's nonentrance into the war.

Russia's mobilization was accomplished with a speed quite unexpected by the Germans. As a result, the Russians, starting a lightning-like advance into German territory, soon occupied a considerable part of the province of East Prussia. According to the plan worked out in

1905, after the Russo-Japanese War, by Count von Schlieffen, then the Chief of the German General Staff, Germany decided to concentrate her main effort on the French front, leaving a relatively small force on the Russian border. This strategy was based on the assumption that Russia had been weakened by the war with Japan and could not mobilize quickly because of the inadequate development of her railways. On the other hand, the German General Staff undoubtedly knew of Russia's plan, in case of war with Germany and Austria, to deploy her armies so as to deliver the main blow against Austria first and, after disposing of the latter, to strike at Germany.

The opening weeks of the war brought brilliant successes to the Russian armies. East Prussia was penetrated by the Czar's cavalry, after which the northeastern part was occupied by the army of Rennenkampf. After having defeated the bulk of the German forces near Gumbinen, the Russians were advancing toward the fortress of Königsberg. In Galicia, on the Austrian front, the Russians were developing a very successful thrust into the enemy's territory. At the beginning of the campaign, the Austrian troops, being ready before the Russians, crossed the Russian frontier, but were soon met by our oncoming armies. Superior in numbers and better equipped, the Austrians stopped our advance for a while; but day by day their attack weakened. Soon we were receiving reports of large numbers of prisoners being taken by our troops and of considerable amounts of war materials falling into our hands.

By August 21, the Russians were at Lemberg, or Lvov, as it is called by the Slavs, and before the end of the month they had occupied that important town. Early in September, notwithstanding the terrific fire of superior enemy artillery, the Russian troops crossed the swampy valley of the River San. The resistance of the Austrians was now broken. They continued to retreat, and the Russians advanced toward the Carpathian mountains and the fortress of Przemysl.

But on the German front a tragedy awaited the Russians at the end of August. While Rennenkamp's First Army was advancing in East Prussia, the Second Army, under General Samsonov, was being concentrated near the southern border of East Prussia. The plan was to close the pincers on the Germans with simultaneous attacks by Rennenkampf from the east and by Samsonov from the south.

At this time, after a short and unsuccessful advance by the French, the German drive to the west began to develop rapidly. Paris was being menaced. The French continued their retreat. The government was moved from Paris to Bordeaux. We were bombarded by the French General Headquarters with demands for help.

To ease the situation on the front of our Allies it was decided to start the pincers movement immediately. But it was too soon. Samsonov's army had not been completely concentrated; its rear was not fully organized. The advance was started with a gap of some hundred miles separating the First and the Second Armies; and there was almost no liaison between the two forces and their mutual Headquarters. The Germans, in the meanwhile, after the defeat of their troops at Gumbinen, had decided on a change of leadership. General Hindenburg, who was retired before the War, was appointed to command the eastern front, and Ludendorff was made his Chief of Staff. To reinforce their armies in East Prussia the High Command, on August 25, ordered the transfer of at least four regular infantry divisions, and some Landswehr and cavalry from the western front. This was the relief sought by the French.

But to help the Allies the Russians paid a ruinous price. Troops unprepared for such an operation had to be sacrificed. Paris was saved. The German attack was checked on the French front, but we paid for it dearly.

The German Command, having intercepted and deciphered the orders wirelessed by Samsonov, was able to set a trap. The splendid net of railroads made possible the quick maneuvering of fresh German troops. The battle started on August 28, near the town of Tannenberg. Being surrounded before achieving the concentration of their forces, the Russians suffered tremendous losses. Vast numbers were slaughtered or drowned in the near-by Mazurian Lakes. The remnants of two of Samsonov's army corps were taken prisoners. The battle of Tannenberg practically erased the brilliant beginning of the Russian campaign and turned it into a defeat.

Rennenkampf, whose dashing advance into East Prussia was already slowing down, having been performed without proper organization of its rear, now started a retreat. The German troops which had successfully fought Samsonov were presently pressing on Rennenkampf, and the latter was forced to evacuate the territory he had occupied in such a spectacular manner and to retreat to the Russian border. This was a severe blow to the morale of the Russian people. The eagerly awaited news from the front was read with tears in many eyes, and crowds who gathered on the corners to read the dispatches displayed on the walls were bitter in their criticism of our leadership.

At that time a new army, the Tenth, was being concentrated between the First and Second. Originally it had been designed as the reserve for the entire group, but this plan had miscarried with the movement that ended in the Tannenberg catastrophe. Now the Tenth Army had to take care of the entire front. It was with this army that my lot was shortly to be cast. For, when one of the young officers of the Tenth Army General Staff was killed while reconnoitering, the vacancy created by this sad casualty was offered to me.

Within a day or two I was on the train to Bielostok, where the Headquarters of the Tenth Army were supposed to be. Before reaching Bielostok, however, I learned that my destination was a small town, called Sokolka. With some difficulties, for there was no porter service and very little order at the station, I arranged for the unloading of my baggage, saddle and all, and was escorted to Headquarters.

From the very first it looked like bedlam. In an enormous hall, filled with smoke, long tables all around, sat the officers of the General Staff with the Chief at their head. Apparently they were working, or trying to work, while the Chief rushed from one to another and shouted instructions or whatever he wanted to shout. The Commander of the Army, General Pflug, wisely remained in the separate room adjoining the hall, for obviously the atmosphere was not conducive to calm thinking. But in a couple of days the shouting Chief of Staff was removed—I think to an insane asylum. His successor arrived, Headquarters were moved to a near-by monastery, and sanity was restored, making work possible. My assignment was to the Division of Operations, and I was made Assistant to its Chief.

As the concentration of our troops progressed, the Tenth Army prepared to resume the advance interrupted by the calamity at Tannenberg. By early October the Grand Duke Nicholas Nicolaievich, the Generalissimo, had amassed seven armies under his command and ordered a general offensive. The man power of the country was so enormous that even such heavy losses as those suffered in East Prussia were easily replaced at once. The preparation of the Tenth Army was carried on under new leadership, General Sivers replacing Pflug as our Commander. And a few days after this change I was made Chief of the Division of Operations.

The advance began. Soon the Germans were retreating before the Russian "steam roller"—to use the foreign catch phrase of the moment—and we re-entered East Prussia. Our Headquarters moved accordingly to Marggrabowa, a clean little town which we found practically abandoned by the inhabitants. Only a very few quite old men and women, who were unable to move, remained. The rest had been ordered out by the German authorities or had voluntarily left for the interior.

I remember an episode which occurred on the first day we were at Marggrabowa, which may serve as an illustration of the peculiar psychology of wartime. Looking out of the window of our quarters into the backyard, my Chief, Baron Boodberg, observed a soldier busily repacking his knapsack. This soldier was an elderly man called to arms from the reserves. Throwing out of the sack some of his own things, he tried to pack in two pairs of woman's shoes. Boodberg was indignant, for those shoes had obviously been stolen by the soldier somewhere in the town. He wanted to call in the "marauder" for an explanation, to be followed, undoubtedly, by a severe punishment. But I suggested that he consider the matter from another point of view. The man was not a thief, I argued, but in his primitive, illiterate way had most likely considered it the conqueror's right to get some booty—especially as the owners had run away, leaving everything behind unprotected. Besides, the very articles taken showed, in a rather touching way, that the man was not selfish. He had not stolen anything for himself but obviously wanted to send something to his wife or daughter. Most likely they had never owned such things as shoes, and almost certainly they had never had such elegant footgear as that which he was now packing for forwarding to his beloved ones. Moreover, to make room he was even now throwing away articles of his own, whose absence he might regret later. Boodberg, who was a very kindhearted man, left the office without doing anything to the "marauder."

War is a peculiar time, and morality a relative conception. It is said, even of ordinary times, that when a man steals a loaf of bread, being hungry, he is a thief; when he appropriates a thousand dollars from funds entrusted to him, he is an embezzler; but when he makes a million by "clever" machinations, he is a highly respected financier. One should not, I think, be too harsh with soldiers living under constant threat of death, even when they do things which would be considered criminal under the normal conditions of community life. On the other hand, lawlessness which leads to the breaking of discipline cannot be tolerated in time of war. Strict military discipline is indispensable; and, of course, looting or any other forms of abuse of the civilian population, which are apt to occur in the unhealthy atmosphere of war, will lead to deplorable results if they go unchecked. So there are times when those in command have to be severe. But at the same time it is necessary to be very sensitive to the unusual psychology that is produced at the pathological time called war. Leniency should be exercised when there is no danger of contagion in criminality, and extreme caution taken in the evaluation of individual acts.

While in East Prussia, for example, I heard of several cases when soldiers had used pianos for firewood. Many people did not hesitate to call this vandalism; they condemned the perpetrators as barbarians. Again I was not so sure. It was too bad, of course, that pianos or any furniture should be destroyed to keep a few men warm. But they were cold and could find no other kindling. Moreover, they were men who had been torn out of their homes and brought to kill other people whom they had never known before and with whom they had no quarrel. They might themselves be killed today or tomorrow. Some of them had never seen a piano, did not know what it was good for, and looked on it simply as a piece of furniture made of wood. Why should they be so particular about the property of those who left the town? Was it not now occupied by these soldiers at the risk of their own life? I do not mean to say that everything is permissible during war. Far from it. I merely say that those in command should not forget that war breeds very peculiar attitudes; and in this connection it is well to recall that the overwhelming majority of soldiers remain quite humane in spite of the horrors around. Sometimes they are more humane during a war than they are at time of peace. Often one sees amidst the horrors of war the most touching demonstrations of man's warm-heartedness, unselfishness, readiness to help others even at personal risk, and strict adherence to accepted moral principles. The crying need, in short, was to prevent, not punish, vandalism. What had been done could not be regarded as a crime.

Soon after our arrival at Marggrabowa, I received a new assistant. General Boodberg had become Chief of Staff, and until the arrival of his successor my duties included not only those of Chief of the Division of Operations, but some of those of the Quartermaster General. There was plenty of work, and an additional aide was welcome. The newcomer was Captain Verkhovsky, a young man with an unusual career. While still in the Corps of the Imperial Pages he had demonstrated in no uncertain terms his sympathy with the cause of the people against the upper-class privileged groups. For this "crime" he was sent to a remote regiment as a private. Later he received a commission as First Lieutenant. In a few years, after graduation from the War College, he was assigned to a Brigade of Sharpshooters stationed in Finland; and since the beginning of the War he had been on the front in East Prussia. During a battle in the very first days of the War he was badly wounded while performing an act of valor that gained for him the Cross of St. George, the highest award for bravery in Russia under the Czars. While still recuperating from his wounds, he asked to be sent back to the front and was assigned to our Staff.

This was the same Verkhovsky, who, after the February Revolution of 1917, became Minister of War in the Kerensky Cabinet and asked me to be his Assistant.

While in Marggrabowa, I became very friendly both with Verkhovsky and with Riabtzeff, a young officer of the General Staff who came with the new Commander, Sivers. The latter considered him, and rightly so, as an exceptionally able man. After the February Revolution, Riabtzeff became Commander of the Moscow Military District. We three easily found much in common, for we were all deeply interested in the fate of our mother country and seriously worried by events at the front. I learned only later that Riabtzeff was active in the political life of the country, and, apparently, belonged to the party of the Social Revolutionaries. Poor man, he met his death soon after the Bolshevik Revolution, while fighting for the Provisional Government, whose mistakes and impotence he fully realized.

After the retreat of the Germans and our reoccupation of East Prussia in the late fall of 1914, our troops were ordered to dig in; and for a while we remained on the same line in trenches, though the other Russian armies were still fighting the Germans in Poland and the Austrians in Galicia. I was of the opinion that this inactivity of such a large number of troops was ill-advised. In order to check some of my contentions about the desirability for an offensive, I personally made reconnaissance on various parts of the front. Once, while in the Twenty-second Army Corps, I asked its chief engineer to accompany me to the trenches and show me where, in his opinion, the German fortifications were less solid and, possibly, open to our attack. We went in an automobile to a certain point and then continued to the trenches afoot. At that period the Russian troops had only just begun receiving barbed wire, and many sectors still remained untangled, leaving free passages through the line.

Walking through a field, we suddenly noticed that a few steps ahead were Germans, looking at us curiously over the crest of their trenches. No one fired. But, naturally, we hastened to a near-by hut, a sort of a dugout. On entering, we found a number of German civilians, some of them wounded, with women and children around.

Coffee was ready, and the inhabitants of that strange hiding place even offered some to us. We declined it, of course, and left immediately without encountering any protest. Why the Germans in the trench did not shoot, is hard to say. Most likely the soldiers on this particular sector were instructed not to open fire without their officers' order, and there was no officer around at the moment. It was certainly a very narrow escape! I did not even ask my guide how it was possible that he, the chief engineer, and responsible for the fortifications, apparently did not know the line of trenches on his own front? How was it possible to bring me right up to the enemy's line? Probably he considered it improper to give me a warning and thought that it was part of my plan to go as far toward the enemy's trenches as possible; and he was not willing to give me the impression that he was afraid. Anyhow, on my return to Headquarters, I was able to give them information which they themselves had not obtained before. The result was that the Chief of Staff reported my "bravery" to Army Headquarters, though there had been none, and I was duly decorated. I had not intended to put my head into the lion's mouth. It had simply happened. It was one of the many cases where an award for bravery was made without any real justification. I had been decorated because the Germans had been nice to me.

In the middle of November, Hindenburg obtained fresh troops from the west, and he was now pressing on the other sectors of the Russian front. By December 15, he had succeeded in pushing our troops which were operating in Poland back to the River Bzura. But the goal of the Germans, Warsaw itself, was not reached, thanks to our resistance and the role played by the old fortress, Ivangorod, which protected the approaches to the River Vistula, on which Warsaw is situated. From that time on most of our armies were forced into trench warfare, as our supply of munitions was almost exhausted, and not enough had been produced as yet to replenish it. Even our armies on the Austrian front were ordered to dig in, though they were still advancing near Cracow.

Once, when returning at dawn to the Headquarters of the Twentieth Army Corps after a night encounter on its sector, I observed an amusing scene. In my group was a young cavalry officer whom I knew as an incorrigible snob. A scion of an aristocratic family, he rarely condescended even to talk to those who were inferior to him in social standing. Obviously he had exhausted his reserve of cigarettes; and the other officers who were with us also had none. I, being a nonsmoker, was unable to accommodate him either. But one Cossack behind him was still smoking. He was a big, bearded fellow, apparently not too finicky in the matter of hygiene. He had rolled his cigarette with some *mahorka* and a piece of newspaper. This *mahorka* was made of the cheapest tobacco, whose smoke was reputed capable of killing not only flies but, as people jokingly said, even larger animals. It was a hard decision for that young man to make, but his longing for a smoke was so strong that he finally turned to the Cossack and asked him for a puff. The Cossack gladly passed him the butt of his cigarette. I had a hearty laugh at the young snob, but I am not certain that this experience helped to cure him of his disdain for what the English call the Great Unwashed.

Before the end of the year rumors began to be heard that not only were the munitions slacking off, but that even rifles were not available to all new recruits. There were instances when recruits used wooden carbines for the period of training. Reinforcements were often sent to the front without rifles. And a little later our artillery received orders to economize on shells to such an extent that replying to the fire of the enemy was forbidden.

In other words, Sukhomlinov had lied when he had boasted: "We are ready." We were very far from ready. Reforms which had been started in the Army in 1910, in accordance with the lessons drawn from the war with Japan, had not been completed. The supply of arms and ammunition was short because the needs had been miscalculated. The result was that already by the end of 1914—that is to say, less than four months after the outbreak of hostilities—the Russian troops were in a tragic situation. The fault lay partly in the fact that estimates of the requirements had been based on the figures of 1904-5, when artillery did not use "barrages," that required such terrific amounts of munition. But it also lay partly in the belief of those responsible for the drawing of plans that modern war could not last long, considering its effect on the economic life of the nation. They therefore found it undesirable to overproduce munitions. Another explanation was corruption. Not all of the money appropriated for defense was actually used for preparedness. To be sure, not all the blame lay with the government. A great number of rifles were abandoned by soldiers in panic. Enormous amounts of war material were lost in retreats and captured by the enemy. Yet St. Petersburg had been able to ship to Serbia seventy million cartridges in December, 1914, when the demands of her own troops still remained unsatisfied.

Russia's industry, incomparably less advanced than that of the other great powers, was unable to cope with the new task of producing munitions on a large scale. And the delivery of replenishments from abroad, even if the Allies had been able to spare any, was rendered impossible by Turkey's entrance into the war on the side of the Central Powers. In December, the Turks struck on our Caucasian front, and though they suffered a defeat that developed into a disaster for Enver Pasha at Sarakamysh, the Black Sea route to the Mediterranean remained closed at the Dardanelles. The northern route was menaced by the German submarines. For a while we were almost cut off from our Allies.

CHAPTER X

THE WORLD WAR

(*The Decisive Years*)

An abortive offensive. Retreat to Grodno. The colonel who was a German spy. Renewal of advance. Visitors. Success on the Austrian front. The Germans intervene. The Vilna operation. Czar in the role of Supreme Commander. Government against the people. Our Allies again ask for help. I am summoned to the Czar's Headquarters. On my way to France.

LATE IN JANUARY, 1915, I renewed my argument for ending a demoralizing inactivity which, in my estimation, was not justified by the supposed weakness of the opposing Germans. Boodberg, very cautious by nature, opposed me. The Commander of the Army, Sivers, was inclined to accept my point of view. Finally, he agreed to let me take a considerable number of troops on a reconnoitering trip through the so-called Johannisburg Forest, which was on our left flank. Accordingly, orders were issued to the general in command on that flank to make all the necessary preparations, and I was given a special train to go there.

I arrived late in the evening, had a conference with the commanding general, and decided to start the next morning at four o'clock. My detachment, consisting of infantry, artillery, and Cossacks, was ready as agreed, and we began our march through the forest. No Germans were seen. But, as our patrols emerged on the farther side of the forest, they were met by fire. Before long our artillery also was fired on by that of the enemy, and a battle ensued.

While riding through the woods, I was suddenly met at a crossing by a young deer, obviously bewildered by the cannonade. Its innocent eyes stared at me as though demanding to know why human beings should kill each other in these woods where no animal is allowed to be killed by hunters.

After about two hours of fighting, we were quite convinced that the German forces on this sector were much larger than we had expected. That was all we needed to find out, and I ordered a return to the village from which we had started that morning.

While the battle was on, I had another narrow escape. At one and the same moment, the commander of the battalion, who was on my right, had his cap pierced by a shot, while the orderly, on my left, was killed by a bullet through his forehead. My place in the middle was, apparently, enchanted.

After a good night's rest, I started back to Headquarters. The weather was not promising. It was windy and bitterly cold, and soon after we had started we were in a terrible snow storm. The train was forced to stop several times. At one of the stations I received information that the Germans had begun an offensive and were advancing on a wide front. Our troops on the left flank were retreating. So now at all costs I must reach my destination before the road was cut. Fortunately, the train managed to plow through and brought me safely to Marggrabowa.

At Headquarters I learned that the report was well founded. On February the seventh, the Germans launched their new operation. They were advancing along our entire front, with an enveloping movement on our right flank. Their numbers were far in excess of our most liberal estimates at that time, and already the resistance of our troops was weakening. Sivers considered withdrawing to a line nearer the fortress of Grodno and gave orders to move Headquarters to Suvalki. Late in the evening of the day after my return, we entrained. On our way, the train was derailed, but without any casualties. Late at night we arrived at Suvalki. Soon it became obvious that our lines had collapsed and the troops were beating a somewhat hurried retreat. The liaison with the Twentieth Army Corps was broken. Reports from the left flank were irregular too. So Boodberg resolved to find out personally what was going on. Sivers decided to move with the Staff to Grodno, leaving me at Suvalki. This was absurd, but not until Prince Kourakin—who represented the Red Cross—interfered, did Sivers change his order and send me word to join the Staff at once.

At this point, it is probably better to return for a while to the story of my reconnoiter in the Johannisburg Forest. Not until much later did we learn why the Germans had increased their forces near that forest, and how they were able to time their advance to the exact moment when we were contemplating ours. At the village from which I started there was stationed a certain Colonel Miassoyedov, whose duty was counterespionage—that is, to watch the German spies and prevent them from acquiring information about our troops and internal situation. This Colonel had served in the gendarmerie and had some strange escapades to his "credit." But he was a close friend of the family of General Sukhomlinov, then Minister of War, and, in spite of certain doubts about his reliability, he was appointed to our Headquarters. Baron Boodberg, knowing of his record, wished him out of the way and decided to send him to this seemingly unimportant place on our left flank. The day I arrived, Miassoyedov was out hunting in the forest. This "hunting" expedition cost us very dear. Apparently he had informed his German friends about our plans; and this not only enabled them to increase their forces and vigilance on this side of our line, but induced them to throw their reinforced troops up on the opposite end of our positon. The Colonel, in short, was a German spy. Later he was court-martialed and executed.

After our arrival at Grodno, we learned that the Twentieth Army Corps had been outflanked by the Germans and was now cut off from the rest of the Army. Around midnight Boodberg returned in a state of great excitement and made his report about the troops on the left flank. He was very pessimistic in his evaluation. But, as it happened, there was no real danger—first, because the main blow of the Germans was directed against the opposite end of the front, and, secondly, because on that flank we had the Third Siberian Corps under a very able Commander, General Radkevitch. We established connection with Radkevitch and found to our satisfaction that on his sector the German pressure was already diminishing.

Grodno was one of the best-equipped Russian fortresses, and, under the circumstances, not a likely object for an attack. Actually, the Germans were stopped by our restored lines a considerable distance from the forts. And a few days later we received reinforcements which enabled us to start a counteroffensive, which not only succeeded in recapturing considerable territory, but pushed the German lines back from the approaches to the forts. A fierce battle near Grodno, at a point called Hill 103, left enormous piles of Russian and German dead, of horses killed, and of material abandoned. Part of the Twentieth Corps which had succeeded in avoiding capture during the German general offensive passed through the Augustovo Forest and rejoined us. For a while our lines advanced, but not for long. The Germans dug in and offered strong resistance. The offensive was discontinued, and both sides resumed trench warfare.

The High Command was displeased with the leadership of Sivers, and his post was given to General Radkevitch. He was the third Commander of the Tenth Army in less than six months. Boodberg also was replaced; and a new Chief of Staff, Popov, was the fourth for the same short period. Both these men remained at their posts up to the time I left the Tenth Army late in 1916.

Another period of tedious inactivity now set in. There was not much work for the Staff officers. But, *"difficile in otio quies"* (quiet is difficult in leisure), and I used my spare time for reading. In the local bookstore I found a copy of the *Critique of Pure Reason* by Immanuel Kant. I read it through with much difficulty, though understanding very little, for my background in philosophy was almost nil. But I labored over it with interest nevertheless. I was much impressed by the way in which Kant reconciled Materialism and Idealism, for I was still under the spell of religion and full of romanticism. His "reality of things in themselves" was in tune with my mental set-up. Next I bought a copy of Max Stirner's *Ego and His Own,* and was rather disgusted by his exaggerated individualism, as in the past I had been by the works of Nietzsche. Somehow this glorification of the superman and the overestimation of the ego never appealed to me.

While staying in Grodno, we had a number of visitors. First the Grand Duke Andrey came for a couple of days. He was a very pleasant man of my age, a graduate of the Military College of Jurisprudence, well educated, open minded, and very reasonable in his judgments, which were usually somewhat tinted with the mild cynicism of a skeptic. I was flattered when he told me that he had heard me highly spoken of in the Stavka, the Headquarters of the Supreme Commander. Whether it was simply vanity or a yearning for approval I cannot say; but it aroused in me a kind of affection for the Grand Duke. This feeling remained unchanged, and I shall always think of him with certain friendliness. He was certainly a far more admirable character than his brother Cyril, who was the self-acclaimed Czar of All the Russias while living in France after the Revolution of 1917, and his brother Boris, of whom it was said that he would appear at any dinner in Paris on consideration of so many francs or dollars paid by those who wanted the "honor" of dining with a person of royal blood.

A number of foreign military attachés also visited our Headquarters. Usually I was assigned to go with them to inspect the troops, for I knew several languages and was better informed on the situation at the front, being in charge of its operations. One of the guests was the British General, Murray, who recognized me as the father of a "charming little girl," with whom he had played in a hotel at Tokyo. I was much embarrassed at having failed to recognize him first. One of the groups consisted of a dozen or so Japanese generals and officers. Naturally, I had to entertain and take them around, for there was no one else who spoke Japanese. At the end of their stay I tendered the group a banquet at which I spoke on the subject of "a friend in need is a friend indeed." The Japanese were allies in this war.

For a while the lull on our front was such that it was even possible for my wife and daughter to visit me at Easter. But although our Army remained stationary, the other Russian forces were seeing plenty of activity. Our men on the Austrian front were striving, under bitter winter conditions, to gain possession of the Carpathian Mountains and to reach the Hungarian plains, the granary of the enemy. By the end of March our troops captured the fortress of Przemysl, with a garrison almost twice as large as our besieging force, and took considerable amounts of war material.

Ludendorff, who advocated more attention to the eastern front, had for a long time wanted to check the Russian advance against the

Austrians. But Falkenhayn, the Chief of Staff of the Kaiser, refused to weaken the western line by shipping more troops to the east. Finally, he had to consent. The British army suffered considerable losses at Ypres and elsewhere. The French were inactive. So, early in May a large German and Austrian force under the command of General Mackensen broke through the Russian lines at the River Dunajec. We did not have enough guns and a very insufficient quantity of munitions. Our positions were not fortified strongly enough and had an inadequate supply of barbed wire. Besides, our reserves were not increased in time. Accordingly, Mackensen continued his advance for two weeks, pushing our armies back to the River San.

On May 15, Italy, the third signatory of the Triple Alliance, who had so far remained aloof, entered the war, but on the side of England, France, and Russia. The Austrians wanted to transfer part of their troops from the Russian front to that of the new adversary, but Ludendorff insisted on continuation of the successful attack started by Mackensen. By June 3, the latter retook the fortress of Przemysl, which we had not considered worth the sacrifice entailed by holding it. In three more weeks we were forced to abandon Lvov also. Again the Russian losses were tremendous—some four hundred thousand men—for they offered stiff resistance and retreated only after some units had lost up to eighty per cent of their personnel. But replenishments arrived quickly, and we were soon ready to start a counterattack on the Austrian front.

The spectacular success of Mackensen was not attained without much bloodshed. The Russians counterattacked several times and inflicted severe losses on the enemy. At Stryj they took almost twenty-five thousand Austrian prisoners of war and great numbers of guns and other war material. The Germans were temporarily compelled to retire to the right bank of the River Dniester, also with heavy losses.

After their success on the Austrian front, the Germans again turned their attention to Poland. With considerable forces at their command, they finally occupied Warsaw, for the Russian reserves were weak, and the arrival of reinforcements was delayed by the condition of the railroads. The situation in regard to ammunition was appalling, and no improvement was in sight. The High Command was anxious to economize on men and arms in anticipation of better times to come. By the middle of August, Poland was in German hands.

In September it was again the turn of our Tenth Army. Ludendorff had long been urging an enveloping movement through Vilna and Minsk, but so far had been unable to persuade the High Command to send more troops from the French front. Finally the reinforcements were sent, for on the western front neither the French nor the British felt inclined to attack. Generals Below and Eichhorn were charged with a combined thrust, one in the direction of Dvinsk and the other toward Vilna.

The operation was started on September 9. Realizing that our lines were weak, for the front was very long, the number of troops insufficient, and the artillery inadequate to stand the renewed pressure, it was decided to draw back our troops. Our Headquarters were moved from Grodno to Vilna, and the retreat was slowly begun along the entire front. The Germans tried to outflank us and concentrated on our right flank. Their cavalry broke through the gap between our Tenth Army and the First, which was on our right, and penetrated our rear, creating a panic. The moment was very tense. Reinforcements were promised but were delayed. Reports from other parts of the front sounded bad, and it was obvious that fear was growing. In our Headquarters practically everybody else favored general retreat at a high speed. I was against it; in my opinion there was no reason to be frightened by the spectacular raid of the German cavalry, which was clearly designed to demoralize our rear. We were in no real danger, I thought, so long as we remained calm. But it was necessary to check the panic by taking appropriate measures in the rear, and we were able to do this with troops coming from other salients. As for the attack of the German infantry, it was quite obvious that their main objective was our right flank. This brought me to the conclusion that on the front their forces must be limited and would become still weaker with the development of their operation. That he who outflanks is himself outflanked is a military axiom. I maintained that we should leave only a tiny thread of riflemen at the front, and withdraw as many as possible from each sector in order to create reserves. Then we should move the reserves, so formed, in the general direction of the northeast, in order to reinforce our right flank.

We had a long discussion of my plan, and practically everyone on the Staff was against me. I continued to insist, however, that my plan represented our only chance of escaping catastrophe. Finally I won over the Commander. My plan was accepted, and I immediately started the work of putting it into effect. One great difficulty was to prevent disorder in the rear through the movement of troops which had to cross the lines of communications of other units in order to reach their new sectors. The danger of this operation was especially serious because of the panic which had previously been created in the rear by the German cavalry.

My calculation proved correct. The Germans took little notice of what was going on before the center of their line. They failed to discover that we had left practically nothing at the front and were withdrawing most of our troops to use them as reserves on the right flank, which they were attacking. No disorder developed in the rear, thanks to the preventive measures taken. The German plan was crushed. Our troops were withdrawn without particularly heavy losses and occupied new positions where they were able to check the further advance of the enemy.

Our Army was safe. Now it could draw back from the net prepared by Ludendorff's stratagem. This was the greatest joy I ever experienced in my life. But the strain under which I worked during the Vilna operation almost resulted in driving me insane. I realized all too well the tremendous responsibility I was taking on myself by insisting on my plan in opposition to the rest of the Staff. But I was so certain it was right that I had to fight for it to the end. When entrusted with its application, I gave it all my energy, all my capacities. It actually became a question of life and death for me. As soon as it was reasonably clear that everything would turn out well, I almost collapsed. Other officers, watching me constantly, realized that it was time to get me away for a while and sent me for an automobile ride. In an hour or so, I was back and at work again.

The whole operation took several days. During that time, again and again we received requests from commanders to permit the withdrawal of their units. Each time we answered by the order to remain in the positions with which they were entrusted. Once, during the night, the demand came from the Corps of the Guards, who were stationed near our right flank. The answer was the same: "Stay where you are." This particular order I signed myself with the name of the Commander of the Army, who had long before authorized me to do so whenever necessary. Next day we had an unexpected visitor. Grand Duke Boris, who was in command of a Cossack Brigade of the Guards, arrived to plead in person for the withdrawal of the Guards. They might be needed in case of disorders in the country. They were the mainstay of the dynasty. And still the order was not changed. After the dinner, to which the Grand Duke was invited by the Commander of the Army, he was brought by him to my office; I was asked to explain the situation and why we insisted on a most stubborn defense of the positions occupied by all the troops, including the precious Guards. The Grand Duke was probably angry with me, but here he was a mere subordinate of the Commander of our Army. He had to comply with the order, even though he did not like it. Soon after the operation was over, the Guards were withdrawn. This at least was accomplished through the Grand Duke's pull, but not before the Guard had fulfilled its duty.

Finally, the retreat was checked. Our lines were reformed, and our Headquarters established on an estate near Minsk. They remained there, or in Minsk itself, for more than a year.

In appraising the Vilna operation, Captain B. S. Liddell Hart, the well-known English military expert, has written: "Ludendorff took the wise course of suspending operation in the face of stiffening resistance of the Russians and the menace to his isolated units from their concentrated forces."

For this operation my superiors recommended rewarding me with the gold sword for bravery and the insignia of St. George. But the St. George Duma, the Committee that decided on new candidates, rejected the plea, quite properly in my opinion, on the ground that no "bravery under fire of enemy" was demonstrated by me while working in the Headquarters. This was a *conditio sine qua non* for receiving this coveted decoration. Instead, I was awarded the "St. Vladimir on the neck," the highest order within reach of a colonel, for I already had all the others. A few months later I was awarded for the same Vilna operation the British Cross of St. Michael and St. George. Promotions and decorations were lavishly showered on us, the "privileged among the privileged," the Staff officers. But this old method of playing on people's vanity was widely used by all armies.

Now again for a long time we were doomed to inaction. Trench warfare was our lot through the entire winter of 1915 and most of the next year. Healing wounds, accumulating new strength, training more recruits, improving fortifications, rearranging positions—such was the business of the day. Only once in a while were we allowed to undertake reconnaissances with a larger use of artillery, when trying to break through the solidly fortified positions on the enemy, entangled by numerous lines of barbed wire. Usually the results of such engagements were quite insignificant. In most cases we simply ascertained that there were no important changes on the other side of "no-man's land." Sometimes we were able to take a trench or two, to advance our own line a few yards. Then once more we would be condemned to remain in the trenches day and night, under constant threat of being killed at any moment, for no lull could continue for ever.

Late in August an important change took place in our High Command. The Grand Duke Nicholas Nicolaievich was demoted to the Caucasian front, and the Czar himself became Commander in Chief in his place. This change was welcomed neither by the Army nor the people. The Grand Duke, though not a military genius, had been an able man, well versed in military matters, and was highly respected in military circles, in spite of his hot temper and occasional eccentricities. His leadership, marked by successes as well as failures, was not considered responsible for the prevalence of the latter, for it was well known that in most cases our misfortunes originated in errors committed before the War. Everybody realized by now how utterly unprepared the Army was, how criminal was the negligence of some officials and the corruption of others. Everybody knew that industrially Russia had been absolutely unable to cope with the demands created by the War, and that our defeats were the price we had to pay.

The Grand Duke was popular also on account of his plea to the Czar to grant the "Constitution" of 1905. He was known for his genuine patriotism, which he proved after the Revolution of 1917 by refusing to associate with foreign intervention in the internal affairs of his country, and by keeping clear of schemes placing him at the head of the movement for the restoration of the monarchy. The sudden change was privately explained as due to the alarm of the Czar and Czarina at the growing popularity of the Grand Duke. Rumor declared that they were afraid of a palace revolution and had decided to prevent it by exiling the possible rival to Caucasia.

There was no doubt whatever that Nicholas II was not a military leader. He was not a leader at all. Kind and pleasant when he wanted to be, he was not an able man. Those who knew him intimately never thought of him as capable of being more than a good colonel, the commander of a regiment. Neither his training nor his interests justified assuming responsibility for the Army at a critical moment. A man of no will power, Nicholas II would have been foredoomed as a military leader, even if he had been surrounded by the most gifted aides. General Alexeieff, his Chief of Staff, was an exceptionally good executive, an able man, and a hard worker, but he was not a military genius. And the outlook at the fronts was dismal. Even the vision of an inspired leader could not have triumphed over our lack of arms and ammunition.

Meanwhile the economic situation of the country was going from bad to worse, the mood of the people grew more and more unfavorable to the regime, and willingness to fight to a victorious end became a hollow phrase. Criticism of the situation as a whole was heard on all sides in the State Duma, as was condemnation of the Czar's action in assuming the Supreme Command. So he dissolved the Duma. This did not react in his favor either. But that did not matter. The government was obsessed with the determination to fight the increasing influence of the parliamentarians and of various civic organizations attempting to do their part in helping to win the War.

In my position as Chief of the Division of Operations I had nothing to do with the policies of the government. But because the Commander of the Army and our Chief of Staff had complete confidence in me and invited me to most of their conferences, I learned a great deal beyond my own field of work. Once they handed me a quite confidential communication from the Minister of the Interior, which opened my eyes to something I could hardly have believed possible. The confidential letter asked the commanders of the armies to take appropriate measures to check the influence which such organizations as the Red Cross, not to mention the representatives of municipalities, especially the *Zemstvos,*[1] were acquiring. Their activities were considered by the Minister of the Interior as harmful to the prestige of the government.

The underlying thought was clear enough. These civic organizations were offering diversified services to the Army, supplying food and other necessaries, tending the wounded, and helping the thousands of destitute refugees in ceaseless flight before the advancing enemy. And with this service the official organizations, hampered by red tape and plagued by corruption, simply could not vie. Yet this was no mere case of jealousy between competing organizations, each trying to gain the approval of the people. It involved as cynical an order as any government ever issued to its minions. To discourage comparisons unfavorable to the bureaucracy, to escape criticism for not doing as well as unofficial agencies were doing, this government of ours was willing to let soldiers suffer more hardships, experience scarcity in this and that, even perish for lack of timely help. What could one think of such a government? How anyone who loved his country and his people could fail to be indignant was beyond my

[1] *Zemstvos* were the voluntary social service organizations formed by local people, and representing various strata of society, though with predominance of the privileged classes. Their functions were centered on matters of welfare of the community, as building of roads, construction of hospitals, schools, and the like. In many instances they were composed of liberals and even sometimes of a sprinkling of radicals. The *Zemstvo* doctors, teachers, and social workers were known for their devotion to and faithful, disinterested work for the common people, but certainly they were not a "hot-bed of revolution."

understanding. I certainly wanted a change, and a change before it was too late.

Despite the many failures on the Russian front, our Allies, who so far had shown few encouraging signs of their fighting capacity, were constantly demanding that we renew our attack in order to secure relief for their own troops. Again and again the Russians proved obliging. In the early spring of 1916 we tried to ease the German pressure on Verdun by starting offensives on our northern and southwestern fronts. Unfortunately, without heavy guns and without sufficient supply of shells our artillery was unable to break the fortifications of the enemy, and no gains were registered. But once more we had done what our Allies asked. Yet this was not all. In spite of the lack of success attending this renewal of our offensive, in March we started preparations for another large-scale movement early in the summer.

This willingness of the Russians to do everything in their power—and often much that lay beyond their real power—has been publicly conceded by French and British writers in their various accounts of the World War. "Though badly lamed (not destroyed)," wrote Captain B. S. Liddell Hart in his article for the *Encyclopaedia Britannica,* "the Russian Army still was able to delay the full concentration of German strength for more than two years, until 1918."

In April, 1916, I was summoned to the Czar's General Headquarters, now removed to Mohilev. There I was given statistical and other material about our armies, our plans and preparations for the coming general offensive, data on our armaments and equipment, and on the various needs which we expected our Allies to meet, and ordered to proceed to France at once.

The evening before I left I was invited to dine with the Czar. Nicholas II lived at the Governor's house in an almost Spartan way. Everything was extremely simple, underlining the need of economy and restraint in time of war. Among those present were all the heads of the foreign military missions attached to the Imperial Headquarters, and I well remember with what easy grace the Czar made the rounds of his guests on entering the great salon, shaking the hand of each and stopping an additional moment to put a few questions to myself, the newcomer. The dinner was far less pretentious than those we were accustomed to enjoy at the Headquarters of the Tenth Army. No wines were served, only some vodka before the meal. Conversation was chiefly with one's nearest neighbor, though from time to time the Czar would interject some remarks, apparently designed for all, and other conversations would stop abruptly. After the dinner, the Emperor left. Passing near me, he smiled and wished me bon voyage and good luck in a most captivating way. He certainly knew how to charm people with his kindly smile.

In a few days I was on my way to France, traveling first by rail through Finland to the newly constructed station of Haparanda on the Swedish border. Next came Stockholm, Christiania, or Oslo, and Bergen. In Bergen I went to see our Consul to ascertain the arrangements for my crossing to England, and sailed from this port to Newcastle-on-Tyne. The rough passage, though otherwise uneventful, was not without its hazards. It was always possible that the Germans had been informed that an officer of the Russian General Staff was *en voyage* with data of extreme importance, in which case they might easily have boarded the ship and taken me as a prisoner of war. Indeed, even if they had boarded the boat without being apprized of my identity, they would have discovered it immediately upon inspection of the baggage. For this particular "courier of the Ministry of Foreign Affairs" had in his valise the complete military outfit of a colonel of the General Staff, with decorations and regalia to match.

After landing at Newcastle and passing a rigid examination by the British passport officers and other authorities, I was allowed to proceed to London.

CHAPTER XI

VISITING OUR ALLIES

(*An Unusual Escape*)

At London. Lord Kitchener. The Russian parliamentarians abroad. Reception at the Embassy. Experiences while in France. Visiting the fronts. "Papa" Joffre does not allow me to visit Verdun. Ambassador Izvolsky and General Jilinsky. My report at Chantilly. Legion of Honor. Versailles and the two audiences. Reviewing the Russian troops. Lunch with President Poincaré. Paris at the time of war. Back to London. How I escaped being drowned with Kitchener. Return to Russia. Another dinner with the Czar. Back to the front. A series of assignments. Appointment to Japan.

LATE IN THE evening of May eleventh, or nine days after leaving Russia, I arrived in London. Next morning I went to see our Military Attaché, General Yermoloff, who promptly introduced me to the Grand Duke Michael Michailovich, uncle of the Czar, who had lived in England for years, having been exiled by Alexander III for marrying without the Imperial consent. A goodhearted romantic, the Grand Duke was never considered brilliant, even by Romanov standards. I was interested to note that in talking with me he very obviously wanted to give the impression of absolute loyalty and devotion to His Majesty, the beloved Emperor, whose titanic work he professed so greatly to admire and for whose success he was constantly praying. He was worried, he said, by news coming from Russia. According to his information the people were becoming restless and dissatisfied with the government.

The following morning I had an audience with Lord Kitchener, then Minister of War to Great Britain. Having been informed of my mission to France and being particularly interested in the status of our armament, he showered me with questions. He proved thoroughly informed on the sad inadequacy of our arms. He knew that for a long time our artillery had had practically no shells and insufficient cannon; and, as an old soldier, he realized what it meant to stay in the trenches with no chance of answering the cannonade of the enemy, which our batteries had been obliged to do again and again. He wanted to know the present situation in regard to our supply of rifles, machine guns, and artillery, and expressed satisfaction at hearing that the situation had improved slightly. And in addition he wished to hear about the progress made by Russian industry in the production of various war materials. It was gratifying to know, he said, that the Russians were doing their best, though it was obvious that they still needed a great deal of help from abroad. He inquired about the spirit of the troops and that of the people at large and expressed a certain anxiety about internal conditions in Russia. Full well he realized that it was dangerous to impose on the patience of a people who were suffering as much as the Russians at that time. In short, Kitchener was genuinely and vividly interested in our conditions. He was so interested, indeed, that the audience lasted a full forty minutes. This was much longer than I could have dared to hope, knowing as I did how busy the War Minister must have been. The result was that when I emerged from his office I found in the adjoining room a long line of visitors waiting their turn and a long line of angry looks directed at my humble self.

My interview with Lord Kitchener left me with the impression that this tall, rather rough man with piercing eyes probably had a good heart, despite his record of severity in India and the Sudan. He was obviously worried about Russia, not merely as an ally in the common struggle, but as a human being who sympathized with the sufferings of other people.

On the evening of the same day I was invited to a reception held at our Embassy in honor of a group of members of the Russian Parliament. Several Senators and Delegates to the State Duma were on a trip to England and France for an exchange of information with the Allies. Among the members of the Lower House was Deputy Speaker Protopopov, who was destined to play an ignoble role in the days that preceded the Revolution of 1917, and Professor Miliukov, the future Minister of Foreign Affairs in the short-lived First Provisional Government. The reception was marked by that wartime restraint which was typical of England in those days. It could hardly be otherwise, for our Ambassador, Count Benkendorf, was correctness and tact personified.

These Senators and Members of the State Duma were the guests of honor. The Grand Duke was there, of course, but made it clear by his choice of partners for conversation that he was not particularly in sympathy with parliamentarism in his own country, however much he might respect it in England. He introduced me to his wife, who was a daughter of the Duke of Nassau by a morganatic marriage, and kept talking to me for a while, obviously to avoid the "nonmilitary elements." I was also privileged to meet a number of prominent English officers, headed by the Chief of Staff, General Robertson, a self-made man who much resembled a husky sergeant with his red cheeks and heavy mustaches, and was quite different from the aristocratic type of British officers I had known before the War. Among others, I again met my old acquaintance, the amiable General Murray, who invited me to his club. But, unfortunately, I was unable to avail myself of this invitation as I had to sail next morning for France.

I crossed the channel, via Folkestone and Boulogne, on a British warship. Though we passed behind the steel net which protected ships from the German submarines, we were ordered to wear life-saving jackets. This was not a particularly picturesque attire, but beauty was not the main consideration, even though there were on board two ladies, wives of French Ministers. Again the Germans paid not the slightest attention to my humble presence; we saw no signs of their submarines and crossed without any excitement.

While waiting for the train at Boulogne, I was surrounded by a group of youngsters, who, recognizing my uniform, asked for all sorts of information about Russia. Chiefly they wanted to know if it was true that one hundred thousand Russian soldiers were coming to help France to annihilate the "Boches," as the Germans were nicknamed by the Allies. I was at least able to answer that some Russian troops were coming and that part of them had arrived at Marseilles a few days before.

Late in the afternoon I was in Paris and went at once to the Hotel

Crillon, which two years later became the headquarters of the American delegation to the Versailles Conference. At the hotel I was struck by the number of crippled Frenchmen serving as elevator boys and in other capacities.

The following morning I reported to General Jilinsky, at that time personal representative of the Czar at the Headquarters of the French High Command. He was especially pleased to hear that I had brought a suitcase full of various decorations for the most distinguished Frenchmen. Medals and ribbons played much the same role in the World War as at the time of Napoleon, who was credited with saying that by giving people old buttons from his pants he could make them die for him. As regards the details of my mission, the General would see me later.

My visits to the French officials and the Headquarters were arranged by our Military Attaché, Count Ignatieff. In a day or two he drove me to the Headquarters of the Generalissimo, Joffre, at Chantilly. Jilinsky, who had at his disposal the entire beautiful estate of Baron Rothschild, near that town, invited me to stay with him. After being introduced to "Papa" Joffre and his Staff, I received a long list of queries which the Deputy Chief of Staff wanted me to answer. I correlated this questionnaire with my ample data, and the next day, after a conference with Jilinsky, I talked for two hours with the senior members of the Staff. This "lecture" obviously satisfied my French colleagues, and the recompense was quite generous. I was made an Officer of the Legion of Honor, without having previously been a "Chevalier." That I received a higher grade at once was probably due to my rank as Colonel; and I was as proud as a peacock. The French have a saying: *"Si jeune et si décoré."* It certainly applied to me, and I heard words to that effect a number of times. And I have to confess that I liked to hear them. Vanity is human.

After my mission at Headquarters had been fulfilled, I was free to visit the front. Unfortunately, not everything I wished to see was "on view" even to the well-accredited representative of an Ally. I was especially anxious to visit Verdun, where the French troops were heroically resisting German attacks. But "Papa" Joffre categorically refused to grant me this permission. Only a few weeks earlier another Russian officer had been killed while visiting the French lines, and "Papa" did not cherish the possibility of another victim from the same allied nation in that hell-like sector. I had to be satisfied with any other part of the front.

While visiting various French and British units from Amiens in the north, through Bray-sur-Somme, Marqueglise, and Choisie-au-Bac, up to the trenches near Soissons, I saw much that made me envy our Allies. Little things will tell the story. For example, after visiting the trenches, I was invariably offered the hospitality of the officers and invited to their mess. The officers' food was excellent, but it was quite good in the trenches too. I was surprised to see what the English soldiers had on their diet. What, I wondered, would my Russian soldiers say if I told them about the chocolate, jam, and biscuits which the Tommies regarded as a matter of course?

Far more important, of course, was the difference in armament, equipment, and war supplies between our Allies and our own troops. The comparison was simply shocking. And to appreciate the difference it is necessary only to recall a few figures. While Russia had at the outbreak of hostilities only seven thousand and eighty-eight pieces of field artillery of all calibers and seven million shells and shrapnel for all, France was able to shoot at Verdun in the two weeks from August 14 to August 27, 1917, four million shells weighing one hundred and twenty thousand tons of metal. During the battle of Flanders in 1917 our Allies were able to concentrate one hundred and fifty cannon per kilometer, or one piece of artillery per seven meters; something of which we never even dared to dream. If we could have had the abundance of munitions and the equipment and fortifications I saw in France, what a difference it would have made!

While in England and in France, I was assured that cannon, machine guns, and rifles were on the way to Russia, together with large quantities of shells and cartridges. Our Allies were anxious to see us well supplied and, as Kitchener said, were doing their best to achieve this end. In France I heard about this from our Ambassador, Izvolsky, and the Military Attaché, Ignatieff. From the French officials

I heard little. No doubt I had myself to blame. I had audiences with the Minister of War and the Chief of the General Staff arranged for a certain date, but missed them. I was invited by the charming daughter of the late Admiral Makaroff and her fiancé for an automobile ride to Versailles, and I simply forgot all about the appointments. When back at my hotel, I was met in the lobby by Ignatieff's aide. He was furious. How was it possible to neglect audiences with such luminaries? But his ingenuity found a way out of this embarrassing situation. He telephoned the respective secretaries, told them that I had a minor accident on the road and was delayed by repairs, and asked for another audience the following day.

The next day, explaining my mishap to their Excellencies, I did not fail to see the twinkle in their eyes. Apparently they had heard of the real cause of my inability to be prompt; and, as real Frenchmen, were probably sympathetic.

Soon after I reached Paris, our parliamentary delegation also arrived from London. A program of entertainment was being planned for them by the French authorities. To arrange for certain details, our Councilor of the Embassy, Sebastopulo, invited two officials of the Protocol of the French Foreign Office to a lunch tendered in my honor. It was quite amusing to hear Ignatieff advising these Frenchmen not to take too seriously the legislators of his mother country. Obviously he had no more respect for the "representatives" of the people than had the Grand Duke in London. Not less obvious was the embarrassment of the two men from the Foreign Office, whose business it was to observe etiquette and preserve good manners.

On one of my trips to the front I visited the Headquarters of General Foch, who at that time was still in command of a group of armies. Everybody, including the energetic Chief of Staff, Weygand—who was then only a colonel but eventually became one of the Marshals of France—was busy with some urgent preparations, and I had to limit our conversation to a few banalities.

During my two weeks of stay in France I also paid two visits to the Russian troops. One brigade had recently arrived by sea at Marseilles and was now getting ready to occupy a sector on the French front. They were included, of course, in a French army corps. When the French Command asked Russia to send some soldiers, they had offered to arm and equip them after their arrival. This evoked bitter criticism in Russia. How was it possible to send "men" and not army units? It sounded as if France were simply demanding additional cannon fodder. That is why it was decided to send complete brigades, armed, equipped, and with their own commanders.

General Jilinsky, naturally, went to review the Russians. I was invited to go with him. A few days later President Poincaré also went to review our troops, and again I was invited to the ceremony. This meant getting up before sunrise, riding in an automobile for six or seven hours, and then standing for another hour or more behind Poincaré, while the troops passed before the Head of the Republic. For this hard work I was rewarded by a very mediocre luncheon with the President in his special car, and by another handshake with the man who became nicknamed "Poincaré the War." I might add that Ambassador Izvolsky, who naturally was present at the review and the luncheon that followed it, was also suspected of "arranging" the World War. The rumor persisted that at the outbreak of hostilities he exclaimed: "This is my own war!"

The personnel of these Russian troops was exceptionally good. Physically, most of them were sufficiently enormous to satisfy that Prussian King, Frederick, who was famous for his giant grenadiers. While fighting on the French front, they acquitted themselves splendidly. After the Revolution of 1917, they expressed the desire to be sent back to their mother country, and on refusal staged a demonstration of protest. For this they were surrounded and fired on by French troops. A number were killed, and the rest were sent to a sort of a concentration camp or military prison. A considerable number of these unfortunates never saw their native land again.

While I was abroad, the Austrians launched an offensive on the Italian front. Their attack developed so successfully that the Italian Headquarters quickly sent a S.O.S., asking for action on the allied fronts. As usual, this request was directed in particular to the Russians. They would not refuse to help if they had the slightest opportunity to do so. The other Allies, apparently, joined in these representations. Russia was asked to start her attack immediately in order to force the Austrians to withdraw some of their troops from the Italian front and transfer them to that of Russia. General Brussiloff, in command of the southwestern group of armies, was accordingly ordered to attack on a large front. The result of this surprise movement —undertaken with little preparation—was beyond all expectations. The Austrians began a hasty retreat and lost more than two hundred thousand prisoners of war, as well as an enormous amount of war materials. Under this pressure, they started transferring troops from the west, and their German allies moved some of theirs from the Anglo-French front as well.

Italy was saved. But this new self-sacrifice again proved costly to the Russian Army. For, as in the days before Tannenberg, the Russians saved an Ally by impairing their own plan for general offensive. The original plan, in connection with which I was sent to France, contemplated starting operations early in July. Our plan was to concentrate large forces, with what was, for us, an unprecedented number of artillery, on a rather narrow salient, and to deliver the main blow in the general direction of Vilna. This blow was to be delivered by seven army corps. Simultaneously, other armies were to start attacks of a supplementary character.

Meanwhile, according to this plan, that unprecedented supply of munitions and other materials had to be amassed within the boundaries of our western group of armies. Naturally, not all the preparations were completed by the middle of May. To start the offensive in another sector, as we were forced to do by the situation in Italy, meant not only confusion in the preparatory period, but also a considerable drain on the supplies which had been accumulated with much difficulty for the general offensive. We replenished them partly through imports from abroad—from the west via Murmansk, and from the Far East via Vladivostok. The diversion on behalf of the Italians meant also a serious drain on our reserves. Several army corps were sent to develop the victory of Brussiloff. The success was great indeed. The Austrians were routed. But our original plan fell to pieces, and when the time for the general offensive arrived, we were unable to undertake an operation of the magnitude expected. In short, the cost of saving Italy had invalidated a plan which Russia, England, and France had been jointly preparing. But of this I learned only on my return to Russia. While in France, I merely heard that the Italians were in trouble and that the Russians were again doing something "very wonderful." Details and results became clear only much later.

Paris in those days was a city of cheer compared with London, which was so much farther from the battlefront. And I do not think this is to be explained merely by the traditional gaiety of the French capital. Rather it was another evidence of the truth of the oft-illustrated paradox that those who are in constant danger take it less seriously than those to whom danger is a threat only realized from time to time. Thus, civilians at home in all countries made a great to-do, perhaps more than they actually felt, about the horrors of war. But in the trenches there was no use pretending. It was better to take things as they came, and keep in a good humor as long as possible.

Another thing I observed during the war was that in the trenches there was no such hatred, if any, toward the enemy, as was cultivated in the rear. Soldiers continued to be human, while propagandists and even common people in the rear worked up a sort of blood lust that almost amounted to insanity.

When I say in Paris the atmosphere was less gloomy, I certainly do not mean that there had been no panic during the approach of the Germans to its gates in the opening months of the war. I do not mean that one did not see many widows and orphans, and people who had suffered in one way or another from this calamity. But there was a healthy desire to keep the chin up; and with the inherent gaiety of the Parisians this was not so hard to achieve, especially in the periods of a comparative lull, such as that which marked the time of my visit.

Theaters remained open and crowded, and the general attitude of the Parisian may be summed up in a story I heard a comedian telling between the acts in one of these theaters. "It may be," he said, "that a Zeppelin will visit us tonight. And again it may not. If it does, it may pass over Paris. And again it may not. If it passes over Paris, it may fly over this street. And again it may not. If it does, it may drop a bomb; and again it may not. If it does drop a bomb, the latter may fall on the roof of this theater; and again it may not. If the bomb hits the roof, it may explode; and again it may not. If it does explode, it may be unpleasant to some of us; and again it may not. But what is the use talking so much about it, when the possibility of such consequences is so remote? Let us be gay, let us talk of anything else." And Parisians tried their best to follow a "keep smiling" attitude.

Londoners, on the other hand, seemed to persist in being serious and even gloomy. Not that the theaters and other places of entertainment were closed or deserted, nor that smiles were never seen; but the general impression left on me from my two short visits there was quite in contrast with what I found in Paris. England was apparently terrorized by the air raids and anxiously expected more of them. The lampposts in London offered a peculiar spectacle with umbrella-like shades to hide the lights and thereby make it more difficult for the German visitors from the skies to find their targets.

When I returned to London on June first, I found the city in particular agitation. The streets were crowded. People were nervously reading the news about the naval battle fought on May thirty-first near Jutland. Small groups gathered to discuss this event.

On my arrival, General Yermoloff told me that he had sent a wire to Paris asking for my immediate return to London and explained that we had to go at once for an important conference with the Grand Duke. Then and there the Duke told me, in a most confidential manner, that Lord Kitchener was ready to start his long-planned visit to Russia. Kitchener had asked the Grand Duke whether it would be possible for me to accompany him on that journey, and therefore I must be prepared to leave with him, probably in a day or two.

To this I replied that, having been sent on this mission by the General Headquarters of the Czar, I had to fulfill my instructions, and they included seeing our Ministers at Norway and Sweden on my way back to Russia. I therefore asked the Grand Duke to be excused from going with Lord Kitchener. That settled the matter. He was not in a position to countermand an order from the Czar. And it was not proper to wire about it. I was free to go alone.

On June third I sailed from Newcastle for Bergen. On the sixth I was in Christiania, and the next day at Stockholm. There I was met at the station by our Military Attaché, and my schoolmate, Kandauroff, who informed me of the tragic fate of Kitchener. He had sailed June fifth on the cruiser *Hampshire* and went down near the Orkney Islands off the coast of Scotland. The conjecture was that a German mine had been responsible.

For me it was another rather miraculous escape. My instructions, after all, had not been so binding as to make it impossible to accept the invitation of Lord Kitchener. It was, undoubtedly, a very flattering invitation too. But for some inexplicable reason I had preferred to decline. Instead, I had sailed alone; and, as a consequence, remained alive.

So far as I am aware, the true story of the *Hampshire* has never been told. Various hypotheses offered in explanation were not convincing. Many years later, when in America, I read a full-page article in the *New York Times* offering one theory. The author, a former chief of the Russian Secret Police, asserted that the Russian Imperial Court knew about Kitchener's coming, and the information had leaked out. This, it was said, enabled the German spies to prepare for the sinking of the ship which carried the British Minister of War. Sensational as it was, this article contained a number of obviously nonsensical assertions. Up to the very last moment neither the date nor the place of sailing were known even to Lord Kitchener himself. To assert, as this article did, that King George V had informed his counsin Nicholas II about these details was unreasonable enough. Why should he? And how could he? But that the Czarina might have been responsible for passing on such information to the Germans was simply absurd. Not that at various times she may not have done something in the interests of her German relatives, but simply because in this particular case the information could not have been available.

It is quite certain that Germany knew many things, and sometimes was informed ahead of others on most important matters. The activities of Herr von Papen, the future Chancellor of Germany, and Ambassador to Vienna and Ankara, who during the World War was Military Attaché at Washington, are too well known to need elaboration. The story of the Black Tom explosion and the fire at Jersey City on July 30, 1916, are well remembered. And they took place very conveniently for Germany at exactly the time when the general offensive of the Allies was planned, and replenishment of war supplies was particularly important.

On my return to Russia I went to General Headquarters to make my report; and was again invited for a dinner with the Czar. Next day I left for Zaslavl, near Minsk, where the Headquarters of my Tenth Army was located.

After the beginning of the brilliant attack of Brussiloff in May, offensive activities continued on small scale on the Russian front through the summer. They were slowed down only on the recommendation of our Allies and contrary to our own plans. We considered it possible to continue them.

In August, 1916, after long hesitation, Rumania entered the war on our side. This was not regarded with approval in all quarters of Russia. There were certain doubts about Rumania's army. The Allies had wanted her to join them in June, when Brussiloff's advance was in full swing; but she had not. It was, however, undoubtedly desirable to put a stop to German use of Rumanian oil and other supplies; and it was better to have Rumania on our side than on the side of the Central Powers. But it remained a question whether it would not result in making our front still longer, in the event the Rumanian army was unable to resist an enemy attack. And that was exactly what happened. The Rumanians started with a spectacular thrust into Transylvania, but were soon in retreat. Our troops had to be sent to reinforce them, and eventually the so-called Rumanian front became a new burden on Russia's shoulders.

Near the end of the summer I was informed that Stavka wanted me to go back to Paris to work on the Interallied Commission. Fortunately for me, this plan did not materialize. A brother of Count Ignatieff, our Military Attaché in France, was appointed instead. In September I was selected to command the Regiment of the Grenadiers of Mingrelia. I was proud of this honor, for the Grenadiers were one of the best units in our Army. But before this appointment was approved, I received yet another assignment.

General Samoyloff, for many years our Military Attaché in Japan, died, and besides myself there was no one available with the required qualifications for the post. At the moment, Japan's attitude was considered particularly important for us. There was no choice but to obey orders. So, in November, after winding up my work, I left Headquarters and was soon on the train, again speeding with my family across Siberia toward the familiar Far East.

CHAPTER XII

FOOL'S PARADISE

(*Diplomatic Career*)

Round of official calls before leaving Petrograd. On the way east. The Diplomatic Corps. Purchasing war supplies. General Tanaka and other high officials. Audience with the Emperor. News of revolution at home. American Railway Mission. The Russian Mission to America. My departure for Russia.

Before leaving for Japan I had to make a number of official calls, including another visit to the Czar's Headquarters. There I again met Protopopov, now Minister for Internal Affairs, thanks to the recommendation of Rasputin. But the other prominent protégé of the "Mad Monk," the Premier and Minister of Foreign Affairs, I did not see at this time; he was very busy, and I merely signed his visitors' book. However, I already knew Sturmer personally, though slightly; for he had been a frequent guest at the home of one of my uncles. At that time, of course, I had been too young to know anything about Sturmer's reputation and record. I simply regarded him as a courteous but obviously very cunning person; and it was only much later that I learned that this Minister of Foreign Affairs was viewed with suspicion by our Allies, especially the English. Count Benkendorf, our Ambassador to the Court of St. James, told Miliukov [1] that after the appointment of Sturmer to that important post the British Foreign Office became definitely more restrained, and even secretive.

Two calls at this time I remember very well. One was on the Minister of War, General Shouvaieff, and the other on his aide, Senator Garin. Shouvaieff was known as a very honest soldier, not brilliant, but a hard worker. He was extremely kind to me, and, after the

[1] Paul Miliukov. *History of the Second Russian Revolution* (in Russian), v. I. Sophia. 1921.

official part of the interview was over, he put his arm around my shoulders and talked with me like a father. But his views on Nippon were peculiar. He found that in one respect at least a striking similarity existed between Russia and Japan; both countries had monarchs, and in both countries, he said, the people adored their Emperors. Fortunately, I was not expected to comment; so we parted good friends. Senator Garin was an entirely different type of person. Very intelligent, keen and able, he was well-traveled and a thorough man of the world. It was Garin who advised me that the surest way to success in my future diplomatic career would be always to read the London *Times,* an "absolutely reliable newspaper." This predilection for and faith in the esteemed and venerable organ of English conservatism was quite in keeping with the Senator's tastes and background. And some might say that it illustrated the adage embodied in the title of Ostrovsky's famous play, *Enough Simplicity in Every Wise Man.* Garin supplied further evidences of this truth, however; he told me, among other things, that I was wrong in my belief that a revolution in Russia was impending. "There are no groups able to lead," he asserted. And this was only four months before the February Revolution!

Perhaps Garin did not entirely believe this; he may well have been better informed on the question of revolution than he considered proper to admit to a young Army officer. Yet I am inclined to assert that he spoke in complete good faith, for it is remarkable how people in comfortable circumstances hate to believe in the possibility of any radical change, likely to endanger their status. Their wishful thinking in the case of impending revolution seems to know no bounds. Whatever the situation, whatever the signs of approaching catastrophe, most of them prefer to believe the most unreasonable explanations, and to invent most irrelevant arguments in disproof.

As a matter of fact, all the usual signs of impending revolution were present at that time. Huge strikes were reported all over the country; indeed, only a month before my conversation with the Senator, such a strike had occurred in Petrograd itself. On the periphery of the Empire the *inorodtzy,* or the non-Slavic nations, rose against the bureaucratic oppression, the War in general, the heavy taxation, the requisition of cattle, and the endless demands for recruits. In 1916 such rebellions had taken place in Turkestan and among the nomads beyond the Urals. The Kirghis and Kalmuks had organized armed resistance to Russian officials. The Uzbeks tore up the rails to prevent the dispatch of troops. Nevertheless, forces were sent to crush the rebellion. Villages were burned, and thousands of people were killed. But while these revolts were certainly put down, discontent was not eliminated. On the contrary, the struggle against the War and the hated regime was intensified. Furthermore, on the front itself it was not difficult to discern that soldiers were tired of the War, disheartened by reverses, indignant at the munitions situation, dissatisfied with food, and generally anxious to see a speedy end to the senseless struggle.

In the country at large, the animosity toward the regime was widespread. The people's representatives, the Members of the State Duma, were losing patience, and few among them continued to entertain any hope for improvement under the Czar and his unscrupulous entourage. At the opening session of the State Duma, Miliukov enumerated the latest blunders of the government and asked his audience, "If that was stupidity or treason?" In his own evaluation, made much later, this session actually marked the beginning of the Revolution itself.

But the bureaucrats were deaf to all demands for change. They continued their policy of fighting the people and showing contempt to the people's representatives. To them war seemed to mean wild spending, accompanied by appeals for the demonstration of patriotism, sacrifices, and then more sacrifices. Ugly rumors about the Czarina's interference in the state affairs and her suspicious contact with the Germans, added to the general nervousness.

I was detained for several days in Petrograd in order to familiarize myself with the work of the special committee, formed under General Michelson, to supervise the procuring of war supplies abroad. My main concern in Japan was to be in connection with this business.

Japan was by now a considerable source of such war supplies. But, it was a source which in the past had been mismanaged, and it was to be my task to straighten out the mess, to place new large orders, to speed up delivery, arrange for transportation, and generally to enlist to the limit the co-operation of the Japanese authorities.

On my way east I had plenty of opportunity to grasp anew the difficulty of transporting goods from Vladivostok to the front. The great Trans-Siberian Railway, more than five thousand miles long, was still a single-track road. Our rolling stock, meager at the best of times, was badly needed at the front. Innumerable freight cars had been lost in the War. Others were worn out by heavy use. As for locomotives, their number was pitifully small. And Vladivostok, though practically the only harbor safe from German submarines and open for incoming goods, was not properly equipped, either for storage or transshipment. Eventually, it became simply a dumping place for enormous quantities of various war materials coming from Japan and America. Most of these supplies were looted during the turbulent days of 1917-1922.

In Japan I found the officials most willing to co-operate in supplying our needs. For this purpose a number of the most important firms participated in the formation of a large corporation, *Taihei Kumiai,* to handle some of our orders. Part, of course, we placed with the arsenals and other military establishments under government permission and approval. But the major portion had to be given to the large private firms such as Mitsui, Furukawa, Okura, Kuhara, and Sudzuki; and here a certain amount of confusion arose. Some of these and other firms had their own representatives in Petrograd who made direct offers there, and sometimes succeeded in obtaining orders at much higher prices than those quoted to us in Japan. This was less a matter of bribing Russian officials than the result of generally poor co-ordination at the capital, the proverbial inefficiency of the Russian bureaucratic machine with its inexhaustible supply of red tape, and sometimes simply poor judgment. In several instances prices agreed upon in Petrograd were fifty per cent higher than those prevailing at the same moment in Japan. It is no exaggeration to say that in nine cases out of ten our difficulties were created by our own clumsy governmental machine. In the tenth case the blame lay with the natives of Nippon.

The private concerns were, of course, primarily interested in making money out of this lucrative business; but, on the whole, dealing with them was quite satisfactory. The attitude of the Japanese government facilitated our task, for in a number of cases the War Office made it a point to guarantee the proper quality of goods contracted by us even through private firms. Obviously this was largely a matter of *amour propre;* but the fact remains that we did succeed in receiving what we needed from Japan and the shipments here were more prompt than those of our commissions in other countries. Partly this might be explained by the fact that Japan was not involved in the War to the same extent as the other Allies. Thus she was able to develop her industry up to our requirements. Her commitments with England and France were limited and left almost all her productive capacity free for Russian orders.

My relations with the Japanese officials were most pleasant; they always seemed willing to help, and in point of fact did help a great deal. Usually every possible assistance was readily rendered to me and my associates. Minister of War Oshima and his subordinates were accommodating. So were General Uehara, the Chief of General Staff and his assistant, General Tanaka, who as Prime Minister later became world-famous for the so-called Tanaka Memorandum, which advocated the conquest by Japan of China, all of Asia, and the whole world. We were quite friendly with Tanaka who as a young officer of the General Staff had been attached for a considerable length of time to one of the regiments stationed in St. Petersburg. He learned the Russian language very well, was friendly with a number of officers in various regiments, and, as the guest of one of these, became thoroughly familiar with Russian life. Thus he was a true expert on Russia and her armed forces, and extremely valuable to his country. And he posed as a Russophile. But he was one of the mainsprings of the armed intervention in the internal affairs of Russia after the

Revolution, and advocated rough treatment of this country which had been so hospitable to him in the past.

Our diplomatic representatives in Japan did their part to make my task easier, but their hearts were not in the work. Krupensky, the Ambassador, was considered a good diplomatist, and his past performances in China probably justified a renown strengthened by his negotiations with Japan, which resulted in the signing of two new conventions. Through these, the two former adversaries became allies, determined to defend their interests in Asia against any third party, which meant the United States. On the interpretation of the word "patriotism," I know, we differed. In his judgment his task was to represent the Emperor. As for the interests of the nation, as I learned full well later on, he was no champion of the people, to say the least. Our relations, always correct, became clearer, but not more friendly after the Revolution.

My colleagues, the other military attachés, were a pleasant group. With the French, Captain Baron de la Pomarède, and the English, Lieutenant Colonel Sommerville, I naturally had the closest contact. Usually we exchanged information, particularly in regard to placing orders and shipments of supplies. After the departure of the American Attaché, Irons, I became the dean, or rather the senior Military Attaché, for I was the only colonel among them. The real dean, in the sense of having been in Japan the longest, was Lieutenant Colonel Herrera de la Rosa, the Spanish Attaché, who was a relative of King Alfonso XIII. He was a most charming man, goodhearted, always gay, pleasant, and a *bon vivant.* His duties were hardly burdensome, and his hospitable home was never closed to his numerous friends, Japanese and foreigners alike. There I came to know many Japanese officers whom I should not have met through official contact. Among them was the young Count Terauchi, who in 1937 became the Commander in Chief of the Japanese armies in North China.

But agreeable as most of the diplomats of my time in Japan were, I had, frankly, to see them too often. The routine included endless luncheons, dinners, parties, in a very narrow circle. One had to see the same faces day in and day out. My day's work was a man-size job, requiring all my energy, and therefore these official social affairs became a good deal of a nuisance. Usually boring because of their extreme artificiality, they were doubly so during the war. Any real gaiety was out of place, the epicurean repasts were somewhat shocking, and the presence of the "neutrals" sometimes was quite embarrassing. While I was at Tokyo, for example, the Swedish Minister was asked to leave Japan on account of his undue co-operation with the Germans. But, *noblesse oblige!* We had to be present at these endless affairs, and the sending of "regrets" was permissible only once in a while. Naturally, we had to keep "open house" too.

Not the least irritating feature of these social functions was that they meant a constant change of dress. In the morning a business suit was worn to the office, only to be exchanged, in all probability, for the military uniform which was *de rigeur* when calling on the War Ministry or the General Staff. Luncheon, or a reception in the afternoon, demanded a cutaway; while further work at office meant that business suit again. And finally one would return wearily home to don dinner jacket or full dress for an evening at one of the Embassies, or at the homes of such high Japanese officials and aristocrats as Count Terauchi, the Prime Minister, or Marquis Motono, the Minister of Foreign Affairs. In my case, furthermore, the normal visiting list of a member of the Diplomatic Corps had been swelled through a number of added letters of introduction supplied by our former Ambassador, Malievsky-Malievich. Such was life! And far away, in Europe, hundreds of thousands were losing their lives, and millions more were in suffering, while we dined and wined in Embassies amid exaggerated courtesy, glittering jewelry, and all the finery of so many human peacocks. It was a fool's paradise indeed.

Officially, my life in Japan dated from my audience with the Emperor. To this function our Ambassador accompanied me, wearing the most fascinating full dress of a high-ranking Courtier with decorations of every imaginable form and color, from practically every country in the world. We were taken to the Palace in a Court carriage, accompanied by horsemen of the Guards. To reach the ceremonial room, where the Emperor gave us audience, we had to pass an endless number of halls, void of furniture in the Western sense, but gorgeous in their ceiling decorations and beautiful screens, and to pass from one master of ceremonies to another. His Majesty, in military uniform, stood under a sort of a canopy, with his aides behind him. The Ambassador was introduced. The Emperor shook his hand and addressed a few words to him through the interpreter. Then came my turn. The Emperor gave me his hand, but, so far as I can remember, said nothing. This ended the brief ceremony. Backing to the door, we were ushered out of sight of the Divine Son of the Heavens. The same Court carriage brought us back to the Embassy and to earthly life.

On another occasion, at a garden party at one of the palaces, my wife was introduced to the Empress. This was a much simpler ceremony. As the Empress and Emperor passed the spot where all the diplomats and their wives were waiting, those who had not yet been presented to Her Majesty were introduced by the wife of the English Ambassador, who was dean of the Diplomatic Corps. A more elaborate affair at the Palace was the celebration of the New Year. On this occasion, the Emperor, Empress, and Princes of Royal Blood were in the throne room; and the entire Diplomatic Corps passed before them, bowed, and backed away from the throne, like so many lobsters or crabs.

Particularly interesting to me was a wild duck "netting party," arranged for us in a suburban palace of the Emperor. On a large wooded estate we tried to catch the ducks with a sort of a net, not unlike those used for butterflies, though, naturally, much larger in size. It was a really difficult thing to do, in spite of the great number of ducks attracted to a certain spot by the domesticated fowl coming for food. Only Motono, the diminutive Minister of Foreign Affairs, in enormous rubber bootgear, looking like puss-in-boots, made an appreciable "bag." He caught a number of ducks. Most of us didn't. However, after the splendid luncheon, served as a reward for our labors, when we returned to the train, we found a couple of fat wild ducks prepared for each of us. So those who wanted to boast about their prowess could show that their bags were not empty.

While we were living in this fool's paradise, momentous events were taking place back in the mother country. Soon after our departure the "Mad Monk" Rasputin, was killed. A strange trio, composed of the Grand Duke Dmitry, Prince Yussupoff, the scion of a wealthy aristocratic family, and Purishkevitch, an ultrareactionary member of the State Duma, were responsible. Undoubtedly they wanted to free the country from the disgrace of its monarch being influenced by this illiterate, immoral, drunken adventurer. Unfortunately, the whole plot was conceived and executed in bad taste. It is true that many attempts made earlier by influential people, even by members of the Imperial family, to put an end to this Court scandal had proved futile. The Czar would brook no interference with his personal affairs; and those who dared to raise this question paid for it by falling into Royal disfavor. But the assassination of Rasputin by a group of indignant habitués of the Palace offered no solution to the main problem. The basic dissatisfaction went far beyond mere Court intrigue, and this *affaire nocturnal* eventually proved the curtain raiser to one of history's most grave political and social dramas.

In other words, within three months of the murder of Rasputin the Romanovs no longer ruled Russia. Events developing in rapid succession culminated in the abdication of Nicholas II on March 15 for himself and his only son, Czarevitch Alexei. His brother, Michael, whom the Czar designated as heir, declined to consider ascending the throne except by popular demand expressed through a Constituent Assembly; and such a demand was not forthcoming. To govern the country in the interim, the Provisional Government was formed under the leadership of Prince George Lvoff, and included a number of well-known members of the State Duma.

News of the revolutionary changes in our mother country evoked a variety of attitudes among the Russians at Tokyo. In the Embassy there was a commotion. Our diplomats, with practically no exception, were saddened by the news. When I expressed my joy, the others looked at me as though I had said something very improper. Apparently it made no difference to them that the Emperor had abdicated and thereby set us free from our oath of the allegiance to him. That the country needed a change badly and now faced a better future was not to be conceded. They were all against a change "by such means." They were full of doubts about the outcome of the Revolution. They could see no good coming out of it. They did not say, of course, "nothing good for ourselves," but they were "worried about the country." And then again, what about the War? The news coming from various sources was not reassuring. Our soldiers wanted peace. Now that the old regime responsible for the War was overthrown, they asked, why should they continue fighting? In their opinion the War had nothing to do with the interests of the people: it was a war of the ruling classes. It must be ended, as quickly as possible. Such, it was said, was the prevailing attitude at the front, and it called forth much apprehension and dismay in the fool's paradise at Tokyo.

As for myself, I was anxious to go back home and take part in events of such importance to the future of my country. But it was not a simple matter. I had to get permission to return. And for a while I had to continue my work in Japan. Our orders continued to be filled and deliveries were running smoothly; but once in a while I received disquieting reports from Vladivostok. The cars available for shipments westward were becoming more and more scarce. I went to Vladivostok to confer with the authorities, but little, if anything, could be done without help from the center. And the center was definitely becoming less efficient. Apparently the Revolution was taxing every government office beyond its capacity for adjustment.

Daily the general situation grew worse, and daily my difficulties about prompt payments for goods delivered according to contracts were increasing. The situation in that respect had been bad enough before the Revolution, but now the delays with the drafts became unbearable. My wires imploring a straightening out of this matter failed to produce any results. Telegram after telegram remained unanswered. Part of our orders in Japan were financed through loans there; others were paid by drafts through Petrograd from the British bankers, Behring Brothers. Since the Revolution, unpaid bills had been accumulating, and by June, I was more than twenty million yen in debt. To be responsible for a business amounting to some three hundred million yen and not able to be prompt in payments was irregular, to say the least. But Petrograd paid no attention to all my appeals. In despair I went to see Junnosuke Inouye, then President of the Yokohama Specie Bank, through which I transacted most of my business. Naturally, he was unable to do anything but console me, and most likely smile at my naïveté. Inouye, who later became Minister of Finance, fell victim of a rebellion in his own country in 1932. He was assassinated in cold blood by super-patriots who disapproved of his unwillingness to encourage the wild spending demanded by the militarists. Indeed, that epidemic of political assassinations in Japan took the lives of a number of those whom I knew besides Inouye. In February, 1936, came the turn of Takahashi, also a Minister of Finance, disapproved of by the extremist jingoes. With him perished Admiral Saito, the former Prime Minister, and General Watanabe, one of the ablest officials in the army.

At last, however, the deplorable condition of the transportation system was appreciated in Petrograd, and a commission of American railroad engineers, headed by John F. Stevens, was appointed to find a remedy. This mission passed through Japan, and I met its members at a luncheon tendered to them by our Ambassador. With the rapidly deteriorating conditions on the railways since the outbreak of the Revolution, the original function of this group was modified. Finally, after the advent of the Bolsheviks, it became concerned, not with the Russian railways, but with the Chinese Eastern, crossing Manchuria.

Another mission born of the Revolution passed Japan on its way to America. This was the special party under Professor Boris Bakhmeteff, the first Ambassador of New Russia to the United States. It included, as the representative of the Ministry of Communications, Professor Lomonossov, who later created quite a furore by joining the new regime established by Lenin. The representative of the Ministry of Foreign Affairs was a young man named Soukine, who later became the Acting Minister of Foreign Affairs in the ill-fated Omsk government of Admiral Kolchak.

While this mission was in Tokyo, we discussed the problem of placing orders for war supplies and came to the conclusion that it would be prudent to curtail new commitments. Until the forwarding of the supplies piling up at Vladivostok was straightened out, and the matter of financing our purchases was clarified, it was foolish to continue on the old scale. Accordingly, a dispatch was sent to Petrograd with our recommendations to that effect. But, to no avail. Demands for new contracts continued to come, but no money was available even to pay for what had already been delivered. So I continued to bombard Petrograd with telegrams, and finally asked to be relieved of my duties in Japan. In reply they sent a draft enabling me to settle all the urgent accounts. Simultaneously, I received a very flattering wire from the General Staff, asking me to remain at my post in Japan, and approving my coming to Petrograd simply "for a conference."

At the end of September, I was ready to leave Tokyo. Ambassador Krupensky gave a luncheon in my honor and in his toast expressed regret that I should probably not return to Tokyo, as he knew that I was anxious to go home. I, certainly, did not think that he was really interested in my coming back. From the moment we first discussed the revolutionary changes in Russia, it became clear that our ideologies were incompatible, that we wanted different things for our country. He, certainly, did not approve of what was going on and never doubted that evil would come of it. I was full of enthusiasm and never doubted the final victory of the people.

Having received my calling cards inscribed P.P.C. (*pour prendre congé*), most of the diplomats came to the station to see me off. But my journey was very short. A terrific typhoon had torn up the rails, and there was no through traffic. So I had to return the same evening. But next day I left, this time without any ceremony, and proceeded quietly to Tsuruga to embark on a boat of the Russian Volunteer Fleet for Vladivostok. My family remained in Tokyo, and I did not wind up my affairs, as, according to the telegram from the General Staff, I was expected to return to Japan in a short time.

CHAPTER XIII

THE FEBRUARY REVOLUTION

(*An Embarrassing Appointment*)

Historic background. Long deterioration of the Monarchy. Military reverses. Economic collapse. Abdication of the Czar. Provisional Government. The Soviets. Duality of power. Kerensky and his vacillations. Lenin and his followers. Army and Navy on the eve of Revolution. Kornilov's revolt. Role of the privileged class. On the way to Petrograd. Unexpected and embarrassing appointment. My mission to Moscow. Meeting delegates. No support for the Kerensky government. Session of the Cabinet in the Winter Palace. General impression.

ALTHOUGH THE REVOLUTION of 1905, which followed the unsuccessful war with Japan, was put down, its causes were not eliminated. The cruelty with which the uprising was suppressed left in its wake a peculiar degree of hatred for the regime, in spite of the fact that from time immemorial cruelty had been the traditional means of curbing popular discontent in Russia. All the former peasants' revolts such as those led by Bolotnikov, Razin, Pugatchev, had been drowned in blood. The rebellions of the Streltzy, the old-type armed forces of Moscow, had met the same fate. So on the whole, did a number of historic revolts among the upper classes, such as the attempt made at the time of the Czarina Anna to secure a voice in the government for the nobility—though some of those rebellions were sufficiently successful to end in compromises. Several palace revolutions, on a smaller scale, were responsible for the making of such monarchs as Elizabeth and Catherine the Great, or unmaking of others; and these, too, involved cruelty. But the brutality and deceit demonstrated by the Imperial government in the case of Bloody Sunday, on January 22 (9), 1905, left in the hearts of the common people a deeper scar than could be erased. Nor was the role played by the intelligentsia in the Revolution of 1905 forgotten. The numerous desertions from the ranks of the revolutionaries did not serve to fortify the trust of the common people in their leaders from other classes. Fortunately, new elements were increasing to strengthen the movement which sought the emancipation of the country from the evils of the decaying regime.

As modern industry developed in Russia, the number of the working class increased. The work of organizing labor commenced in 1871; and for this the ground had to some extent been prepared, shortly after the emancipation of the serfs, by a Populist movement among the peasants, in which social-minded youths from various classes had been active. So now these young people—particularly students from institutions of the higher learning—turned their attention to the industrial workers. Under the influence of Marxism, with their hopes fixed on socialism, they plunged enthusiastically into this new labor, merging their efforts with those of other progressives among the intelligentsia. And for a while they did indeed achieve a very conspicuous success in propagandizing the workers. But mere propaganda, unsupported by power, was not enough, and in due course the collapse of the Revolution of 1905 made it plain that a successful revolution could not be brought about without the aid of an effective organization among the armed forces. Nor was a strong revolutionist sentiment in the rank and file sufficient; for, while it was true that the failure of the Decembrists of 1825 to achieve reforms similar to those witnessed in France had been largely due to the fact that the plot had been solely an officers' movement, it was equally true that the failure in 1905 was at least partly due to the fact that the overwhelming majority of officers had been anything but co-operative. But now the times had greatly altered. By 1917 millions and millions of men from all walks of life were mobilized and hence ripe for organization, and these millions included many officers of the "reserves," active in the revolutionary movement, who became propagandists and agitators, and at the crucial moment leaders of a revolution which was ultimately accelerated, though at first retarded, by the World War. For the first consequence of the outbreak of hostilities had been to put an end to the widespread strike movements of the early part of 1914 and hence postpone the Revolution. Universal and genuine patriotic fervor countenanced no internal dissent. But the reckoning with the decaying regime was simply postponed for three years. Nothing could have averted that final reckoning. It was merely a matter of time.

In those three intervening years, however, the Romanov Monarchy seemed positively to rush toward its doom. The extreme of decay was, of course, best exemplified by the scandalous relations established at Court by the so-called Mad Monk, Rasputin. But a hopeless disintegration had already proceeded far beyond the Czar's immediate entourage. The façade of the Monarchy, the bureaucracy, was speedily deteriorating; and the widespread popular discontent had brought about a "leap frog of ministries"—to quote the bon mot of a contemporary "wag" in the State Duma—so farcical that a repetition of the famous case of the Roman emperor who made his pet horse a senator would not have surprised anyone. No upright man of ability wanted to be Prime Minister. Protopopov, Sturmer, Trepov succeeded to the office, each being worse than his predecessor; until finally the situation became so impossible that an old man, Prince Golitzin, who had no qualifications whatever for such a post, was chosen by the Czar to be pilot of the government. Strangest of all was the part played by the hierarchs of the Russian Church in the downfall of the Romanov dynasty. Headed by the Metropolitan Archbishop, Pitirim of Petrograd, they not only recommended many of the most pernicious appointments made by the Czar, but were able to promote or demote anyone they chose.[1] Dr. E. J. Dillon has said of the Russian Court at this period that its "atmosphere was impregnated with mephitic gases."[2] It was indeed; and a good deal of the stench came from ecclesiastical circles.

Such was the background for 1917, when at last the reverses on the fighting fronts translated the growing indignation of the people into action. It was obvious that these reverses, humiliating to the nation, were the result of the incompetence of the government. The economic condition of the country was nearing a complete collapse.

[1] Extremely interesting and illuminating material on this is found in the seven volumes of the Proceedings of the Special Commission appointed by the Provisional Government, that were published in the Russian, under the title, *The Fall of the Czar's Regime*. Leningrad. 1925.

[2] E. J. Dillon, *The Eclipse of Russia*. Doran Co. New York. 1918.

Fourteen million men had been taken away from a productive work. Stores were empty; imports had almost ceased, for the sole European port of entry, Murmansk, was being used almost exclusively for bringing in war supplies, while Vladivostok, in any case too far away, was also almost monopolized by war needs. The transportation system, always inadequately provided with rolling stock, was breaking down under the load of the requirements of the Army. Even the delivery of food supplies to the large centers, including Petrograd, lagged badly; and, as refugees poured into the capital, the augmented population grew more and more restless. For hours, in the bitter cold, women would stand in line waiting for bread, meat, sugar, or kerosene, only to learn at the shop door that no more goods were available. Mere grumbling turned to open agitation for revolt, an agitation fanned, of course, by the professional revolutionaries. That a change was imminent and necessary could not escape the attention of any class, even of that of certain members of the Imperial family, who pressed for some reform before reform without bloodshed should be too late. The State Duma, which had long since ceased to co-operate with the Czar's futile or disgraceful Ministries, realized the seriousness of the situation and prepared to take the helm of the government into its own hands. And plots in the making—some of them involving Members of the Duma—abounded. The memoirs of Rodzianko, President of the State Duma, of Terestchenko, Minister for Foreign Affairs under Kerensky, of Maklakov, the Ambassador at Paris after the Revolution, and of Miliukov, the Foreign Minister of the Provisional Government, are packed with details and information about such conspiracies. One such plot, in which a number of Army officers participated, contemplated a Palace revolution, the idea being that an internal *coup d'état* was necessary to prevent the common people from taking the affairs of state into their own hands.[3] Another scheme involved the deposing of Nicholas II, the consigning of the Czarina to a nunnery, the crowning of the little Czarevitch Alexei, and the appointment of his uncle, Grand Duke Michael, as Regent.

[3] Grand Duke Alexander in his memoirs expressed the opinion that the idea was traceable to the British Embassy.

These various plans, however, were considerably changed by the assassination of Rasputin. But that deed succeeded in solving no major problem. The assassins of the Mad Monk were of the upper stratum; their interests were not those of the nation at large; and they were able therefore to benefit neither the Monarchy, nor the country. Besides, the situation demanded a radical change, not a mere house cleaning in the Court milieu.

This radical change came, as we know, in 1917. A number of strikes in various parts of the country ushered in that fateful year. At the fronts, we have seen, the soldiers were becoming more and more unruly. Officers openly talked of revolution. And when in February "disorders" started in Petrograd, and the government called on the Army, the soldiers refused to fire.

On March 10, or February 25 by the old-style calendar, the Czar issued a ukase dismissing the State Duma. And the Members of the Duma, knowing only too well the mood of the nation, decided to reply by remaining "on the job." Whether or not they actually remained "in session" is a moot point. Miliukov declared that they did not carry defiance quite that far, but merely retired to a smaller chamber to discuss the situation and to resolve not to leave Petrograd. It makes little difference. In "session" or out, they defied the will of the Czar. The die was cast.

Two days later, on March 12, a number of regiments of the Imperial Guard, comprising about twenty-five thousand men, joined the crowds which had come out on the streets to demand an end to the already intolerable situation; and before long all the armed forces had deserted the Czar. Political prisoners were released by the people from various jails and from the Fortress of Peter and Paul. Police, gendarmes, and former Ministers were put under arrest. The Arsenal was seized, as were the post and telegraph offices. The State Duma now named a Provisional Committee to elect a government and preserve order, while the toiling masses formed the soviets and simultaneously offered their help in establishing and preserving order too. Reports from all parts of the country indicated that people everywhere were demanding political control, and were completely and enthusiastically in support of the movement rapidly developing in the capital. Regiment after regiment arrived at the Taurida Palace to express their loyalty to the Duma. This procession included the sailors of the Guards, headed by their commander the Grand Duke Cyril, with a red ribbon in his lapel. He came to declare himself at the disposal of the people, "whom he loved" and "with whose aspirations he was in complete accord." Later, in France, he proclaimed himself Czar of All the Russians, but died in exile twenty years later without having been recognized by the "ungrateful" nation.

When the question of abdication was raised, no resistance was offered from any quarters. There was no choice left. Even the highest commanders of the Army, without an exception, advised the Czar "to do immediately what the interests of the country clearly demanded." So on March, 15, 1917, Czar Nicholas II signed the manifesto of abdication and monarchy was ended in Russia.

The First Provisional Government, formed by the State Duma to rule until a Constituent Assembly could meet, was greeted buoyantly by a majority of the people.

On March 16, Miliukov, its Minister of Foreign Affairs, informed the world by a wireless of the change in government. In this message he stressed Russia's determination to continue the struggle on the side of her Allies. Following this, he listed as the most important agenda of the new regime the granting of a general amnesty; assurance of freedom of assembly, organization, religion, and the press; preparation for the convocation of the Constituent Assembly; abolition of national and religious discrimination; and the granting of civic rights to those serving in the armed forces. A promise was made not to remove from Petrograd the military units which had been there at the moment of the Revolution and which had taken part therein.

Foreign governments, one after another, hastened to recognize this new government and to offer their help in the continuation of the War. The United States was the first to greet the new member of the family of democratic nations. Not long before the February Revolution had broken out in Russia, the United States had severed diplomatic relations with Germany, who had begun her unrestricted submarine warfare. From April sixth a state of war existed between the two countries. Anxious to see Russia continue fighting with the other Allies but appreciative of the appalling economic conditions in the new democracy, Wilson's administration offered generous financial help. For a while the impression prevailed that, after this change, Russia would enter a new era of happiness and success.

But the damage created by the decaying regime could not be remedied simply by a change in the form of government. Profound economic and social changes were necessary, and, naturally, such changes could not be accomplished overnight. The February Revolution, though almost bloodless, was incomplete; and it quickly became clear that the population at large would not be satisfied by the simple replacement of a corrupt group of ministers by one more honest. The soldiers wanted peace; the Revolution, they insisted, had been carried on under the slogan of peace, and they demanded to see this promise translated into fact. The peasants were impatient at the delays in the redistribution of land. The urban population was not satisfied with the tempo of the "improvement" in the economic situation. Bread was still scarce, and the ruble was rapidly becoming worthless.

Thus, the first government formed after the Revolution soon became the target of attacks from Right and Left alike. The task of governing in the circumstance would have been difficult in any case, but it was infinitely aggravated by a curious duplication of power. For, along with the Provisional Government formed by the State Duma almost exclusively of the representatives of the privileged classes, other parallel organs had been formed by the working people. These were the "soviets" or councils, modeled after the soviets which had been formed during the Revolution of 1905 by industrial workers in various manufacturing centers, such as St. Petersburg, where they had functioned briefly until abruptly dissolved by the Czar's regime. Naturally the coexistence of two such organs of political power did not augur well. "Two bears cannot live in one hut," says the Russian proverb. The truth of this saying was soon to be proved.

In April it became known that Miliukov, Minister of Foreign Affairs, had assured the allied governments that the Russian people were determined to continue the War to a victory. Constantinople and the Straits connecting the Black Sea with the Mediterranean were promised by the Allies as a reward for Russia's part in the War. This offer of spoils was, of course, quite out of keeping with the tenets of the Revolution, and it had the effect of arousing popular indignation to a high pitch. How, everybody asked, was it possible for a revolutionary regime to consider annexation of territory belonging to other nations? Had there been no revolution? Why should the people fight for the aims of the imperialist Powers? A demonstration was staged in protest. Not less than one hundred thousand people came out to the streets with placards reading "Make public all secret treaties," "Down with the War," and "All power to the soviets."

As a consequence, both Gutchkov, the Minister of War, and Miliukov were forced to resign. A ministerial crisis followed, and on May 18, the first Coalition Government was formed. Prince Lvoff, the Prime Minister of the First Provisional Government, had already asked the Petrograd Soviet to participate in his Cabinet, in an attempt to consolidate the power and at the same time weaken the soviets. The offer had been rejected, but the soviets were willing to co-operate with the government. Now, six Socialists entered the Cabinet along with nine non-Socialists. Early in June a Congress of the Soviets was held at Petrograd. Still moderate in its political composition—there were only a few Bolsheviks in the soviets at that time—it passed a resolution to support the Provisional Government, and approved its decision to start an offensive on the front. But on July 1 (June 18 by the old style) a demonstration was staged by some four hundred thousand people around the grave of the victims of the Revolution. There, on the former Champ de Mars, with the British Embassy in the background, the slogans, "Down with the War" and "All power to the soviets" were heard again. And that same day, Kerensky, who by that time had become Minister of War, ordered a beginning of the offensive on the front. It proved a complete fiasco. The Russian lines were broken by the Austrians at Tarnopole. The only result was a marked increase in the bitterness against the Provisional Government.

On July 16 (3) and 17 (4) new demonstrations took place in various parts of the country. Hundreds of thousands protested against the senseless attack with such enormous losses. The demonstration in Petrograd was peaceful and orderly, but the government met it with bullets. Asserting, in spite of denial, that this demonstration had been organized by the Bolsheviks, the authorities decided to strike at their enemy and ordered the arrest of their leader, Lenin, who, however, escaped into hiding. And so began the decisive struggle between the Provisional Government and the Bolshevik Party. The latter was seeking control over the soviets in order to overthrow the impotent and vacillating Provisional Government, which now, after the resignation of Prince Lvoff, had been intrusted to Kerensky.

To carry on the struggle, Kerensky needed above all things military support. But his chances of wholehearted co-operation from the Army were already none too good. He had earned the animosity of the officers by a haughty attitude and many tactless attacks. And while in the beginning he had been very popular with the rank and file—he was a golden-tongued orator and could play the role of master of persuasion to perfection—his former prestige as idol of the masses had waned almost to the vanishing point as a result of the disastrous offensive which he had ordered in June. So now, as Prime Minister, his main concern was to overcome the growing influence of the Bolsheviks in the Army and the country in general. Miliukov, in his history of these days, has decribed the period as one "when the Socialists in the Cabinet were defending the Bourgeois Revolution against the Social Revolution." It was a critical struggle, and the fortunes of the bourgeois leaders could scarcely have been at a lower ebb.

A number of steps were taken to strengthen the opposition to the Bolshevik influence, and these inevitably resulted in strengthening the reactionary elements. Numerous congresses and conferences which were held in Moscow during the summer by such groups as the landed proprietors, the various bourgeois and semibourgeois political parties, the All-Russian Commercial and Industrial Congress, the All-Russian Peasant Union, the Economic Council, and the like, offered an opportunity for promoting the "handcuffing" of the Revolution. The

Congresses of the Bolshevik Party, on the other hand, deliberated on achieving the opposite aim. Meanwhile, the infiltration of Bolshevik propaganda in the ranks of the Army rendered discipline by the officers increasingly difficult. The restoration of the death penalty in July did nothing to check disintegration at the front. The Commander in Chief, General Kornilov, who succeeded Brussiloff at the end of the month, attacked the interference of the soviets and demanded dissolution of the committees in the Army units. But no such measures could arrest the rapid bolshevization of the soldiers and sailors.

The middle of August arrived. In spite of the protests of the Leftists, a session of the Council of State was convoked at Moscow. General Kornilov openly demanded the dissolution of all the soviets. His resolute stand against "anarchy" rallied to his support people of various classes and persuasions who for one reason or another wanted "order restored," and in due course a plan was evolved to establish a military dictatorship. Kornilov was to be the leader.

Kerensky's attitude in relation to this plot was, to say the least, suspicious. It was charged that he knew far more about this conspiracy than was possible for a mere outsider; and in his book *The Prelude to Bolshevism,* published in New York two years later, he prints the minutes of his examination by a Special Commission of Inquiry as part of a far from convincing attempt to refute this accusation. In any event it cannot be denied that he carried on negotiations with the conspirators, and ordered the arrest of Kornilov and his collaborators only at the last possible moment. The deathblow to the Kornilov revolt came when General Krimov, sent with troops to seize Petrograd for the rebels, committed suicide when his own soldiers refused to obey his orders. They had learned from Bolshevik propagandists the true aim of the expedition, and they had no intention of helping to strangle the Revolution.

In view of what followed, it is interesting to take a glimpse into the mind of Sir George Buchanan, then British Ambassador to Russia. He held no flattering opinion of the Prime Minister, nor was he anxious to see him win in the struggle with Kornilov. In his memoirs, published several years later, he writes that "Kerensky, whose head has been somewhat turned of late and who has been nicknamed 'the little Napoleon'... cannot hope to retrieve the military situation without Kornilov, who is the only man capable of controlling the Army; while Kornilov cannot dispense with Kerensky, who, in spite of his waning popularity, is the man best fitted to appeal to the masses and to secure their acceptance of the drastic measures which must be taken in the rear if the army is to face a fourth winter campaign." [4] (Actually, after Kornilov was arrested, Kerensky himself became the Supreme Commander.) Nor were Sir George's activities at this time confined to making notes in his diary. In the Proceedings of the United States Senate one may read the statement by Colonel Raymond Robins, who at that time represented the American Red Cross in Russia, that General Knox, then Military Attaché of Great Britain in Russia, had said to him: "You ought to have been with Kornilov," to which Raymond Robins had answered: "Well, General, you were with Kornilov." Whereupon Knox "flushed, because he knew that I knew that English officers had been put in Russian uniforms in some of the English tanks to follow up Kornilov's advance, and very nearly opened fire on Kornilov's forces when they refused to advance from Pskov." [5]

Tidings of this abortive attempt of Kornilov's first came to me when I was still in Japan. I was definitely on the side of Kornilov. I knew enough about him to consider him a good soldier and an ardent patriot (in the sense we had learned to apply to this term in our school days, and continued to believe in without any considerable revision up to those days). From the information I had in the newspapers I was unable to learn much, either of the details of the Kornilov affair or of the Revolution in general. It was natural, I think, that under such circumstances my evaluation of the episode was dictated partly by my esteem for the man, Kornilov; partly by

[4] Sir George Buchanan. *My Mission to Russia and Other Diplomatic Memoires.* Cassel & Company. London. 1923. V. II, p. 172.

[5] Hearings of the Judicial Committee of the Senate. 65th Congress, 3rd Session, 1919. "Bolshevik Propaganda," p. 780.

my belief in the necessity for order and discipline and therefore a strong regime; and partly by certain doubts about the other man in the drama, Kerensky, whose treatment of my fellow officers I did not approve. Anyhow, I expressed my conviction that it would be better for the country to see Kornilov succeed. As a matter of loyalty, too, I was still in favor of continuing the War on the side of our Allies until victory was assured. Had we not been fighting for three years? Was it not natural to seek victory, not defeat? Could we forget the sacrifices of those three years? Had we no moral obligation toward the memory of those who had died on the field of honor?

Two years later, in Kerensky's apologetic presentation of the Kornilov affair,[6] I read the following quotation from a letter written a few days after the attempted coup had been frustrated:

> The Kornilov affair was not the affair of a group of adventurers, and you know to a certain degree that certain circles of our society not only knew all about it, not only sympathized with the idea, but helped Kornilov as far as they could.... I have one more question: I do not know the addresses of Vishnegradsky, Putilov[7] and the others. The families of the imprisoned officers are beginning to starve, and I insist on their coming to their aid. Surely they will not abandon to their fate and to starvation the families of those to whom they were linked by the common bond of an idea and preparation.... In that case (i.e. if this demand is not immediately satisfied) General Kornilov will be forced to declare in detail before the court the whole plan of preparation, all the conversations with persons and groups and their participation, in order to show the Russian people with whom he was working, what real aim he was pursuing, and how, abandoned by all in his moment of need, he had to appear before an improvised court with only a small number of officers.

This informing letter was written by General Alexeieff, former Chief of Staff of the Emperor, and later on Supreme Commander, to Paul Miliukov.

Just a few days after the Kornilov revolt was crushed, I sailed from Japan. On my way west I observed many things which worried me a great deal. There was no order in the country, and chaos prevailed on the railways. Trains were packed with soldiers whose behavior told of the disappearance of discipline; and on the platforms one no-

[6] A. Kerensky. *The Prelude to Bolshevism*. New York. Dodd, Mead & Co. 1919. p. 278.

[7] Well-known Russian financiers who stood at the head of a group of banks.

ticed too many soldiers. They could not belong to the local garrisons. At one station in Siberia I remember having a strange dialogue with a guard on duty, rifle in hand and bayonet affixed. After I lamented, in a very friendly manner, about the unbecoming conduct of the other soldiers on the platform, he looked at me in my civilian dress, as though I were his worst enemy, and said: "What do you want of them? They should kill you and all your kind"; and to make his idea more comprehensible he pointed his gun at me. Unfortunately I found soon that this mood of animosity towards other classes was widespread among the soldiers, workers, and peasants. The atmosphere was filled with hatred. Kornilov's revolt, as I learned later, had aggravated this state of mind to the point where it became quite difficult to converse with anyone calmly and amicably. The common people suspected every "bourgeois" of plotting counterrevolution. Clearly the country was heading for a civil war. No longer were there any signs of rejoicing in the achievements of the Revolution. On the contrary, there were plenty of signs of discontent, gloom, suspicion, and determination to fight for whatever one considered one's due.

On my arrival at Petrograd I found more evidence confirming this general impression. Those who were informed predicted worse to come in a few days. Officials were no more reassuring than were the people on the street. I went to see many of those officials and was shocked to find that the governmental machinery was already cracking and performing hardly any useful work at all.

One of my official calls was on my former aide, Verkhovsky, now Minister of War. He greeted me in a most friendly way. He had wanted to summon me from Japan, but learning from the Chief of the General Staff that I was already on my way to Petrograd, was waiting for my arrival. Now he wanted to hear my opinion of the general situation. The very first thing I told him in reply was that, in my opinion, Kerensky should publicly apologize to Kornilov, and probably resign. Verkhovsky did not start arguing, but told me next that he wanted me to be his assistant. I could only smile at this. I thanked him for the honor, but declined the post. How could I accept it? I was in no way qualified. I had never occupied any administrative positions of that kind. Nevertheless, he insisted that I was the man he wanted and asked me to consider it seriously and give him my consent as soon as possible.

This amounted to a command. What was I to do? First of all I went to see several of my friends on the General Staff. They were unanimous in approving Verkhovsky's choice and insisted that it was my duty to accept the responsibility. So next day I returned to Verkhovsky and became Assistant Secretary of War. This was not a matter of routine work in this office, but of co-operation with the man who trusted me, and whom I had learned to admire for his integrity. It was a revolutionary situation, where unity in judgment or at least similarity of approach, was more important than the office details. In short, I was needed not for my experience in the War Ministry—I had none—but as a man with definitely liberal leanings in political matters, a man long in sympathy with the aspirations of the common people, and open minded enough not to be afraid of any new situation.

Nevertheless, I had my doubts regarding the ultimate wisdom of this promotion, and I asked Verkhovsky not only to consider my new appointment as temporary but to keep my old post at the Tokyo Embassy vacant for a while. To this he agreed.

That I was justified in doubting my adequacy to cope with the muddle which existed in the War Office at this time is borne out by the experience of Kerensky himself during his brief tenure of the post occupied by Verkhovsky. "From the very beginning," he writes in his apologia already quoted, "when I became Minister of War, it was evident, without expending much time in one's survey, in what an inextricable confusion Gutchkov, with his preposterous reforms, had thrown the Ministry.... In fact, the statute which defined the nature of the committees and organizations elected by the soldiers was sanctioned by Gutchkov and appears in his famous order No. 213. The much-discussed Commission of General Polivanov (former Minister of War) which worked out the declaration of the rights of the soldier, and generally has cost the army so dear, existed during Gutchkov's term of office, but was, as soon as my authority enabled me to do so, set aside by me." [8]

A day or two after I began my new duties, Verkhovsky asked me to report on the situation in Moscow, where my other former aide, Colonel Riabtzeff, was in command. On my arrival there, I was met at the station and brought to Riabtzeff's quarters in the Kremlin. It was a small, very unpretentious apartment, probably occupied in the past by some minor official or a servant of the Court. Riabtzeff was a very modest man, utterly unlike Kerensky, who now lived in the Czar's apartment in the Winter Palace and traveled in the Imperial train.

Following a very simple meal, visitors from all walks of life were admitted one by one. There were deputies of the Soviet, delegates from the soldiers and the workers, teachers and doctors, privates and officers. Practically all were emphatic that Kerensky no longer deserved their support. His vacillations, they declared, had demonstrated his inability to cope with the situation. His role in the Kornilov revolt had left a bad aftertaste. He would have no popular support in case of a showdown. The officers came to ask my help in their plan to organize an officers' union. I flatly refused. In my opinion it was wrong to segregate officers from the soldiers; at this moment, it seemed to me, the most important problem was to bring them closely together, to bridge the gulf separating them. I had no doubt that a considerable percentage of the officers sincerely supported the Revolution, and that they could only gain by co-operation with their soldiers. It was dangerous to form a separate officers' union. So I could not approve of their plan. But the chairman of the group, General Prince Drutzkoy, Professor of the Military College of Jurisprudence, whom I knew as an extreme reactionary and a good friend of the famous Procurator Pobiedonostzeff, could not and would not agree with my arguments. As for the younger officers in the delegation, and especially those with the insignia of universities, that is to say officers for the duration of the War only, they obviously were on my side.

[8] A. Kerensky. *The Prelude to Bolshevism*. Dodd, Mead & Company. New York. 1919. p. 71.

Some of them came to Petrograd a few days later, saw me in the Ministry, and demonstrated their approval of my stand in no uncertain terms.

Late that evening, between appointments, I visited my sister, whom I had not seen for a long time. She had heard of my appointment and was sorry that I had accepted. How, she asked, could I co-operate with revolutionaries? No good could come out of it, in her opinion. We had always been good chums in spite of our disagreement on certain matters, and we parted chums, I am glad to say; for this was the last time I saw her. She died during the typhus epidemic that ravaged Moscow during the horrible years that followed.

The next morning Riabtzeff asked me to review the troops. On the Red Square, in front of the Kremlin, for the first and the last time in my life, I reviewed the garrison of that beautiful ancient city, the former capital of the pre-Romanov Czars, and soon again to be the capital of the country under the coming Soviet regime. After the parade was over—and there was little to differentiate it from a parade of Czarist days—Riabtzeff and the mayor of the city, Dr. Rudnev, asked me to drive with them. The ostensible purpose of this excursion was to give me an idea of living conditions of the people, but actually my guides were more interested in explaining to me the possible use of various heights in case of an uprising. They expected one, and before long. No one knew what spark might start the conflagration, but all were certain that a flare-up was inevitable.

I hurried back to Petrograd that evening. My report was not unexpected by Verkhovsky; he had already heard from various places that people were turning away from Kerensky, and that the present Coalition Government as a whole had little support in the country.

One afternoon, Verkhovsky, who was not feeling well, asked me to go in his place to that evening's Cabinet session at the Winter Palace. There, for the first time, I met the Prime Minister, Kerensky, and most of his Ministers. My impression of Kerensky, like Sir George Buchanan's, was not very flattering: he impressed me as a rather young lawyer playing a role to which he was ill-suited, and playing it with more bravado than efficiency. Indeed, the whole session of the

Cabinet depressed me deeply; I could not help feeling the unnaturalness of the situation, so like an *opéra comique* with a tragic ending. After a few minutes of the deliberations one began to suspect that the members of this conclave were nervous and obviously uncertain how to govern a country where new outbursts of popular disapproval were expected at any moment. There was also a touch of grotesque melodrama. In the splendor of the Imperial Palace, the Ministers of the Republic were seated around a huge table, while servants of the defunct regime, in pompous liveries, served tea in glasses and pieces of black bread about one cubic inch in size. I do not remember whether there was any sugar, but probably not. The food situation continued to be as bad in the revolutionary capital as before the abdication of the Czar. As for the agenda of the session, they were of no particular interest or importance: just routine business. I left the palace a sadder and wiser man. It was obvious, even to a newcomer, that after six months of revolutionary government, Russia was on the verge of a new change.

The following day, near the Hotel Astoria, I met my old acquaintances, Generals Prince Bielosielsky and Count Shouvalov. Both informed me, in a confidential manner, and with twinkling eyes that betrayed their satisfaction, that in a few days the Bolsheviks would stage an armed uprising. In their opinion Kerensky "hadn't a chance." In this they were right, even though they were deceived in their obvious hope that the coming change would bring them back the power and wealth they had enjoyed before the Revolution. Less than a month after my return to Petrograd, Kerensky was no longer in power. An entirely new situation, completely unexpected by me, was created by the advent of more radical elements than those ushered into power by the February Revolution.

CHAPTER XIV

THE BOLSHEVIK REVOLUTION

(*Disillusionment and Confusion*)

War aims. Political parties. Meeting the leaders. Members of the Cabinet. Military experts. The Pre-Parliament. The Bolsheviks' armed insurrection. The fall of the Provisional Government. Chaos. My departure for Japan. My arrest at Harbin. Free, and speeding to Changchun. Through Manchuria and Korea to Japan.

ONE OF THE main issues between the moderates and the radical wing of the political battlefront concerned the prosecution of the War. We have seen that when the First Provisional Government—that included only one Socialist, Kerensky—was formed, the determination was reached to continue fighting until victory was achieved. Miliukov proclaimed as much in his first message to the world in general. A little later he announced that Constantinople was promised by the Allies to Russia as her share in the forthcoming spoils. We have also seen how popular disapproval of this violation of the spirit of the Revolution forced the resignations of Gutchkov, the Minister of War, and of Miliukov himself, leading to the formation of a series of Coalition Cabinets in which Socialists were included in increasing numbers. But this made no difference. The cry was still "On to Victory."

And so the fundamental incongruity remained. The ideas and ideals underlying the Revolution were so utterly incompatible with an Imperialist war that a conflict would inevitably arise if the new regime looked forward to indemnities and annexations. Those political adversaries of the Provisional Government who relied from the very outbreak of the Revolution on the toiling masses and their soviets, did not fail to see the opportunity offered by the bellicose stand of the Cabinet. They comprehended very well the mood at the front; they realized the strength of the sentiment for peace and turned that sentiment to their advantage. Thus the antiwar elements found resolute support in the Bolshevik Party. And the Bolshevik Party found in those elements their most powerful weapon against the Provisional Government.

The unsuccessful attempt of Kerensky to renew the offensive in June resulted in a tremendous upswing of prestige for the Bolsheviks. Propaganda among the soldiers was well organized and the determination of the military people not to support Kerensky developed rapidly. When I arrived in Russia from Japan, this trend was so plain that it did not require any high political acumen or even any particular intelligence to foretell a new crisis. The Kornilov affair was but the last and most conspicuous signpost pointing in that direction.

Open warfare between Kerensky and the Bolsheviks was inaugurated in the middle of July with the order to arrest Lenin. The Bolshevik leader, as we know, was not arrested, but was sent by his followers into hiding. There he continued to direct the preparations, first to acquire control of the soviets, and then for an armed uprising designed to place full power in the hands of the reconstructed "soviets of the toiling masses and soldiers." With the slogan of "Peace, Bread and Land!" the Bolshevik Party grew by leaps and bounds from a membership of some eighty thousand members in May, 1917, to one of two hundred and forty thousand in August. It continued to grow; and, as it grew, the moderate, vacillating group of Kerensky rapidly lost ground throughout the country.

I was very poorly informed on the details of the struggle and its underlying causes. All I could learn in Moscow and elsewhere was that after Kornilov's abortive attempt at a *coup d'état* the feeble Provisional Government had lost the support of the masses. From my friends and associates and from the press I learned that "all the troubles originated with the Bolsheviks," who were said to belong to a "criminal type of demagogue." It was openly asserted that some of them were even agents of Germany, and that "their leaders, including Lenin himself, were sent to Russia, through Germany, in order to disrupt the work of the revolutionary government and thereby facilitate the defeat of Russia by the armies of the Kaiser."

The truth of the matter was that I had neither the time nor the means to learn the real facts through wider contacts. I had to rely on what I learned in the circles in which I moved at the moment. But whoever the opponents of the government may have been, it was evident to me that some of their slogans were highly effective, not without reason. The broad masses, I could see, looked on the Revolution as the emancipation of Russia from the evils of the past. They could not see why the war of the Imperialists should be carried on any further. They wanted peace. Peasants whose main concern was to get rid of the *pomiestchiki* (the landlords) and to receive more land, were impatient at the policy of the Provisional Government; they demanded immediate confiscation of the estates and their redistribution among the toilers. It was self-evident that something drastic had to be done without delay to restore the faith of the people in the new regime, to regain their support, and to calm the soldiers, if the country were to be brought out of chaos.

At precisely that time plans were being laid for a mission to Paris to discuss with the Allies the aims of the War and Russia's role after her Revolution. The composition of that mission, which was to be headed by the Socialist, Skobelieff, was such as to leave no doubts that it would uphold the assurance of the new regime that Russia would continue her stand behind the Allies. This was, to say the least, a dangerous stand at utter variance with the actual situation. Yet it was considered disloyal to question our unaltered determination to fight, when actually we were unable to do so. I could not agree with this attitude. It seemed to me misleading, and likely to misdirect our Allies in their further plans. In my opinion we would be doing a far more decent thing if we told the Allies the truth about the disintegration of our armed forces, instead of promising our support.

With this in mind, and knowing that the mission was getting ready to start for Paris, I suggested to Verkhovsky a meeting of the leaders of the political parties. Then a session of the Cabinet could be arranged to discuss the instructions to be given to the mission. It seemed to me at least advisable to review our war aims in the light of the actual situation created by the Revolution. Verkhovsky agreed with my plan. A meeting of the leaders of political parties was arranged and took place the next day in my office.

Avksientiev, Gotz, Dan, and a number of lesser leaders of the Social Democratic and Social Revolutionary parties were present, but not a single representative of the Constitutional Democratic Party (the Cadets) appeared. Miliukov and Vinaver excused themselves by citing another meeting elsewhere. The leaders of the Right were also absent, for they were in hiding. All those present declared themselves in sympathy with the idea of re-examining our war aims. There was no dissent on the necessity for telling the Allies the whole truth, instead of making promises which could not be fulfilled. It was agreed to ask for a Cabinet meeting on the morrow.

Most of the members of the Cabinet and several military experts, whom we had invited in order to bear witness to the actual status of the armed forces, gathered in my office the following day. Neither Kerensky, the Prime Minister, nor Terestchenko, the Minister of Foreign Affairs, deigned to come. Clearly they were no more in sympathy with our plan than were Miliukov and his colleagues.

The discussion opened with my report on the general situation. Professor Prokopovich, the Minister of Food Supply, then gave a sad picture of the utter disorganization of the transport and the pitiful inadequacy of the food supply, both at home and at the front. Minister of Finance, Professor Bernatzky, gave a picture of the status of our finances, which were far from good. The military experts, Generals Golovin and Michelson, confirmed the utter disintegration of the armed forces and the shocking inadequacy of our munitions and other supplies. From the figures presented to the gathering, it was evident that our front was not held by a force capable of withstanding any serious attack. Already thousands of soldiers had deserted their units, and the thin line left along the enormously long front was but a poor guarantee against a break and consequent invasion of the country. There was but one logical conclusion to be drawn from the sum total of these reports. Not only was a re-examination of the war aims imperative, but also this re-examination would have to face the fact that for the time being Russia was practically *hors de combat*. The Allies would do well to consider their chances of fighting without her further help—particularly now that America had joined with them and was preparing an army to be transported to the European battlefront.

Unfortunately, no results were achieved by these two meetings. Of course, we did not deceive ourselves by thinking that it would be easy to influence public opinion merely by declaring that a re-examination of the war aims was contemplated. We had hoped, however, that a declaration to that effect might start a new trend in the policy of the government, which would reconcile the revolutionary masses and gradually win back lost confidence. In short, we hoped that it might lead to more genuine co-operation by the contending parts of the dual government. For my part, it was quite clear to me at that moment that only by reaching a better understanding with the people at large could the government function efficiently henceforth. Without listening to the demands of the people, no government could survive. I did not question that the government was composed of honest people, even though they were not experienced in the intricate business of governing, especially under the double strain of war and revolution. These people, I told myself, were known for their progressive trend and their intellectual integrity. They deserved respect. Therefore I was sure that a compromise with the more radical groups, "in spite of their unreasonable demands," was more desirable than the withdrawal of the present government and its replacement by the Bolsheviks. Even if they could not last long, as was said, their advent would be costly.

Was it naïve to expect that a compromise was possible and that its results might be beneficial? I do not know. Even now that I have become wiser in these matters and probably better equipped to understand them, I am inclined to think, as I did in 1917, that a compromise still could have been arranged, that the clash could have been postponed, if not averted, and that thereby many lives could have been spared and much horror avoided. But dream or plan, it did not materialize. Kerensky was set on fighting. At least, so he said when addressing the Pre-Parliament a day or two later. He declared then that the government was determined to re-establish order and to act resolutely in curbing the extremists.

The Pre-Parliament was designed as a rostrum for the public discussion of national affairs—now that the State Duma had ceased to exist—until such time as the Constituent Assembly could begin to function. It was, in short, a palliative. Nevertheless the Central Executive Committee of the Bolshevik Party declined participation, for in the opinion of Lenin and his closest collaborators it could only detract the people from the real issues of the moment. They insisted that the preparation for a showdown on the political front was in order, not compromise and the lulling of the nation by fruitless debates. Only a few members of the party, such as Kamenev and Todorovich, still attended the sessions, while a few others, like Zinoviev, gave it their approval. But the Party as a whole was busy organizing the Second Congress of Soviets convoked for the end of October.

After the failure of our plan for re-examination of the war aims, Verkhovsky decided to make an appeal at the session of the Pre-Parliament. There he delivered a passionate speech, but unfortunately the result was not what we sought. His speech was distorted by the newspapers opposed to the idea and represented as a demand for peace at any price and the abandoning of our Allies. To disavow this, Kerensky "offered" Verkhovsky a "leave of absence." Next day he left. But before leaving, he asked me to go to the Pre-Parliament and continue the fight for our stand. This I did.

The Pre-Parliament convened at the Maryinsky Palace, where the State Council used to meet before the Revolution. The session was not expected to be of any particular importance. Nothing seemed to be particularly important then. All plans were in abeyance, for everybody expected something to happen at any moment, and no one was sure whether he would have a chance to play a decisive role.

When I entered the hall of sessions, Professor Miliukov was speaking. To my bewilderment I heard him talk about the knapsacks and belts which were, or could be, included in the equipment of the soldiers. It sounded out of place and truly shocking; to me it smacked of a demonstration of contempt for the gathering. I asked for the floor immediately afer Miliukov had finished, and began to talk on the general situation and on the actual condition of the Army. This was my first speech in such an assembly, and, very likely, it was not convincing. When I was through, Miliukov again asked for the floor and protested that they had already heard all this the day before. This was an obvious reference to Verkhovsky; and the session closed without any discussion of whether or not it was desirable to re-examine the war aims, and without formulation of instructions to the Paris mission. Perhaps we were wrong; possibly it was already too late to talk about plans for fighting. But I, certainly, was not aware of this.

A few days later I saw the background more clearly. On November 6 (October 24) the Petrograd garrison, reinforced by the Red Guards, or armed workers, led by Lenin, who had emerged from hiding, began well-prepared armed insurrection. Next morning they occupied the central postal, telegraph, and telephone offices and various other strategic points. Next they attacked the Winter Palace, where the Cabinet was in session, and occupied it on November 8, after breaking the gallant, but weak, resistance of the Junkers and a Women's Battalion. The Provisional Government capitulated; most of its members were arrested—as a few months earlier they had themselves arrested the Ministers of the Czar—but Kerensky escaped. Resistance was hopeless in the face of an overwhelming majority of soldiers backed by the almost united workers and some representatives from other walks of life.

And thus the storm that had been gathering so long broke out and swept away the vacillating Kerensky regime, the reactionaries, the moderates, the liberals, and even those revolutionaries whose ideas did not concur with those of the extreme Leftists, the Bolsheviks, and their sympathizers.

On the very day of the proletarian revolution, November 7, the Second All-Russia Congress of Soviets of Workers' and Soldiers' Deputies opened its session at Petrograd. The Mensheviks, the members of the Jewish Bund, and some of the Social Revolutionaries adjourned from the session, declaring that they disapproved of the "mutiny." When Lenin introduced the drafts of three decrees, one on peace, another on land, and the third on the political structure of the country, they were accepted and confirmed. The first decree authorized immediate negotiations with all belligerents for stopping the War and concluding peace on a basis of equality. The second abolished private ownership of land and placed lands to be confiscated from the landlords and monasteries at the disposal of the toilers. And the third one transferred all power in the country to the soviets. Russia was declared a "Soviet Republic." Then the Congress elected a Council of People's Commissars, under Lenin, and this new executive organ took the place of the former Cabinet of Ministers.

Kerensky, leaving Petrograd in a hurry, left no instructions, and those of his colleagues who still remained at liberty had no idea either of his whereabouts or of his plans. His aim, as we learned afterward, was to muster an armed force sufficient to reoccupy Petrograd and restore his authority by might. He failed because there were no troops in sufficient numbers, who were willing to fight for him. What I had learned several days earlier at Moscow now proved true: there was no support for the Provisional Government either in the Army or in the country.

At the time of the storming of the Winter Palace, my wife's cousin came to the Astoria, the hotel where I was staying, packed my trunks, and moved them to the home of my mother-in-law. On November 8, I went as usual to my office and even wore my uniform. The streets were almost deserted; a strange calm prevailed in the city for a short while. I reached the office without interference. But while I was still there, I had a telephone call announcing that a Commissar was coming to see me. Instead of waiting for the visitor, I left the office never to return. There was no question in my mind of submitting to the new regime, and the alternative was arrest and death. The power was in their hands. Obviously, discretion was the better part of valor. For that same morning the other Assistant Secretary of War, General Prince Toumanov, was found drowned in the canal near our office. He was met on the street by sailors, and, apparently for no other reason than his uniform, was shot and thrown in the water.

Since the Kornilov affair, officers were no longer trusted; a great number of them fell victims to the enraged soldiers. And very likely most of these victims merited neither distrust nor such a cruel reckoning. But one cannot deny that a number of officers, partly as a result of erroneous understanding of their duty, but mostly as result of political ignorance, acted contrary to the aspirations of the nation at the time of the Revolution. In a number of cases counterrevolutionary plots or deeds of the officers resulted in cruel acts of retaliation by soldiers and sailors. In the fortress Kronstadt, and in Finland and other places, officers were killed in appalling numbers and sometimes in the most outrageous fashion.

Next morning I went to the Headquarters of the General Staff, which was one of the departments under my jurisdiction; but this time I wore civilian clothes, for the place was opposite the Winter Palace, where only two days earlier the members of the Provisional Government, to which I belonged, had been arrested. There I met a number of my colleagues and discussed with them the new situation. Most of the other Ministries had decided, I was informed, to sabotage the new regime. But for us sabotage was unthinkable, in my opinion. The Army, especially its units on the front, had to be fed and supplied regularly, whatever the new situation might be. The others concurred with my opinion. Consequently I gave the order that no department of the Ministry of War should be closed and no officer who could get civilian clothes should stay away from work.

It is probably necessary to explain here that neither the Minister of War nor his Assistants, as purely administrative officers, had any troops under their command. We were all functionaries without direct contact with the armed forces. In the confusion of those days, even some very important orders issued by the commander of the garrison did not reach me; and, as a result, I was not even informed about the preparations being made for "crushing" the Bolshevik uprising.

With the departure of Verkhovsky, the assassination of Toumanov, and the arrest at the Winter Palace of General Manikovsky, the Senior Assistant, I became acting Minister of War. To me it was more than obvious that, with no experience in this field, I was not qualified for such a role, especially at such a moment. A newcomer in Petrograd, only recently arrived from abroad and not properly versed in the intricate and confused situation, I was not the man to disentangle this situation. And lacking any previous acquaintance with the troops stationed in the capital at that moment, I was not the man to appeal to the soldiers either. Under the circumstances it was decided that I should at once return to my post in Tokyo.

The Chief of General Staff immediately issued the necessary document, authorizing my departure to Japan. After signing a number of papers which were waiting for me, I went down to the lobby, ready to leave the Headquarters. On the stairway my secretary met me with some more papers for signature. So as not to go back to the offices, I suggested using a little table that was in the lobby, near a window. The doorman immediately pulled down the shade, explaining that it was not safe to expose me to those on the street.

Before I was through with the papers, the door leading to the street was opened with an uproar and a number of armed sailors entered the lobby. My secretary signed to me to get out, and out I went. Fortunately I was again in mufti, and thus escaped meeting the fate of some of my colleagues. My turn "to face the music" had not come yet.

To arrange for my departure I went to see the general who was the chief of military transportation. But he was unable to do anything for me; nobody would heed his orders. So I had to make whatever arrangements I could as an ordinary passenger. I went to the central ticket office and joined the longest line I had ever seen. There was no choice but to stand and wait my turn. In the line I discovered the Rumanian diplomat with whom I had traveled from Japan on my way to Petrograd only two months before. We did not manifest our acquaintance in any undue manner; it was better to be inconspicuous. Finally, I secured a ticket for the next through express to Vladivostok. It proved to be the last such train for years to come.

While waiting for my train's departure, I stayed with my mother-in-law. Apparently, no one knew of my whereabouts, and I was unmolested. The streets were no longer deserted, nor were they particularly calm. Groups of armed workers, the Red Guards, were marching toward the outskirts of the city. There was some fighting with the troops of General Krasnov, who for a while co-operated with Kerensky. But this was soon over. An attempt, led by Social Revolutionaries, to start fighting in the city also was frustrated. Rumors of other counterrevolutionary plots were common, but the workers were industrious in discovering where danger existed and dealt with it effectively. In Petrograd, at least, there was not the slightest likelihood of the new order being overthrown.

Exactly one week after the Bolshevik Revolution, I was accompanied to the station by my brother-in-law, a young doctor, and one of his friends. To be sure about my baggage I went to the baggage car, and discovered that my trunk was not there. Fortunately, I found a porter who was able to arrange things for me, and my baggage was not left behind. I jumped on the train when it had already started moving. So far everything had worked smoothly. But I had a long distance to cover before reaching safety. On the way eastward we found that the struggle was still undecided; in some places the Soviet power was meeting resistance, in others it was slowly establishing itself. The further we went, the more obvious was the confusion and even chaos. Newspapers were scarce and gave little information. Further east there was no news whatever; all wires had been cut.

Train life reflected the unrest and uncertainties. Many of the passengers clearly preferred not to disclose their identity. Some were too talkative, nervously discussing events. Others were too silent. The cars were crowded to capacity by soldiers, who filled every available space including the corridors. The cars on the Russian railways, especially those on the through trains, were arranged with compartments on one side and a corridor on the other. Now those corridors were used as sleeping quarters for the luckier of the soldiers. The less fortunate had to stay on the platforms, but those migrating peasants, in uniform, and with arms in hand, were so numerous that even on the platforms it was not too cold, in spite of the Siberian winter. One way or another they were moving toward home. Discomfort, cold, and even hunger were cheerfully endured.

At Irkutsk the space in the corridor opposite my compartment was stormed by a soldier. Before long his behavior became quite objectionable. In the next compartment were my acquaintances, the Rumanian diplomat and his family. In an attempt to protect the latter I suggested to the soldier that he should at least consider the ladies, especially since they were foreigners, and as such should not be made to suffer unduly from our upheaval. He reacted in a most unpleasant manner. There was no use arguing, and certainly it was better not to have him discover my identity. But this young man was a troublemaker. Somehow or other he found out my name and determined to revenge himself for having been reprimanded. Nothing was easier under the circumstances.

When the train pulled into the Manchuli, on the border of China, a group of local authorities came to my compartment and asked me, "as a member of the Provisional Government, to inform them on the events in Russia, and instruct them what to do." I answered that I was not a member of the government, for the Provisional Government itself no longer existed, and that I had no authority to give instructions. They left me alone.

But this was only the beginning of my troubles. We crossed the Manchurian border, and at the next large station, Hailar, the Russian commandant entered my compartment and wanted to know why I was on my way east? I showed him my papers, which were in order, and he went away. When the train started moving, I overheard two soldiers, rifles in hand, asking the whereabouts of "the general they had to watch." They had been assigned to this pleasant duty by the commandant. I may add they kept out of my way and did not annoy me in the least.

On arrival at Harbin the situation became more serious. Two porters, accompanying an agent of the local police, entered the car, picked up my baggage, and invited me to follow them. When I asked for an explanation, they answered that I was under arrest and must see the commandant. Fortunately, in the station waiting room I met two officers who had known me well when I was attached to the Staff of the Far Eastern Military District at Khabarovsk. They explained who I was; I showed my diplomatic passport and the order of the Chief of the General Staff for my return to Japan. A number of passengers also interposed, indignantly protesting my arrest; and after a short consultation the authorities decided that there was no reason for detaining me. I then asked them to arrest the young trouble-maker instead, and this they did.

I was free but decided that it would be safer not to proceed via Vladivostok, as originally planned. I was in no mood for a repetition of this experience. Accordingly I changed to a southbound train for Mukden and Korea. That night I was in a comfortable bed at the Yamato Hotel in Changchun.

Next evening I reached Mukden. Here I was met by our Military Attaché, who plied me with questions about the situation in Russia. And the following day I was in Keijo, formerly Seoul. Fusan came next, and the boat for Japan. I lost no time on this latter part of my journey. I was too eager to reach "home."

And how good it was to be "home" in Japan, after this short but very eventful visit to my mother country. It was good to see my family again. And it was good to have leisure for thinking over the spectacular, strange, and sad events I had just witnessed. Dizzy as I was from watching the kaleidoscope of change, I did at least appreciate that something of immense importance was going on. At present I felt sick and disillusioned by what I had witnessed in Russia. And I felt utterly confused. I could not comprehend or analyze the significance of what had occurred. Still less could I draw correct conclusions.

CHAPTER XV

CIVILIZATION ON THE DECLINE

(*On the Right Track*)

Back at Tokyo. Meeting of the Russian colony. New Year's reception at the Imperial Palace. News from Russia. An envoy from Semenov. Kolchak's visit. Brest Litovsk. My attitude. Wires from Petrograd. Intrigues brewing. Japanese warships at Vladivostok. My uncompromising opposition to any foreign intervention in the internal affairs of my mother country. Decision to leave for America. A temptation that failed. Moving to a suburb. Curiosity of a chief of police. On the boat to the New World.

TIDINGS OF THE latest developments in Russia greeted me on arrival at Tokyo, but to say that they made me much wiser would be anything but true. Confusion might have been expected in any case, owing to the swiftness of the changes, the unparalleled nature of the happenings concerned, the great distance of Moscow from the Japanese capital, and the wretched organization in the news service. But the intense partisanship on the east side of the arena rendered confusion worse confounded. Misinterpretation, distortion, and even wholesale concealment of the news was so much a matter of course that to keep abreast of events—much less preserve a sensible perspective—was almost hopeless.

One thing only was clear, Russia was in the throes of a much more serious revolution than that of February; and the predictions of the "well informed" that the Bolsheviks would not last more than "twenty days" were already being taken with a grain of salt. Skepticism was growing. Something was seriously wrong, and Russia, apparently, was not to be the only country affected by the storm. To the gloom and weariness generated by war, and the sufferings it had brought to many people, uneasiness, fear, and despondency were now added. Personally, I was more grieved than stupefied by the news from my mother country. More deeply than anything else I felt the disappointment of not having seen that rebirth of my country through revolution, which I had expected to see. But I was not only depressed, I was utterly confused.

Soon after my return, the Russian colony, which had steadily increased since the February Revolution, held a meeting at one of the hotels. I was asked to speak on my impressions of Russia. I made a very short report and, I am sure, a far from clear one, for I was in the dark myself. I expressed the hope that this period of chaos, created by the advent of the Bolsheviks, would soon be over, for they were an alien element whose ideas could not appeal to the nation at large. In this I simply repeated what I had heard and been unable to digest; for the story that Lenin and his followers had come to Russia via Germany in order to disrupt the work of the Provisional Government was still in vogue. The information given out by newspapers in Japan was, as I now know, anything but reliable. Similarly the interpretations offered by members of the Diplomatic Corps were colored by their disapproval of the radical trend of the Revolution, and, in some cases, the mere idea of revolution. Information supplied to the Embassy came from interested sources, and it took no particular perspicacity to see that it was incomplete, to say the least.

But little incidents around me, conversations that I heard, the gradual formulation of opposing groups of opinion, and the opinions of these different groups, slowly but surely opened my eyes. My people became the target of attack, and this shocked me. My country became the object of numerous plots, and that shocked me even more. Soon it became an urgent matter to decide with which group I was going to stand, with what line of conduct to identify myself in the future.

It was a vexing and difficult dilemma. News from Russia indicated that the Soviet regime was not accepted by all classes. In various places resistance had been offered. In Moscow, my old friend Riabtzeff paid with his life for his loyalty to the Provisional Government. At Orenburg another schoolmate, Dutov, headed the local Cossacks' anti-Soviet movement. To the south, in the territory of the Don Cossacks, their Ataman, General Kaledin, was gathering forces for a campaign against the Bolshevik "usurpers." Generals Alexeieff, Kornilov, and

Denikin joined the venture, and a large number of officers of all ranks, as well as Junkers and Cadets, flocked to its standard. Rodzianko, the former Speaker of the State Duma, Miliukov, and other well-known persons were reported backing the movement. Civil war was inevitable, and I was not in sympathy with civil war; the idea of fratricide appalled me. It dismayed me that so many of my friends, and so many good people like Alexeieff, whom I had learned to esteem and respect, were turning to this method of defending what they considered the good of the nation. In any case I was by no means sure that their ideas of good coincided with those of the people at large.

I had been for Kornilov against Kerensky in September because to me he stood for a strong authoritative government in the time of war, not a reactionary movement designed to crush the revolution. Now I was not with Kornilov and his followers. This new civil war, I perceived, was very definitely planned against the revolutionary aspirations of the masses, not for them. The elements on which its leaders relied, the privileged classes, the rich Cossacks, and kulaks,[1] were openly counterrevolutionary.

Soon it became even more obvious to me that I could not and should not have anything to do with this civil war. On the border of Siberia, a certain Cossack officer, Semenov, had established himself with a band of Cossacks and mere adventurers and had started his career of "defending civilization" with wholesale slaughter of all those of whom he disapproved. Already he was killing and plundering on a large scale and in a large area. And very soon after that another Ataman of the same sort—namely the infamous Kalmykov—appeared in the Far East "to save Russia from revolution." But General William S. Graves, commander of the subsequent American Expeditionary Force to Siberia, called Kalmykov and Semenov "murderers, robbers, and cutthroats"—not heroes! [2]

Before long the "saving of Russia from revolution" ceased to be a purely domestic pastime. Japan was demonstrating her concern and

[1] Kulaks, or fists, were the well-to-do peasants, whose interests were for *laisser faire,* not for any radical changes in political, social, and economic structure of Russia.

[2] William S. Graves. *America's Siberian Adventure.* Jonathan Cape and Harrison Smith. New York. 1931. p. 90.

eagerness to interfere in the internal affairs of my mother country. I entertained no illusions about the meaning of this touching solicitude. Nor did other foreign officials with whom I discussed its possibilities. Externally the life of the Diplomatic Corps presented few changes. But in the privacy of their chanceries diplomats were nervously discussing the urgent necessity for curbing the Revolution in Russia. At New Year's we all attended the brilliant Imperial audience at the Palace, where ladies of the Diplomatic Corps swept past in gorgeous trains, some of which represented fortunes; and later at the British Embassy we admired the same pageant of trains and the gracefulness of those who wore them. But the debonair faces did not express serenity. They were deeply troubled by the uncertainty of things to come.

Early in January I had an unexpected visitor in the person of an emissary from Semenov. The Ataman wanted my co-operation in arranging for arms and munition for his troops. Japan, he was informed, would gladly supply him, if I would approach the authorities. I offered the visitor a good lunch, but flatly refused to do anything for his chief. Then, after my guest left, I went to the Ambassador and told him about the mission of this envoy. I told him, too, what I had answered and added that in my opinion to ask Japan to arm such a man as Semenov would be highly dangerous. In the first place, available reports on his activities inspired no confidence, and in the second, it could lead to Japanese help on a larger scale, which might mean Japanese troops. Krupensky listened politely, and on the following day quietly arranged for everything that Semenov asked.

It was about that time that Admiral Kolchak arrived from England. I met him in the Embassy and later entertained him at my home. But our conversation was neither fruitful nor marked by any real congeniality. Kolchak disapproved of the Revolution in general and of the new order inaugurated in the Navy in particular; and in the early days of the February overturn he had accordingly resigned as Commander of the Black Sea Fleet. When the sailors confronted him with a demand for the surrender of his saber, he threw that weapon into the sea. Of my short-lived connection with the Provisional Government, I am sure, he thoroughly disapproved. So our meeting established no relations between us, and we never met again. Before long, however, I learned that Kolchak had become a tool in the hands of foreign and Russian plotters, who placed him at the head of a movement designed to crush the Revolution, with Siberia as a base.

Complications continued to accumulate. Early in December the Soviet regime started negotiations for peace with Germany and her partners. The Allies were not disposed to take seriously the Bolsheviks' appeal, addressed to all the belligerents, immediately after their advent to power, to start negotiations for stopping the War. Germany, Austria, Turkey, and Bulgaria, on the other hand, expressed their readiness to discuss terms of peace. So, on December 15, an armistice was signed with these countries, and preparations for a conference were set in motion. Brest Litovsk was selected as the place of conference.

This sounded as if Russia were seeking a separate peace, in spite of her solemn promise given early in the War and repeated by the Provisional Government. I declared myself decisively opposed to any such discussions. Accordingly, I sent a telegram to Petrograd "protesting the negotiations, undertaken by the group of self-appointed persons, and which had no approval by the people." I added that I could not and would not recognize any government but that instituted by the Constituent Assembly, soon to meet. In reply I received a telegram from the General Staff, signed by Potapov, its Chief and a general of the old regime, asking me to refrain from interference in affairs of which, obviously, I was not informed.

On January 18 the Constituent Assembly was convoked in Petrograd. Its members were mostly from the Social Revolutionary Party and from the Mensheviks.[3] The Bolsheviks were a minority in the Assembly, but they were in control of the political power in the country. There was no chance for reconciliation of the two groups. Therefore the Bolsheviks decided to act in a revolutionary way, as their understanding of the situation dictated, and dissolved the Assembly.

[3] The branch of the Social Democrats which advocated reform, recommended co-operation with the bourgeoisie, and disapproved of the October *coup d'état.*

Ten days before these events President Wilson submitted to the Congress in Washington his Fourteen Points Program for ending the War. It was almost a replica of what we had discussed before the Bolsheviks came into power. Now it had become respectable in Allied circles to talk about peace, and even on the same terms as the Russians had suggested a few months earlier.

But peace was not yet in sight. Indeed a new war was in the making. On January 12, the Japanese cruiser *Iwami* arrived at Vladivostok, to be joined two days later by the British warship *Suffolk*. They came "to protect their nationals and their property," of course. There was no open talk of "intervention" yet, but only rumors. Nevertheless, I was seriously worried both by the possibility of an invasion and by the even more disheartening news from the European front.

Negotiations at Brest Litovsk ran into a series of deadlocks. Finally, on February 10, Leon Trotzky, who was chief Russian delegate at the Conference, declared that he could not accept the arrogant terms offered by General Hoffmann of Germany; and the negotiations were broken off. Lenin was furious, for he realized the utter impossibility of resisting the Germans, who would now inevitably renew their attack. But at the moment he had insufficient support in the Soviet to take a stand on this question. So the German armies marched again, and easily occupying a number of Russian towns, such as Minsk, Lutzk, Pskov, and Reval, continued their advance until they were checked near Narva. On March 1, Lenin issued an appeal to the nation calling for readiness to defend the mother country from the Germans, and in order to save the Revolution. The Congress of Soviets now expressed its concurrence with Lenin's recommendation to accept the German terms. But the new terms proved to be even more severe than those Trotzky had rejected. On March 3 the Treaty was signed, and on the fifteenth of March it was ratified by the Special Session of the Congress of the Soviets.[4]

On receiving this news, I called a meeting of all Russian officers then in Tokyo, to discuss the situation. A resolution drafted by me,

[4] On November 13, immediately after the capitulation of the German armies and the signing of the Armistice on the western front, the Brest Litovsk Treaty was annulled.

expressing our indignation at the abandonment of the Allies, was passed and its contents wired to Petrograd. It was a futile and despairing gesture, to be sure, but I felt that as a Russian, and especially as a representative of the Russian Army abroad, I had to make at least a protest. Duty and patriotism seemed to demand that a statement should be made to the effect that Russian officers did not necessarily concur with those who, "unrecognized by Russia as her lawful spokesmen, had given their signatures to a document that reflected on Russia's honor."

Now that many years have passed since the humiliating Treaty of Brest Litovsk was consummated, one can see, in the light of subsequent events, how farsighted Lenin had been. The utter inability of the remaining fragments of the Imperial Army to offer any resistance to the onslaught of the Germans should have been self-evident. The Allies paid no heed to the requests for help coming from Moscow. Indeed, after the Rada, the autonomous government of Ukrainia, headed by antisoviet elements, was tricked by the Germans into signing a peace treaty with the Central Powers independently of Russia, the latter was faced with a situation in which no other solution than that advocated by Lenin was possible. And in spite of all the disadvantages of the terms imposed by Hoffmann, Russia did gain thereby a respite that enabled her to concentrate on the more urgent problem of saving the country from further chaos and disintegration.

As for the territorial losses, they were temporary. Germany herself experienced much more serious consequences of aggression at the time of Napoleon, only to regain her lost territories and to take sweet revenge. In the middle of October, 1806, the Prussians were routed by the Corsican. The Emperor himself led the attack on Jena, his Marshal Davou, that on Auerstadt, and forced the Prussian armies into a retreat which proved to be the beginning of the complete annihilation of the German military machine. One after another, garrisons of large German cities and strong fortresses capitulated, most of them even without resistance, to the triumphantly advancing French armies. Within a few days' time Napoleon entered Berlin. But less than seventy years later the German armies had their revenge. In 1870 they defeated the French, and in 1871 their leaders were dictating arrogant terms of peace at the same Versailles, where in 1918, the triumphant Allies dictated a still more humiliating treaty to the Germans. By that treaty, among other things, they were deprived of what they extorted from the Russians at Brest Litovsk.

Organized opposition to the Bolshevik regime spread quickly after Brest Litovsk, both within and without the borders of Russia. Dutov was active in the Orenburg region. The Volunteer Army in the south was growing, and armed clashes had already occurred. Semenov and Kalmykov were causing trouble in the Far East, while other groups were forming under Baron Ungern in Dauria and under Baron Tirbach in Trans-Baikalia. Our information about the troops in the European part of Russia was sparse, but news from Manchuria and from the Russian Far East told a detailed and horrible story. The Atamans were staging a wholesale slaughter. Plundering and burning of villages suspected of harboring Bolsheviks or their sympathizers, were common.

To would-be interventionists all this was most opportune, and foreign interest in Russian events developed noticeably. One week before the arrival of the Japanese cruiser *Iwami* at Vladivostok a raid on the local hotel, the Versailles, took place. Most of the guests were robbed, but it was interesting to note that not a single Japanese was molested or lost any of his belongings. The old technique was still afloat—that same technique which became so familiar to the postwar world, when excuses for various irregular acts could always be found in curiously appropriate "incidents." Without delay the various consuls began posting protests, complaining of chaotic conditions in the country, and demanding more adequate protection for foreigners.

In March a conference of representatives of the Powers took place at Peking. Worried by the trend of events in Russia and its effect upon the Far East, they discussed possible methods of interference. The deluge of telegrams about means of "saving civilization" at this time seemed to denote something very like panic. Nerves already rasped by the protracted War were apparently shattered by this new calamity, the Russian Revolution, which seemed to menace the very basis of the old order. Was it possible that defenders of the latter were beginning to doubt a civilization which was ever more corrupt, rapacious, and vulgar? Was it not on the decline?

Vladivostok, where the Japanese and the British warships were already "guarding civilization," had enormous stores of war materials. More than one million tons, worth hundreds of millions of rubles, were piled near the piers or along the coast. Shells, cannons, powder, shoes, knapsacks, and what not were stacked under the rudest kind of covering, or under none at all. The gunpowder alone amounted to almost three million five hundred thousand pounds; and then there were thousands of tons of valuable metals of all descriptions. It was necessary to protect all this, especially because part of it had been delivered from abroad without payment.

A considerable percentage of these goods, possibly most of them, had been shipped by my office from Japan. Bills had remained unpaid, for it was long since my current account had been augmented by a new draft, and I could not expect another for some time. And what I had at my disposal was certainly not enough to pay in full our outstanding obligations. The last draft entered on my accounts was of October 25, the day of the Bolshevik Revolution. But this was a minor amount, covering only the salary of one of my affiliates; no considerable sum had been received since October 15. When I left for Petrograd, only one million and five hundred thousand yen remained. While in Petrograd, I had arranged for several substantial drafts, and on my return to Tokyo there were over seven millions on my accounts, but even that was very far from my requirements. I decided to divide this money between all the firms with whom we had business, and reserved only a modest sum for the expenses of the office. On March 1, when I decided to resign and to leave Japan, I transferred 250,000 yen to the account of my aide, Colonel Podtiagin, whom I designated, with the Ambassador's approval, to take over my duties. But, by agreement with my successor, almost one half even of that small amount was used, before I left Japan, to cover a few more outstanding bills.

I decided to resign because the preparations for intervention in the internal affairs of Russia were developing at high speed. My old friend, General Tanaka, was a most ardent advocate of foreign interference. I could not and would not have anything to do with it. No country has any right to interpose in the internal affairs of another. And in any case I should certainly have disapproved of the kind of machination which was carried on around me regarding intervention. So before the end of February I made all arrangements for leaving Japan. We moved to a suburb of Tokyo, in order to dispose of everything that we had: furniture and various collections of bronze, china, brocade, and arms. Now, in lieu of other better amusements, foreigners in Japan were fond of attending auctions. We did not go to see the spectacle but heard that it was an interesting one. The French Ambassador was anxious to have our oriental rugs; collecting them had been my hobby, when still in Caucasia. But a wealthy Englishman outbid him. They brought considerably higher prices than I had paid for them originally. Our automobile was sold even before the auction was started for almost twice as much as we had paid more than a year earlier. The importation of automobiles had been practically stopped by the War, and even second-hand cars were at a premium. It was certainly a bit of luck for us!

My decision to resign was strengthened by the signing of the Brest Litovsk Treaty. A telegram received from the General Staff in reply to my protest informed me that I must report at once to Petrograd to face the Revolutionary Tribunal. But the same communication informed me that all officers above thirty-seven years of age were allowed to resign if they wished. I was below that minimum age, but one could resign "on consideration of health." Another wire informed me that General Baron Boodberg, my former chief, was coming to take my place. When Krupensky learned this, he declared very emphatically that he had no intention of recognizing Boodberg or any other appointee of the new regime. The whole situation offered a technical justification for my leaving Japan. I wrote out my resignation, pleading ill health, although my health was never better, and, as a matter of formality, mailed it to the General Staff in Petrograd. To Krupensky I explained that I could not remain at my post for I was utterly opposed to any foreign intervention in the affairs of Russia. He, certainly, did not protest my decision. Anyhow, according to the Russian rules, I was not under his jurisdiction; he was only the senior representative, and I was independent of him, and directly subordinate to the General Staff.

The coincidence of these events resulted in various untoward interpretations of my decision. A rumor spread that I had decided to return to Russia and make peace with the new regime. This was not true. I did not even contemplate the possibility of such a step; so partly to refute this rumor, and partly to explain my stand, I wrote an article for *The Japan Advertiser,* one of the largest English language papers in Nippon. The following extracts may give an idea of my attitude at that time:

PRESENT CRISIS WILL REVEAL REAL FRIENDS OF RUSSIA[5]

The communication which has appeared in the local press that I am leaving Japan in the next few days and that I am going through America and England to Russia is correct as to the fact, but leaves ground for different comments. I think it therefore my duty to give some explanation of this departure. I am certainly going to Russia, as every Russian who sincerely loves his country will sooner or later return home and try to do for his country all that is in his power. Before returning home, however, I intend to stay in America and Europe; but as to the term I cannot decide for the moment and it is possible that I shall stay abroad until the end of the war.... I am willing to offer my knowledge, experience, and even life for the common cause of the war which had been begun so well and beautifully by us Russians shoulder to shoulder with the Allies for aims which were and are so dear to every Russian. I shall certainly try by my work first in America and then in Europe to demonstrate as forcefully, as my weak abilities will permit, that the Russian people has not betrayed the common cause and that the Russians have not renounced and do not refuse now to fulfil the duties which have been imposed upon them not only by inviolable treaties, but also by the sincerity of their sympathy for the ideal which animates the Allies in this war.

Of course, the acute and prolonged illness of the country has absolutely excluded the possibility of continuing the fight on the same battlefields which have been moistened by the blood of millions of Russians....

Everybody who knows the history of Russia is acquainted with her manyfold crises when the country was on the verge of ruin, being torn by civil war and menaced by partition. *From each of these crises Russia emerged successfully by her own inherent strength,* and remained not only intact but also renewed her life with even a stronger vitality....

[5] *The Japan Advertiser.* 1917, No. 8506.

On rereading this opus of mine, the title of which was supplied by the editor, I am not particularly proud either of my ignorance about the interest of the Russian people in the aims of war, exposed by this article, or by its literary "qualities." But it was written with the best of intentions and the possibly naïve sentiments were quite sincere. It was dictated by a genuine resentment against the lowering of Russian prestige by the Brest Litovsk Treaty, and by my desire to express a personal loyalty to the Allies by offering my services in their ranks. At the same time the article was an opportunity to stress Russia's ability to muddle through her crisis, without any foreign "aid" in restoring order.

My decision to leave the country was known to the Japanese officials long before the publication of this article. Everything that went on in my office and home was reported regularly to the proper authorities. My "first boy," the butler, sometimes did this very unceremoniously over the telephone in the hall adjoining my office. One afternoon, during office hours, the telephone rang and a voice asked for one of my assistants. Someone at the Ministry of War was curious to know which Japanese decorations I had, explaining very obligingly that the authorities were anxious to see me decorated properly. I have always looked upon this as a clumsy subterfuge to tempt me into canceling my departure. But they did not succeed, and my collection of medals was not augmented by a new decoration from Japan. After we had moved to the hotel in the near-by small town, actually a part of Greater Tokyo, the local Chief of Police paid me a visit. He wanted to know why I had decided to leave. Was I dissatisfied with something? Did I disapprove of something? No, everything was fine! Just that I had decided that with the new developments I was unable to remain at my post: it was simply a personal matter. I was ready to sail for America.

Baron Boodberg arrived several weeks before we sailed. I paid him all due respects and greeted him warmly as an old friend, but explained that he could not expect to become Military Attaché at the Embassy. He understood the situation, of course, and explained that he had accepted the assignment simply as a means of leaving Russia, where, as he asserted, he could not be of any use at that moment.

One more problem remained before sailing. This concerned the fate of the sanatorium which had been opened not far from Tokyo by the Russian Ladies' Committee, of which my wife was president. Originally, it had been planned as a modest rest home for a dozen or so convalescent soldiers. But after the Revolution, when the lot of the officers became extremely unhappy, it was decided to invite officers, not soldiers. The change produced all sorts of trouble. Not only were the officers more particular in their demands, more difficult to satisfy and harder to handle, but they were politically intolerant. This was not surprising. Many of them had suffered keenly from the atmosphere of suspicion and even hatred which was felt from the very outbreak of the Revolution, and this had been greatly increased by the Kornilov revolt. Usually unversed in the interpretation of events, for they had been artificially kept from politics by the design of the old regime, they reacted in a most violent way to changes which seemed to them unjust and irrational. The result was that many of the officers developed not only an antipathy toward the Revolution, but also a passionate desire to punish the "culprits" and avenge themselves.

To these gentlemen I was a symbol of the hated Kerensky regime, and hence an object of their scorn. This made my position uncomfortable in the extreme, for, as Military Attaché, I was responsible for all Russian Army men residing in Japan. And when, in the line of duty, I visited the sanatorium shortly after my return to Tokyo, I felt a draught almost instantly. The attitude was deliberately correct—and deliberately cold. This was my first experience of the kind. In all the years of my service I had always enjoyed the most friendly relations with my fellow officers—superiors, equals, and subordinates alike. I was deeply hurt; I could not see that I deserved such treatment. Yet this sort of reaction to my prorevolutionary tendency soon proved to be a growing, not a diminishing, phenomenon, and I was faced with the alternative of dissociating myself from what I considered right, or facing the consequences of not being what in the American collegiate parlance is called "a regular fellow." Regular or not, I made my choice. I could not align myself either with outsiders who were trying to strangle my mother country, or with any class or group of my compatriots who had a similar aim.

On March 20, 1918, we sailed from Yokohama on the Japanese boat *Korea Maru*. Endless bouquets, plants, and flowers from various friends and firms with whom we had had business, were showered upon my wife. Among them was an enormous bouquet brought by the officers of the sanatorium. They had come to wish her "bon voyage"—but not me, as I was told about a year later.

The boat was filled with American missionaries from China, homeward bound on furlough. It was a mixed crowd. The number of children was amazing, which was pleasant for our daughter. As for my wife and I, we did not lack agreeable company. My Assistant, Colonel Aivazoglou, and our friends, an engineer with his wife, who acted as governess to our daughter, went with us to America to seek new opportunities. We spent most of the time on board making plans for the future. Our companions insisted that we should join in buying a farm and settle in California. I shook my head; I had other plans, and I was not made to be a farmer. No, I was going to Washington to see what could be done to fulfil the plan of which I wrote in my article for *The Japan Advertiser*. As for my family, I was certain that they would be happy in the New World, even if left alone for a while. My faith in America was unlimited. I had always thought of it as the land of justice and universal opportunity.

CHAPTER XVI

DEMOCRACY ENDANGERED

(*In the New World*)

Expectations and impressions. San Francisco. Eastward ho! Boston is the center of America for a professor from Harvard. Still I am going to Washington, Chicago, and New York. Consuls, and my shocking suggestion. Russian officers and their strange tutors. Ambassador Bakhmeteff. Audience with Secretary Baker and General March.My plan for Russian volunteers. There is no chance for a general. Pamphlet by request. Committee of "prominent" Russians. Dr. Masaryk's arrival. America is interested in the Far East. My return to Russia. Kolchak's *coup d'état*. Back to America.

OUR ACQUAINTANCE WITH the New World began while we were still on the Pacific; for to break the monotony of the seventeen-day journey, the boat was allowed a one-day stop at Hawaii. And here, strangely enough, what impressed me most was not the natural glory of the Islands, their surroundings, nor even the wonders of the aquarium, but a certain sugar mill we visited. The complete mechanization of its process of production gave me my first glimpse at the industrial progress of the country as a whole. This was the first characteristic which impressed me. To be added, before long, was the boundless energy and remarkable efficiency of the people, offsprings of pioneers, or themselves pioneering immigrants in search of what has since been called "the more abundant life" and ready to work hard to attain it.

Our first visit to the Western Hemisphere promised to be an exciting experience. We expected something quite different from the familiar sights of Europe, something quite incomparable to the Asiatic scene. And in this connection I remembered well my conversation with the American engineer years before in Japan. I should have liked to check him on his comparative opinions as to the evils of the

Russian system under the Czars. Now, at last, I should be able to see democracy at work, to compare, and draw my own conclusions. But first we would go sightseeing and thus acquire a rudimentary knowledge in the geography of the country.

After a few days in San Francisco, I left my family and our friends, and started eastward via Los Angeles. First of all I wished to pay a visit to Hollywood, for I had heard so much about the importance of the movie industry; and next I longed to see the Grand Canyon. That unique, majestic panorama, or rather kaleidoscope of ever-changing colors, fully repaid the little detour. I remember that in the hotel there I met at breakfast a fine elderly gentleman, who, on learning that I was on my first visit to the United States and going to New York and Washington, most strongly disapproved of my itinerary. In his opinion I should first go to Boston, for only there, he said, would I get a "taste of the real America." This gentleman was a professor from Harvard. Yet, strange to say, I persisted in making the mistake of going to New York instead. Boston I did not reach till eight years later and only then did I discover wherein lay the indisputable advantage of the capital of Massachusetts over the Empire City with its tall skyscrapers. People do not push you in Boston as much as in New York, and apparently are not in such a hurry.

While speeding through the desert on the Santa Fe train, I was fortunate in my fellow travelers. Two ladies from Kansas City, apparently curious to find out who was the lonely, un-American-looking passenger, began to talk with me. Having discovered that I was not only a foreigner, but was on my first visit, they volunteered to enlighten me on their hospitable country. When there was no better way of killing time, they asked me to read a magazine—I think it was the *Cosmopolitan*—which contained an article by Theodore Roosevelt. This was interesting to me not only because the author was a former President of the United States, but because the article dealt with the Root Mission to Russia. This Mission was sent by President Wilson to my mother country almost immediately after the February Revolution to study conditions, and incidentally to ascertain what opportunities the Revolution might have opened up for American business. Theodore Roosevelt severely criticized Elihu Root for his failure to grasp the real meaning of what was going on in Russia. Facts, of course, justified the stand of the Colonel.

On arrival at New York I called first at the Consulate, and then visited the Flatiron Building, where the Purchasing Commission had its offices. Here I was astonished to find a staff of probably ten times as many officers as I had in Japan, although the volume of orders actually executed here was possibly slightly less. But everything in America must be "bigger and better" than elsewhere, and I assumed that this explained the multitude of highly paid functionaries. They had an officers' society, and its president asked me to come and give a talk on what I had seen in our country during the Revolution. From even a casual acquaintance with this group it was easy to conclude that most of the officers were not only discouraged but in complete confusion about the prospects of Russia. Unfortunately, being poorly informed politically, if not simply ignorant, they had to turn for guidance to someone supposed to be better versed in these matters. The result was that the officers' society fell under the influence of a lawyer and a civil engineer who had their own plans and obviously were not particularly interested in the fate of the officers as human beings. The result was deplorable. A majority of the officers had been induced through propaganda to hate the Revolution; but what lay behind the Revolution they neither knew nor cared to know. In such circumstances I realized that, as a former member of the Kerensky Cabinet, I could not be *persona grata* in that milieu. The "lawyer" even asked me point blank if I had not been disgusted by all that the Revolution represented. I certainly was not, and that finished me with the officers' society.

There was no doubt in my mind about the patriotism of the overwhelming majority of these officers, but I also suspected that it meant loyalty to the Czar and readiness to die for him and for the glory of the country. It seemed to me that in their lopsided glorification of monarchy these old-style military men failed to recognize that a nation consists, not of the figurehead, but of an entirety of people living on a definite territory under the rule of one or another political system. The main element of patriotism, in short, eluded their notice. They had no conception of loyalty to the nation as a whole; the common people, in their view, were put on this planet to work or die as ordered. It would have surprised and shocked them profoundly to learn that they subordinated the interests of the country to the fate of a system, that they were classbound. Indeed, I am sure that the majority never thought of themselves as members of a class, or that their class was already engaged in a losing battle with the newly risen proletarians. Differentiation of classes? The class struggle? There was no such thing, according to the best authorities. Those behind the Revolution, or even in sympathy with it, were either self-seeking, stupid, or positively criminal.

Here I am reminded of the case of a former captain of a Caucasian regiment, whose little book I sent to Hoover's library on the Russian Revolution at Stanford University. A gallant officer, who had fought at the front with distinction and been wounded a number of times, he was completely bewildered by the coming of the Revolution. When that calamity arrived, the young man complained, he and his fellow officers instinctively looked to some general for guidance. They were used to receiving and blindly following orders, and were helpless without them. So they simply did as best they could and followed the dictates of their wrongly conceived patriotism. Casting in their lot with a regime which could no longer save their country, they lost, in the end, both cause and country. It was surely a greater punishment than most of them deserved.

From New York I went to Washington. Ambassador Boris Bakhmeteff, himself an appointee of the First Provisional Government, naturally did not show any animosity toward me. On the contrary, I found in him a kind and understanding listener. After dinner at his home, we spent several hours talking about our country and discussing the probable trend of events; I think, when we parted after midnight, he concurred in my opinion that foreign intervention in the affairs of Russia was inadvisable, to say the least. But the next morning, when discussing the same question with the Counselor of the Embassy, Soukine, I was told that I was utterly wrong; the only proper solution was to ask for the intervention, not to oppose it. This young man, I may add, soon afterward became Minister of Foreign Affairs in the so-called Siberian government, and later on Assistant Minister of the ill-fated Kolchak government. Still later he became its acting Minister of Foreign Affairs, for Sazonov, his chief, remained in Paris to direct negotiations with the Powers. Their work added nothing either to the welfare of their country or to their own glory.

While in Washington, I was introduced by our Military Attaché, my good friend Colonel Nikolaiev, to the U. S. Secretary of War, Newton D. Baker, and to the Chief of Staff, General Peyton C. March. This was merely a courtesy call; but it led me to present them with my memorandum on the further effective participation of Russians in the War. My personal desire was to be allowed to serve with the American army. After a short while I received a letter signed by General William S. Graves, then Assistant to the Chief of Staff, conveying Secretary Baker's "appreciation of the valuable suggestions submitted" in my memorandum; but in regard to my own services I was told that there was no place for a foreign general in the ranks of the American army. I could enter as a private; but, as I did not consider that in such a capacity I should be particularly useful, I dropped my idea of military service for the time being. However, I did go to the nearest registry office, and after answering all the questions they asked me there, received a certificate. That ended my still-born career in the American fighting forces. The time when Lafayette, Kosciusko, and other foreigners were welcome, was gone.

Having decided to remain for a while in the United States, I went back to California to get my family, and immediately returned to New York. From then on New York became our headquarters.

In the mean-time I was doing what I could to be useful to my own country. Ambassador Bakhmeteff, who was forming a "Committee on problems of rendering help to Russia," invited me to participate with a number of other "prominent" people. Professor Baron S. Korff, former Deputy Governor General of Finland, who later became a lecturer in history at Columbia University; A. Bublikoff, a brilliant engineer and Member of the Duma during the revolutionary days of

1917; Bashkiroff, a wealthy merchant, who was Assistant Minister of Supplies under Kerensky; Sergius Ughet, the Commercial Attaché; and a few others, were members of this Committee. We used to meet once in a while to discuss the events, but it was a mere futile exchange of ideas, and nothing ever came of it.

News from my mother country at this time could scarcely have been worse, for a new peril had been introduced by the problem of some forty thousand Czechs, former prisoners of war, who were allowed by the Provisional Government to form their own units, and later allowed by the Soviet government to return to Europe. On their way through Siberia the Czechs turned their Russian guns against the country which had treated them so well; a move in which they were instigated by those foreign residents of Russia whose activities in co-operation with the various counterrevolutionary groups have been so vividly pictured by His Britannic Majesty's onetime chargé d'affaires, Bruce Lockhart, in his revealing book entitled *British Agent*. Thus, by the end of May, the Czech troops were in occupation of Cheliabinsk, Penza, Syzran, and Kazan, where they seized six hundred million rubles worth of bullion belonging to the Russian State gold reserve, which had been transferred thither from Petrograd when the Germans menaced the capital. This was a serious blow of far-reaching consequences, for a large percentage of this gold never returned to the Bank, which, whatever its new name and management, still rightfully belonged to the Russian people. As a result the latter were permanently deprived of a considerable portion of their wealth. Such was the price of the "intervention."

By the end of June the Czechs were in control of practically the entire railway from the Volga River to Vladivostok; and in the east they were not alone; for some Japanese had already landed, and more were expected. Other foreign expeditionary forces followed the example.

In Samara, on the Volga River, a number of members of the Constituent Assembly, which had been dissolved by the Bolsheviks, gathered to set up a provisional authority in the form of a committee called *Kochum*. At Omsk, yet another group was functioning under the name of the Siberian government, only to be replaced by a Directory composed of five members of the Social Revolutionary Party, with Avksientiev as its head. In the southern part of European Russia likewise a number of antisoviet governments were active.

It was at about that time that Thomas Masaryk, the national leader of the Czechs in their emancipation movement, and later the first President of their Republic, arrived at Washington. His coming posed a pretty problem to our Embassy: should they welcome or ignore him? It was at length decided that he should be officially met at the station pending developments. And before long the stand of this venerable old man became quite clear. His first and utmost concern was the liberation of his people; he completely approved the acts of the Czech Legionnaires. Thereby, he became *persona grata* to our Embassy and to all who advocated the sending of troops to curb the Russian Revolution. These interventionists, incidentally, were dominent in influence when later on the future of the Czech nation was discussed.

Early in July, at exactly the time when the Fifth Congress of the Soviets discussed and adopted the Constitution of the Russian Soviet Socialist Republic, uprisings organized by the Social Revolutionaries and the so-called "White Guards," occurred in Moscow, Yasroslavl, Muromsk, and Rybinsk. All these revolts were crushed, and the net result was to strengthen the Soviets, for more people of the lower strata became convinced that the privileged and their collaborators were against this regime.

Soon after my arrival I was asked by the Embassy to write a pamphlet on the role of the Russian Army in the World War. This pamphlet was published by the Russian Information Bureau in New York and mailed to the members of the Government, and to Congress, as well as to various diplomatic agents, and to the press. It was a short outline of the gallant service rendered by the Russians from the outbreak of the War up to the Revolution, and it stressed the fact that, even after our collapse, the Germans and Austrians found it necessary to keep about forty-seven divisions, or more than seven hundred thousand men, on the Russian front. "These figures," I said

"... will grow, for to restore order in Ukrainia the Germans will have to reinforce their garrisons...."

What I meant by this was that the Germans, who had tricked the Ukrainians into signing a separate peace treaty about a whole month before Brest Litovsk, and had then invaded their country, were now plundering it. Naturally, the population, when they realized the real meaning of the German visit, rose en masse against the marauders from Berlin. Finally the Germans were forced to retreat, leaving behind them ruins, gallows, and the undying hatred of the Ukrainian people.

On all the borders of their country the Russians were gradually learning the price of intervention, friendly and unfriendly alike. But few of those living abroad realized or even bothered to think about its meaning. I remember being invited, soon after my arrival, by our Consul General at New York to a dinner at his club. There, after we had adjourned to the sitting room for coffee and a resumption of our conversation, one of the party asked me what in my opinion we should all do in the circumstances I had described. My reply was that we ought to try to understand the other side too, and to gain a better understanding of the deep causes of the Revolution, and that we should regard foreign intervention, of which all the offices were already talking, not from the point of view of possible restoration of the privileged classes in Russia to their old position, but in the light of the price which might be demanded for such a service. Quite obviously the gentleman decided that I was a fool, if not actually a knave.

In the middle of July a world famous tragedy took place at Ekaterinburg, the town in the Urals to which the ex-Czar, Nicholas II, and his family had been exiled. After the abdication they were allowed to remain in the Palace at Tsarskoye Sielo under polite supervision. Later on, under pressure from the Soviets, Kerensky ordered them removed to Tiumien, a small town in the Urals, the plan to allow the Imperial family to leave the country and go to England having failed to materialize because King George V, the cousin of the Czar, was unable to obtain the consent of His Majesty's Government. After the

Bolshevik Revolution of October, the supervision over the Imperial family was made considerably stricter, for there were rumors that monarchists were planning their release, and, when the moment seemed propitious, the restoration of Nicholas to his throne. The rumors became more persistent as the Czechs approached the neighborhood, and finally the local Soviet, fearing the possible flight of the Czar, decided to take the law into their own hands and kill not only the former Emperor, but his whole entourage. On July 16 the entire Imperial household were brutally assassinated and their remains burned in the cellar of the house in which they lived. So died Nicholas II, last Czar of All the Russias, and with him were exterminated practically all the Romanovs who remained within the Empire which he once had ruled.

This horrible news shocked me to the depths. Personally I had only the most pleasant recollection of the Czar.[1] I remembered his kindness, his gentle voice, and his captivating smile, though I also heard of his weaknesses and shortcomings that made him unfit for the role of a monarch. And so, while I was relieved to learn of his determination to abdicate and concurred in the wisdom of removing him from Petrograd, I had sincerely hoped that he and his might be allowed to live out their lives peacefully and happily in England. It was sad enough to know that he must remain a prisoner; but to learn that he had been killed with his whole family, with his four daughters, who did as much good as they were able in their circumstances, not to mention the little Czarevitch, was almost unbearably ghastly. But did this mean that my faith in the people should be killed by an outrageous act of a few individuals? Certainly not. How could the people be held responsible? But this assassination increased the animosity of many outsiders toward the new regime. In it they found a new and strong point for denouncing the regime, for enlisting more support for the plan of sending foreign troops to Russia to crush the Revolution.

[1] Only later, from the *Memoires* of Count S. Witte, from the *Eclipse of Russia* by E. J. Dillon, and especially from the correspondence between Nicholas II and his wife, the Czarina, and his cousin, Wilhelm II, I learned what kind of a man the late Czar actually was.

As soon as the Czechs had established themselves on a fairly solid basis in Siberia, the advocates of "intervention" began to press the American government to join in it. In this Japan was the most energetic of the Powers, though Britain was by no means passive. But for a long time Washington resisted the pressure; and in March, 1918, President Wilson even sent a telegram of greetings and good wishes to the Congress of the Soviets then in session at Moscow, as follows:

> May I not take advantage of the meeting of the Congress of the Soviets to express the sincere sympathy which the people of the United States feel for the Russian people at this moment when the German power has been thrust in to interrupt and turn back the whole struggle for freedom and substitute the wishes of Germany for the purpose of the people of Russia? Although the Government of the United States is, unfortunately, not now in a position to render the direct and effective aid it would wish to render, I beg to assure the people of Russia through the Congress that it will avail itself of every opportunity to secure for Russia once more complete sovereignty and independence in her own affairs, and full restoration to her great role in the life of Europe and the modern world.
>
> The whole heart of the people of the United States is with the people of Russia in the attempt to free themselves for ever from autocratic government and become the masters of their own life.

In other words, Woodrow Wilson pledged the United States to respect the complete sovereignty of Russia in her own affairs, and mastery of her people's life; and it cannot have been easy to convert him a few months later to the principle of armed intervention. But British diplomats were equal to the task; while Japan, the first of the Allies to land troops on Russian soil, even went as far as to suggest later that sending troops to Russia was America's idea. The formula for intervention was found in the desire to help the Czechs to return home—whatever that meant—and a still more far-fetched excuse was discovered in the necessity for preventing the German and Austrian prisoners of war, held in Russia, from forming a new fighting front endangering the Allies.

As a matter of fact, if anything was endangered by this development, it was the cause of democracy. The decision reached in August to send expeditionary forces to Vladivostok and to Archangel, in the North of European Russia, was scarcely in accord with American ideals. Furthermore, this participation in what proved to be simply an attempt to strangle the Revolution in Russia not only led America further away from her traditional policy of keeping out of foreign entanglements, but put her squarely in association with those who wished to see democratic ideals trampled. America is thus not wholly free from the responsibility of preparing the groundwork for that series of aggressions later carried on by the fascist states under the pretext of fighting communism. It is only right to add, however, that at the time this decision was taken the normal processes of American representative government were in abeyance. This was "time of war," and the President's power amounted to dictatorship.

The first American troops to land on Russian soil reached Archangel on August 3, 1918, and Siberia, on August 16. The Commander of the American Expeditionary Force, General William S. Graves, landed at Vladivostok on September first. And I should like to add here that, thanks to the strict fulfillment of the instructions issued to General Graves by Secretary Newton D. Baker, not to take part in political controversies while in Siberia, and his refusal to be swayed by those who wanted it to be otherwise, the American troops were never accused of doing anything wrong in Siberia, and left no bad feeling behind them.

By that time I had decided to go back to Russia, for the government that had been established at Omsk seemed to me altogether deserving of support and respect. Its leader, Avksientiev, enjoyed the best of reputations, while his associates included such well-known leaders of the Social Revolutionary Party as Zenzinoff and Argunoff. This party, with its populist sentimentality and reliance on the peasantry, appealed to me more than any of the others of which I knew. In addition, General Boldyreff of the old General Staff was a member of the Omsk government, which, I felt, had at least a chance of restoring "order" without further bloodshed, now that the Bolsheviks were reported to be retreating on all fronts and very near collapse. Furthermore, the group was said to support the Revolution and hence, I felt, might be counted upon to defend the interests of the people.

The fact that Siberia was in the hands of the Czech troops was interpreted as an indication of the anticommunist sympathy of its population; while the situation in Europe promised a speedy end of the war in the west. Almost on the eve of leaving New York I gave a talk before a large group of liberals on "the Role of Army Officers in the Social Movement in Russia," in which I stressed on one hand the patriotism of that group and their unselfishness in serving their country, and on the other hand the unfortunate lack of political understanding, which had resulted in an appalling death roll of officers during the Revolution. My address was widely approved, published in the local Russian Socialist paper, and issued in pamphlet form. Yet some extreme Radicals suspected it of being an appeal for a "General on a White Horse," or military dictatorship.

Late in September I sailed on a Japanese boat from San Francisco. My fellow passengers included the French Mission, headed by my old acquaintance, General Janin, who had been attached to the Czar's Headquarters and was now appointed to command the Czechs in Russia. In our frequent conversations while crossing the Pacific, Janin and his Staff made no secret of their intention to bring "revolutionary nonsense" to an end. In Janin's opinion Boris Savinkoff, who had been responsible for various terrorist acts in the Czar's time, was most likely to be of help in attaining this end. After the Revolution, Savinkoff had become one of the trusted lieutenants of Kerensky; for a short time he had even been his aide in the War Department.

I remained in Japan only until the next boat sailed for Vladivostok, and in the middle of October I landed in that port. I found Vladivostok nominally under the control of anti-Soviet Russians. But foreign troops were very much in evidence. To say that order prevailed, would be an overstatement. The atmosphere was charged with electricity. There was no feeling of certainty about anything. No one seemed at ease.

On arrival I lost little time in reporting to General Ivanov-Rinov, who was Minister of War of the Siberian Government. To his question what kind of a position I would prefer, I replied that I preferred to have time to acquaint myself with the situation. Emerging from his office, I met my former Commander of the Army, General Pflug, who was not particularly optimistic about affairs of State. Then I went to see my old friend, Kurenkoff, who was an official of the Foreign Office in prerevolutionary days, and was in charge of foreign affairs in Vladivostok. In the evening we both had dinner with the local British Consul and discussed the situation. The following day I paid my respects to General William Graves, but to no other foreign officer. Altogether my impression was not a happy one. Something was brewing.

After a few days in Vladivostok, I wrote to our Military Attaché at Washington, as follows:

On my arrival here I find that the formation of a power acceptable to the majority is far from being completed...hopes for a reconciliation between the Directory and the Autonomous Siberian Government are very slim...the dissolution of the local Siberian Duma has not only split these two groups, but, still worse, brought to almost naught all the work for bringing the people together. This state of mind, naturally, has also infected the new army, which is still in the process of formation. Already there are very disquieting rumors about disunity developing among the armed forces. There are troops that refuse to support the government which showed its contempt of the people's representatives....

Particularly here, in the Far East, suspicion and even animosity toward the Directory is taking the place of the recent warm approval of it...to make the story short: it looks as if the establishment of an authoritative government is still far off....Naturally a strong power is essential: to continue under the existing conditions is impossible; but, it would be a grave mistake to imagine that the people will accept just any sort of a political organization. Shortsighted, indeed, are those who are in a hurry to celebrate the coming of the reaction.

At present the democratic elements of Vladivostok are very gloomy; but the followers of General Horvath are strangely jubilant. The other day there was a parade here...some three hundred soldiers and many more officers...in the crowd some one said: "Look, there are officers of General Ivanov-Rinov; Horvath has his own officers; but the Russian people has none."

The union between the military and civilian intelligentsia observed while the common enemy, the Bolsheviks, were present, is disappearing. Everyone who is more to the Left is now called semi-Leninist, or semi-Bolshevik. Already there are demands for the arrest of those citizens whose speeches only recently had been greeted with applause.

If this trend continues, it is possible that a new Bolshevik period will arrive. Again there will be bloodshed, again the restoration of an orderly life will be postponed....

Workers, and especially the peasants, so I have heard, disapprove of the policies of Horvath; some of them are openly antagonistic to him. Warnings are sounded that a dictatorship of the military officers may be attempted soon....The broad masses do not trust the officers....

One evening, at a theater, I saw the two Atamans, Semenov and Kalmykov. My friends proposed to introduce me. But that honor I declined, for I had nothing in common with those two, and never could have anything. As for the numerous other representatives of various movements, parties, governments, and simply groups, I was careful not to become involved in any combinations and intrigues, and resolved to associate only with those whom I had known before, and of whose stand I was certain.

Early in November I received a letter from my old friend, Baron Boodberg. He had left Japan soon after me and now lived in Harbin, a "more neutral place under the enlightened rule of General Horvath," the General Manager of the Chinese Eastern Railway. Boodberg informed me that he had written to General Pflug, who had become the Commander of the Far Eastern Military District, recommending him to invite me to be his Chief of Staff. But fate decreed otherwise.

Three days later I was awakened early in the morning by one of my former associates, with news of the *coup d'état* engineered at Omsk by the supporters of Admiral Kolchak. The Directory was arrested, and Kolchak was proclaimed the Supreme Ruler. This brought a radical change in my plans. I had not returned to Russia to co-operate with a dictator, so that very day I went to the offices of the Governor, and asked that my diplomatic passport be exchanged for an ordinary one, and that I be allowed to leave the country. The passport was issued immediately, and I was free to go. The next problem was to obtain permission from the Japanese to land on their soil. Fortunately, among the Japanese officers in Vladivostok I found a colonel with whom I had transacted business in my Embassy days. He was very kind and obliging, and through his good offices I was enabled to sail, just as the rest of the world was rejoicing over the Armistice signed by the belligerents in France. The War was over, but not for the Russians.

Before I left the territory of my native land, English troops were already operating near Archangel. They were also present in Turkestan, in Central Asia, in Siberia, and, most important of all, near the famous oil fields of Baku, which were obviously of more interest to some Englishmen than was the future of the Russian people. The Japanese troops continued to pour in. Instead of the seven thousand men agreed upon—a force equal to that of the Americans—they had massed twenty-three thousand by October, and continued to bring more until the total reached over seventy thousand. French, Italian, Portuguese, American, Japanese, British, and other soldiers representing fourteen flags, were gathered on Russian soil ready to do anything asked of them in order to return the remnants of the Czar's regime to power.

There was no longer any need to help the Czechs. They knew very well how to take care of themselves and incidentally how to help themselves to Russian wealth. The Japanese, too, according to the testimony of General Ivanov-Rinov, who should know, were doing wholesale plundering.[1] There was no longer any justification for the presence of foreign troops to prevent the German and Austrian prisoners of war from forming a fighting front. Indeed, there was never any such intention, as has been made clear by General Graves in *America's Siberian Adventure*. This remarkable book mercilessly exposed the distortion of facts and the misinformation which was presented, as official reports, to the State Department by its Consuls and other representatives then stationed in Russia. In other words, there remained no pretext for keeping the foreign troops on Russian soil. Nevertheless, they remained there, fighting an undeclared war, and continued to interfere in the internal affairs of Russia in a most shocking manner, until the resistance of the Russian people forced most of them to return ingloriously home.

As for the rumors about the reverses of the Red Army, they were all wrong. By the end of September it had reoccupied Kazan and Simbirsk, forcing the Czechs and the "White" Russian troops to retreat. And in the south of European Russia the pressure of the General Krasnoff's army was also checked near Tsaritsyn on the Lower Volga. Along with reports about these successes on various fighting fronts, newspapers printed horrible stories about the Red Terror. This terror actually was inaugurated early in September after a number of

[1] *Tihii Okean*. Moscow. 1938. No. 2, pp. 132-150.

assassinations of Soviet officials, such as Volodarsky and Uritzky in Petrograd and the attempt on the life of Lenin made by a Social Revolutionary at Moscow.

The end of the World War had been prompted by the revolutionary movement in Germany, where early in November the first soviets were formed. Thereby the Russian Revolution acquired a certain support beyond its own borders. Gradually its waves reached not only Germany and Austria, but other countries as well. In that sense the Russian Revolution was instrumental in speeding up the defeat of the Central Powers by the Allies. Furthermore, not only the vanquished, but some of the victors, too, experienced in the postwar period serious reverberations from the Russian Revolution. Their governments, concerned with these repercussions at home, had to shape their activities in Russia accordingly.

The democratic elements of various countries began protesting against the extralegal activities of their armed forces in Russia. Voices were heard demanding their recall. Naturally, such voices were heard in America too. But it was a long time before the withdrawal began; and when at last it started, it was due less to the insistence of the protesting voices than to the resistance which the armies met in Russia, which was unexpectedly strong. The Russian people were demonstrating their support of the new regime in no uncertain terms. To the activities of the Red Army, guerrilla warfare was added. This was conducted by the population on a large scale and with increasing success.

CHAPTER XVII

THE WINNING SIDE

(*It Is Hard to Lose One's Mother Country*)

Return to Japan. Waiting for a visa. Breshkovskaya. On the boat to Canada. The Prinkipo episode. The *Cordon Sanitaire*. The struggle for power. Kolchak, Denikin, Yudenich, Wrangel. Who backed them and why? Why did they lose? The role of the American Expeditionary Force in Siberia. Bullitt's mission. Colonel Raymond Robins. Results of Versailles. The RSFSR's treaties. Decision to stay in America. My trip to the Middle West.

TSURUGA, WHERE I disembarked on a November morning, looked much the same as on a dozen previous landings. But how greatly my own condition had altered! Only two years had elapsed since I first arrived in Japan as Military Attaché to the Imperial Russian Embassy and was greeted with all that elaborate courtesy to which diplomats are entitled. Now I was without official status. Nay more, I was a "man without a country." With no government to stand by, I was at the mercy of any functionary who cared to make himself unpleasant. To be alone and "just a human being" sounds great, but in practice it may be not so attractive, in this world of ours where there are too many frontiers, too many restrictions for the "aliens" or simply foreigners, too many methods of discrimination, and too many stiff-hearted bureaucrats, who have no trace of humaneness left in them. Certainly it is not what the advocates of complete freedom of the individual would like to try on themselves.

In the Russia of the Czars it used to be said that everyone was composed of three parts: Body, Soul, and Passport. Travelers in the postwar world have learned to know full well what this means, and no one thinks anything nowadays of having his passport examined at the point of entry into another country, or of being plied with silly personal questions. It is a matter of well-established contemporary international "etiquette" for greeting visitors from foreign lands, especially those who are "nobody." But the examination I had to undergo at Tsuruga that day was uncommonly thorough and unpleasant; for while the Japanese police are famous for their politeness, so long as there is nothing out of the ordinary, they can be probably the nastiest in the world when confronted with something they do not understand or which arouses their suspicions. Now the local agent of police had apparently been instructed to find out in what capacity and with what intentions I was visiting Japan, and he was obviously unprepared to find that I no longer carried diplomatic credentials. He wanted to know why I traveled as a simple citizen; why I had not kept my diplomatic passport, which would be so much more convenient. My reply that I had resigned all my posts and was on my way to America with no other plans but to join my family, evidently was not convincing. But finally he declared that, as my documents were in order, I could proceed wherever I desired.

In Tokyo, too, I found that the Russian Revolution had already created serious obstacles in the way of one's freedom in traveling. When I had left Japan the previous March for my first trip to America, my visas were all granted in the shortest possible time and signed by the respective Ambassadors themselves. Now it was an entirely different story, and not simply because I had resigned my post and was no longer entitled to special consideration. No, it was a matter of being a Russian. Besides, as I discovered on my return to the United States, my political sympathies had become objectionable to certain groups. The lawyer I met at the Society of the Russian Officers on my first visit to New York, and who was in some way connected with the Department of Justice, had tried his best to prevent my return to America. Fortunately thanks to our Embassy at Washington, the visa was granted, though only after a most unusual procedure. The American Ambassador at Tokyo was authorized to decide my case himself and applied for advice to his Russian colleague, Krupensky. The Russian Ambassador had nothing against my going to the United States; I think he was even anxious to be rid of my presence in Japan, for our political differences had by then become quite obvious. So, with much delay, causing anxiety to my family in New York as much as to myself, the visa was granted, and I embarked at length on a Japanese boat for Canada.

Among my fellow passengers was the "Grandmother of the Russian Revolution," Madame Breshko-Breshkovskaya, whom I already met in Japan, and with whom I had formed a pleasant friendship. Madame Breshkovskaya was one of those Russians of "good families" who had devoted their lives to the emancipation of the people from the evils of monarchy, and she had spent most of her long and fruitful life in prison or exile as punishment for her devotion to the common people. She was a most charming lady, with a warm understanding heart and a genuine gift for narrating her fascinating experiences. So it was a real pleasure to spend several days with her in Japan and to be with her again on the boat. Madame Breshkovskaya was bitterly opposed to the Bolsheviks for she did not approve of their use of violence; and this seemed to me a surprising attitude in one who was a member of the Social Revolutionary Party, for this party had a terrorist organization and was proud of its deeds. But, the "Grandmother of the Russian Revolution" insisted that individual terror, which involved the risk of the terrorist's own life, was entirely different from the mass terror inaugurated by the Bolsheviks.

Undoubtedly there were profound differences between the programs of her own party and the Bolsheviks. The struggle between the two was of long standing. But I am not convinced that Breshkovskaya would not have preferred to stay in Russia even after the defeat of her own party by the Bolsheviks, for she loved her mother country more than any doctrine. Years later I thought I discovered one of the special causes which had made her leave Russia at a time when the revolutionary changes for which she had striven her whole life were becoming a reality. This was her "maternal love" for Kerensky. She could not forgive the downfall of her idol. Freud would probably record it as a case of "mother complex."

I had a strange confirmation of this theory in 1921. Madame Breshkovskaya was then visiting my old friend, General Shokorov, who had formerly commanded the Czech troops in Russia, and for these services had been invited by President Thomas Masaryk to the new republic. Shokorov, now a General of the Czechoslovakian army, lived in the villa of a former Austrian aristocrat, which had been confiscated after Czechoslovakia became an independent state. I was at that time on a short visit to Prague and was invited by Shokorov to a dinner at which both Madame Breshkovskaya and Mr. Kerensky were present. After the dinner we all went for a stroll in the park surrounding the villa. Soon, having tired of walking, the old lady wanted to rest, and we adjourned to the bowling alley. Kerensky and I decided to play a game or two. I won the first tilt. We played another, and I was the victor again. Then something touching happened. Madame Breshkovskaya came near me and whispered: "Why don't you give him a chance to win?" I thought instantly of a mother whose first concern is to see her child happy. Was it not possible, I thought again, that the boundless affection of the great old lady toward her disciple and devoted friend, Kerensky, had been a prime factor in her departure from Russia after the October Revolution?

At Vancouver we parted; for Madame Breshkovskaya went straight to the United States, where she had many friends among Americans who knew and loved her as I did. I decided this time to cross over Canada. On the train I learned of an extremely interesting development. Representatives of the former belligerents had gathered in Paris to settle the various questions arising from the World War. The Peace Conference extended an invitation to the Soviet Government and to the numerous regional governments formed since the Revolution on the boundaries of the former Russian Empire, to send their delegates to the Prinkipo Islands, near Constantinople. This was an attempt to legalize the deliberations of the Versailles Conference on matters pertaining to Russia. The plan failed to materialize. The Soviet Government accepted the invitation and even expressed its willingness to make serious concessions, "provided that these would not menace the future development of Soviet Russia."[1] But after my return to New York, I learned that the other "Russian governments" had de-

[1] Professor Malbone W. Graham, on "The Peace Policy" in the symposium, *The Soviet Union and World Problems.* Chicago University. 1935. p. 169.

clined to meet the Soviet representatives, so the conference did not take place either at Prinkipo, or anywhere else.

It is interesting to note the kind of concessions Soviet Russia was willing to make at that early stage of its existence. The note of the Narkomindel, the Foreign Office of Moscow, dated February 4, 1919, listed these as follows: "(1) the repayment of privately held debts, on bases to be negotiated; (2) the guaranty of payment of interest on its loans by the Soviet government through delivery of a certain amount of raw materials; (3) the grant of concessions in mines, forests, and other resources, so long as these involved no violation of the new Soviet economic order; (4) territorial concessions, if need be; and, if necessary (5) a pledge to be included in the general agreement with the Entente Powers, not to interfere in their internal affairs." [2]

At that time the anti-Bolshevik elements in Russia, and especially abroad, were sure that the Soviet regime had no chance of survival. "Not longer than twenty days" had been the original formula. This was now revised, but still there was no doubt in their minds that the downfall of the Bolsheviks was a matter of a very short time. Indeed, plans to intervene in Russia's fate had been formulated as early as December, 1917, by certain French, British, Italian, Japanese, and other statesmen. The ruling classes did not relish the possibility of the advent to political power of the lower strata in their own communities if the Russian movement were not arrested. The old idea that some people were born to be leaders, and the rest created by the Almighty to satisfy the needs of those superior beings, was too strong to disappear without a fight.

Personally I had never accepted this convenient interpretation; I always entertained the belief that it was lack of opportunity to develop their mental abilities, not heredity, that handicapped the common people in rising to positions where their talents could be demonstrated. The principal loser by this abnormal arrangement, I thought, was the community as a whole.

Early in the spring of 1919, I wrote a series of articles under the

[2] Quoted from Professor Malbone W. Graham's "The Peace Policy," ibid., p. 169, as the terms appeared in the original.

general title "The Centuries-Old Discord," which were published in the Russian newspaper, *Russkoye Slovo,* then appearing in New York. The basic thesis was that the abyss which separated the upper classes of Russia from their own common people was created by the systematic denial of education to the latter. The result, I argued, was that the so-called intelligentsia, and most of those who enjoyed formal education, had lost contact with the people at large. They spoke a different language, cherished ideas alien to the broad masses, and strived for other ends. Mutual understanding became difficult, and suspicion was born. Out of suspicion animosity grew. The two revolutions through which Russia had passed demonstrated this clearly, and it was high time to start remedying this tragic situation. "But," I said, "those who are planning to find the way toward this goal should remember that it is not a question of teaching the people, but helping them to learn. It would be wrong to attempt to force on them what one considers right, without considering what may seem right to them." Nor was it a matter of seeing justice prevail, for who should decide the meaning of justice? The most practical, earthly consideration was what mattered. The main consideration was to eliminate the mutually painful and unpleasant distrust.

The year 1919 was full of activity. But, if it witnessed a number of spectacular successes for the "interventionists," it was also marked by the final collapse of their efforts, the withdrawal of practically all foreign troops from Russian territory, and the confinement of the civil war in Russia to the Crimean front.

In the spring of 1919 a combined onslaught by all the anti-Soviet forces was planned. The main attack was to be led by Admiral Kolchak, who was well supplied by the foreigners, and Czech troops were to participate. General Denikin was expected to join the troops of Kolchak somewhere near Saratov, on the Volga, and then continue his triumphal march on Moscow. General Yudenich was to attack Petrograd. At the same time the British would advance in Turkestan and the Archangel region. But the plan failed. Kolchak was repulsed beyond the Urals. Denikin was stopped far south of Moscow on the Kursk-Liski-Balashov line. Yudenich retreated to Yamburg.

Another concentrated effort was made in the fall, and ended in a rout of Kolchak's forces. But on the southern front Denikin met a temporary success. Well armed and supplied by Great Britain, and to a certain extent by the other partners of the Entente, his army succeeded in penetrating far inland. By October, Ukrainia was under Denikin's control. His cavalry made a raid up to Orel and approached Tula, the center of munition factories. But at that time the Red Army concentrated every available force; and, before the end of October, not only succeeded in checking Denikin's advance, but also in inflicting a serious defeat on him near Voronezh and Orel. The brilliant cavalry raid led by Budyonny, a sergeant of the Czar's Army, resulted in a smashing defeat of the forces led by his former commanders. Early next year, 1920, Ukrainia returned to the control of the Soviets.

In his attempt to capture Petrograd, Yudenich reached the outskirts of the city, but was also forced to retreat by a timely organized resistance followed by an effective counterattack, in which workers and other citizens joined in the gallant fight of the Red Army. By that time the armed man power of the Soviets exceeded two million and a half. The lack of arms and ammunition was counterbalanced by the determination of the people to stop the antirevolutionary forces—forces drawn from their own privileged classes and foreign assistance, unjustified by even the most elastic interpretation of international law.

By the end of 1919, Kolchak was captured, with General Janin of France playing an unsavory role in surrendering him to the Reds. The following year, after a trial at Irkutsk, Kolchak was executed. Denikin's career was also over. Soon, another leader took his place, in the person of General Baron Wrangel, who continued the fight for almost another year. Finally, on November 7, 1920, he was routed at Perekop by the Red General, Blucher, and forced to discontinue the war and to retire, together with part of his troops, abroad.

Disappointed by the results of their venture, the foreigners were gradually withdrawing their forces from Russia. The French started the evacuation soon after their sailors, led by André Marty, refused to fire on the Russians. English troops were driven out of the

Murmansk and Archangel region in August, and before the end of 1919 had withdrawn from practically all other parts of Soviet Russia. In January, 1920, under pressure from home, England, France, and Italy decided to lift the blockade instituted early in 1919 and known as the *Cordon Sanitaire,* a phrase coined by Clemenceau. January, 1920, was the time, by the way, when the League of Nations came into existence. It was rather embarrassing to have this international conclave, created for the purpose of promoting good will among nations and preventing wars, in session while the Great and lesser Powers were demonstrating in Russia their utter disregard for international law. Their interference in the internal affairs of that country and toleration of its plunder by some of their partners seemed incompatible with the principles of the League. Besides, affairs at home were not quite reassuring. Soviet regimes were formed in Bavaria and Hungary. Workers in many lands were restless, demanding certain improvements in their working and living conditions. Furthermore, the chances of defeating the Bolsheviks obviously were none too good. On consideration of all these developments, the troops were evacuated from European Russia by the beginning of 1920. By April second the American troops were withdrawn from the Far East as well.[3] Only the Japanese continued the stubborn attempt to "save Russia" from her own people; though the Poles also made a move to show their hand in the same direction between April and October of this year.

When in December, 1917, Clemenceau, Pishon, and Foch, representing France, discussed with Lord Milner, Lord Robert Cecil, and others, representing England, how to organize the armed intervention in Russian affairs, they divided their national spheres of action in a way which left little doubt about their ulterior motives in the attempt to strangle the Russian Revolution. French troops were dispatched to the Don Basin region, where the "metallurgical appeal" to French capital was strong. The British were allotted the Baku oil fields.[4] In *The World Crisis,* by Winston Churchill, then the Minister

[3] The American troops on the Archangel front were evacuated late in June, 1919, after ten months of their activities in that region.

[4] Denikin, in his *Outlines of the Russian Revolt* (in Russian), wrote: "But the French policy and the Polish strategy unfortunately did not take into consideration the interests of Russia." (v. IV, p. 31.)

of War and the main advocate of intervention, one can find many pages that reveal the role played by Great Britain in that inglorious adventure, so costly and fruitless to all concerned. For Japan, the expenses amounted to almost one billion yen; for Great Britain, undoubtedly, even more. One can judge this from the British objectives listed in Churchill's book, as of November 30, 1918, when London decided: to continue the occupation of Archangel and Murmansk; to press forward the Siberian expedition, while trying to persuade the Czechs to remain there too; to occupy the Batum-Baku railway; to render every possible assistance to General Denikin in the south; and to send war supplies to the Baltic states.

The pretense that the Entente was concerned with helping the Czechs and feared the organization of prisoners of war has been completely refuted by such authorities as General William S. Graves, and the British Chargé d'Affaires at Moscow, Bruce Lockhart. "The Czechs were never in danger from the aggressive acts of the Soviets ... the Czechs were the aggressors ..." wrote General Graves, relying on the reports of Colonel George H. Emerson.[5] "As for the armed German and Austrian prisoners of war, there were none," wrote Bruce Lockhart.[6] And in his straightforward style General Graves also wrote as follows:

> If the Allies were really trying to get the Czechs to the Western front in France, it seems peculiar that no arrangements had been made for ships to take them from Vladivostok. I am clearly of the opinion that as early as May 28, 1918, there was no intention of sending the Czechs to the Western front. I am unable to say exactly when this decision was made, but it was at least two months and six days before I received my instructions, in which appears the sentence: "For helping the Czecho-Slovaks, there is immediate necessity and justification." [7]

[5] William S. Graves. *America's Siberian Adventure*. Jonathan Cape & Harrison Smith, New York, 1931. pp. 51-52.

[6] R. H. Bruce Lockhart. *British Agent*. G. P. Putnam's Sons. New York. 1933. p. 251.

[7] William Graves, ibid., pp. 44, 45.

Commenting on the following statement of Professor Schuman: "Military intervention was undertaken under the guise of rescuing the Czecho-Slovaks, and assisting the Russian effort at self-government," General Graves said: "I take this to mean that Dr. Schuman charges the United States with lack of sincerity in announcing the reasons for intervention, and I have come to the same conclusion." (Graves, ibid., p. 350.)

Trying to reconcile the contradictions between the professed aims and the actualities, Graves came to the conclusion that: "The United States, therefore, had its representatives of the State Department and War Department working at cross purposes from the beginning of military action in Siberia." (William S. Graves, ibid., p. 54.)

The assistance rendered by the Powers to the various counterrevolutionary Russian groups was multiform and generous. Arms, munitions, clothes, food, medicaments, loans poured in from all directions. As for the foreign troops, they were not very numerous, for only the Japanese concentrated in Siberia over seventy thousand soldiers. This was doubtless because the Powers believed that Russia was disorganized by the Revolution, and had no troops with which to resist. They were certain that the Reds had no military leaders, for the majority of the former officers had joined the various counterrevolutionary formations. They were sure that the new regime of Russia would be unable to arm its soldiers and supply them with necessities for war; there were no factories to speak of in its hands. And there was also the blockade. Those whom the Entente Powers supported so lavishly, on the other hand, were in an incomparably better position: they were better armed and had no particular difficulties in receiving what they needed from abroad. They occupied the richest parts of the country: the Don Basin with its coal and metals, the fertile fields of the south, which had always been the granary of Russia, and for a time the oil fields of Baku, which were not so important as a source of oil for themselves, but as a trump card for winning over the powerful Sir Henry Deterding of the Royal Dutch interests.

But, the calculations of the "interventionists" proved to be wrong, and their efforts futile. Their stratagem failed utterly and ended in a complete fiasco. Their troops had to return home with nothing to brag about. Their protégés were forced to leave their own mother country and begin life anew as refugees. Their own national economies suffered in a number of ways; for financially the intervention in Russia had been very costly. But what was still worse for the economic health of the Powers was the universal dislocation of economic life inaugurated by the blockading of Russia, or one sixth of the earth surface of the globe. For thereby Russia was forced to become self-supporting and to develop branches of industry which she would not otherwise have needed to develop.

To see the "whys" of the outcome of the "intervention" may be simple enough today, but at the time of these events few people actually appreciated the forces behind the Russian Revolution and the weaknesses of the rest of the world. The Red Army won because the new regime commanding it stood for a policy obviously in accord with the aspirations of the people, and was loyally supported by an overwhelming majority of the people. Indeed, Colonel Eichelberger, the Intelligence Officer of the American Expeditionary Force, stated in a report that "probably 97 per cent of the people in Siberia are anti-Kolchak." [8] Workmen and peasants formed detachments of "partisans" and carried on guerrilla warfare against the counterrevolutionaries; while to the rear of the fighting forces the inhabitants could be counted upon to supply the defenders of their common interests with whatever they needed. Very often the population deprived themselves of the most necessary goods, but gave to the Red Army men everything they needed. Besides, the Soviets found support abroad among the workers and the progressives in various lands. Often, workers in the countries whose ruling groups carried on the struggle against the Soviets would refuse to load ships destined to deliver war supplies to the White Armies; and workers and progressives everywhere protested against interference in the domestic affairs of Russia.

Such were positive reasons for the Red victory. But there were negative reasons also. In no circumstances, probably, would the peasants and workers of Russia have stood for the Whites, whose treatment of the lower strata of the people was very often shocking. We know this, among other sources, through the testimony of such impartial observers as Colonel John Ward, Member of Parliament of Great Britain, who spent a number of months in Siberia, and of General Graves. Colonel Ward has described with horror "the contempt which the officials of Kolchak's government demonstrated towards the common people." General Graves goes further: "How could one think," he writes, "that the Russian peasants and workingmen would take arms and fight and put in power the Kolchak supporters, who were committing such atrocities against the people to whom they looked

[8] William S. Graves, ibid., p. 290.

for military support...." [9] "By changing names and places and individuals the atrocities committed in Siberia could be made to apply in the country dominated by Denikin," according to a report from a British officer who was in the south of Russia.[10] An opinion also held by Dr. Girsa, the Czech representative, who later became a high official in the Foreign Office at Prague.

"The 'Reds' are cruel," argued the peasants. "They are merciless to their enemies. And the 'Whites' are cruel and merciless to their enemies. But the 'Whites' are killing our kind of people, the common people. We cannot be with them. If we have to make a choice, we shall stand by the 'Reds.' "

Again and again the population received object lessons at places captured by the White troops. The first result inevitably was the return of the landlords, who demanded the restoration of their properties and the chastisement of those who were, or were supposed to be, responsible for their unlawful occupation. Gallows and whips were everyday implements of punishment. Of course, in every civil war one finds examples of abuse of power by the military victor; in the Southern States, for instance, one can still hear shocking stories about the march of General Sherman. But the reaction to the counterrevolutionaries in Russia was a result of an accumulation of hatred. This hatred united the people behind the new regime, which was fighting those who had abused them.

Early in the summer of 1919 I wrote an article under the title "What Makes the Bolshevik Army Strong?" [11] in which I expressed the opinion that it was extremely dangerous to underestimate, as many of the Whites had done, the forces of an adversary. I pointed out the falsity of the assertion that the Bolshevik Army was composed of bands of Chinese, Hungarians, Letts, and other mercenaries. Their armed forces already were strong—more than two millions—as I later learned. And reports from various impartial sources indicated that these troops were well organized and sufficiently well armed. Being

[9] William S. Graves, ibid., p. 337.
[10] William S. Graves, ibid., p. 338.
[11] *Narodnaya Gazeta* (People's Newspaper), published in New York. June 5, 1919. pp. 5, 8.

based on compulsory service, they, naturally, represented the country at large. They were led by a number of old officers who were fighting for their country; and while some of them disagreed with the new regime, the majority considered that it was their duty to fight because it was not simply a civil war, but a war against foreign invasion. So far the fighting capacities of the Red troops had been proved good, for they had succeeded on a number of occasions in defeating their adversaries. The Red Army of today, I said, would inevitably be simply the Russian Army of tomorrow.

In the same article I severely condemned the vengeance practiced by the Whites, citing examples from Denikin's army, and saying: "Is it not obvious that one must look for means to break down resistance, and not for more and more victims for the gallows?" The policy adopted by the anti-Bolshevik groups in dealing mercilessly with those who fell into their hands, prompted a large meeting of officers in Moscow, at which a resolution was passed "to continue the struggle at whatever cost up to the bitter end." I closed my article by an appeal to stop the executions and the sowing of hatred, and for a promise of wide amnesty instead, not only to those who were misled through lack of knowledge, but even to those who had committed certain crimes in the pathological atmosphere of revolution.

As for myself, I made another attempt to return to Russia in the summer of 1919. This was not exactly my own idea. In this case I acted under the influence of a friend, a former Socialist, who, as I discovered later, became a defender of everything that was supposed to harm the Bolsheviks, and an advocate of a policy of rough treatment, in spite of his good nature and his long career as a fighter for the betterment of the lot of the masses. At that time I valued his opinion very highly, and, therefore, after a certain amount of hesitation, wrote to our Military Attaché at Washington that I wanted to go to Omsk. The reply arrived late in September, 1919, and informed me that there was "no objection" to my return, provided that I was "willing to start with a minor position as a Chief of Staff of a Division." It was more than evident from this reply that those in authority were not interested in my services, to say the least; they made it clear that my participation in the Kerensky regime was not forgotten, and would not be forgiven by those who were trying to curb the Revolution and eradicate everything recalling it. This was another unpleasant lesson I had to learn from my old colleagues. It served to confirm my decision to remain in America, much as I wanted to go back to my country. For it was clear that those at the helm in Omsk had learned nothing and were simply continuing the Czarist policy of opposing their own people. There was no way home for me.

Here is what the most reputable of the White leaders, General Denikin, has said in his memoirs:

> They wrote us again and again from Paris that the assistance from the Allies was insufficient because the struggle carried on in the south and in the east was not popular among the European democracies. To acquire their sympathy we should have pronounced two words: "Republic and Federation." We did not pronounce them. But if some other Russian government would have allowed such dictation from abroad, and therefore have started settling basic problems of the political structure of Russia without awaiting the popular vote, would there have been any difference in the events? Would those who were poisoned with the sweet dream of complete independence have joined us sincerely and unselfishly? Would the English regiments of General Walker have marched on Tsaritsyn, and the sharpshooters of the French General Anselm, on Kiev? Finally, would the Russian armies have become inspired by the idea of fighting for the Federated Republic? Certainly not.[12]

But, naturally, it was not only the stubborn stand of the counter-revolutionary leaders against the aspirations of the Russian people, that made their efforts vain.[13] The clash of interests among the foreigners also contributed; and the difficulty they had in co-ordinating the plans may now be seen in the extensive literature, in various languages, covering this period. But, in addition to the disagreements and sometimes even quarrels between the partners in the "intervention," there were the intrigues between the Russian leaders; and some of them were supported by the Allies. The role played by Japan in this respect was probably the most detrimental. Tokyo did not approve

[12] General A. J. Denikin. *Outlines of the Russian Revolt.* Jonathan Cape. London. Quoted from the Russian edition. Berlin. 1925. v. IV, p. 245.

[13] Once in a while, of course, it was asserted that "there is no question of going back to the old regime." Such was the reply of Kolchak, in May, 1919, to the "demands" presented by Clemenceau. But these were words completely contradicted by the acts of the same people, as one can see, for example, from the confidential correspondence between Kolchak and Denikin.

of Admiral Kolchak, the protégé of Great Britain, and not only supported the insubordination of her pet, Ataman Semenov, but even insisted on his continuing the outrageous policy of interfering with the traffic on the only road supplying the Omsk regime. Semenov, at Nippon's behest, continuously disregarded the demands of Kolchak and his officials, thus often creating insurmountable difficulties for the Kolchak government.[14]

Japanese activities in Siberia have been vividly described by General Graves, who found numerous occasions for becoming indignant at their deeds. Not only did the Japanese break their agreement with the United States by bringing in ten times as many troops as agreed upon with Washington, but by ubiquitous interference they made themselves objectionable in general and to the American commander in particular. One example will suffice. In writing about the Japanese attitude toward their pets, the Atamans, Semenov and Kalmykov, General Graves stressed the fact that Japanese troops would not interfere with them "no matter what they did in sections of the railway guarded by Japan, and as a result of this policy Semenov was permitted to force indignities upon some members of the American Railway Service Corps, in the sectors guarded by the Japanese. He was also permitted to stop an American train, loaded with rifles destined for Kolchak, and demand fifteen thousand of the rifles, which he threatened to take by force unless the officer willingly gave them up."[15]

As for General Graves himself, his exceptional tactfulness was appreciated by the Russians. After the restoration of diplomatic relations between Washington and Moscow in 1933, the Soviet Commissar for Foreign Affairs, Litvinov, who was sent by Moscow to negotiate with President Roosevelt, declared that his government had decided to waive its claims for the damages inflicted by the American participation in the "intervention" in Siberia.

Fairness and truth dictate the assertion here that the attitude of

[14] Valuable material relating to this and other handicaps to the Omsk regime may be found in the extremely interesting diary of Baron Boodberg, who was for a short time acting Minister of War under Kolchak. Published in the *Archives of the Russian Revolution,* in Russian. Berlin. 1922-23.

[15] William S. Graves, ibid., pp. 185-186.

the United States and its citizens toward the Russian problem in its initial stages was incomparably better than that of any other nation. It is enough to recollect the report of William Bullitt on his mission to Moscow in 1918, in which he recommended negotiations with the government headed by Lenin as one supported by the people. It is true that, when Bullitt returned to Paris from Russia, he was not received by Wilson although the President himself had sent him there to obtain first-hand information. But by then the atmosphere had changed in European official circles. One must also remember the report made by Colonel Raymond Robins, who represented the American Red Cross in Russia during the War, and remained there for some time after the Revolution. In his opinion, too, the American Government would do well to take the new regime of Russia seriously. But Washington had already made up its mind, and instead of negotiating with Moscow, joined the interventionist policy.

This was a difficult time for me. Counterrevolutionary *émigrés* from Russia had the ear of Washington. So it seemed better to stay away from official American and Russian circles entirely. To kill time, I accepted the invitation of a representative of the old Russian co-operatives to join him in a trip to the Middle West, where he wanted to get acquainted with the co-operative movement in America. We toured Minnesota for the grain elevators, Michigan for the potato growers' associations, Wisconsin for the cheese-producing co-operatives, and Illinois for the work of the fruit exchanges. Thanks to this, my mind was occupied for a while by other things than the Revolution in Russia and foreign intervention. But not for long.

CHAPTER XVIII

CRYSTALLIZATION ACCELERATED

(*New Experiences*)

Committees, schemes, and intrigues. The Collegiate Institute. Lecturing among the Russians. Adventure in printing. The Soviet-Polish War. The International Committee of the Y.M.C.A. The great famine in Soviet Russia. "Scouting." Prague selected for the publishing venture. Paris and the Russian "Ministers." The Washington Conference. The Russians at Prague. Books for whom? An unusual financial transaction. Back to New York. Jobs and enterprises. Crystallization goes on.

FOREIGNERS OF THE privileged classes who live abroad are nearly always less united than one would expect considering their common origin and language; and among the Russians in the United States after the Revolution of 1917 this phenomenon was particularly striking. To social incompatibility and minor or major differences of political opinion was added that extreme bitterness known only to those who have lost their country and their privileges and have been torn from the only environment in which they could feel at home. Furthermore, most of the Russian immigrants since 1917 had come to the United States from necessity rather than volition, and those in particular who had arrived as refugees from the Revolution were apt to be utterly unfitted for facing life in the raw. Many of them had never worked before, had no profession or trade on which they could depend for a living; and in the circumstances, it was only natural for them to concentrate their enforced leisure on political argument and indulgement in wishful thinking. Indeed, their most popular pastime seemed to be hoping for an early collapse of the Bolshevik regime and their own return to Russia and their mansions, estates, and privileges. They combined in countless kinds of organizations for the restoration of the old order in their mother country. Politically ignorant, they very often became the easy prey of more enlightened, but not necessarily scrupulous, "leaders," and unwittingly served as pawns in their schemes and intrigues. And this is easy to understand.

It seems to be human nature for people to believe themselves experts in political matters after reading a few newspapers and hearing a few orators whom they accept as well-informed and reliable interpreters. To become an engineer one must study some fifteen years. To become a physician one must go through a schooling quite as long or even longer. But to become an expert politician it seems enough to read the headlines in a couple of papers. Few people stop to think how complicated are the matters pertaining to the political, economic, and social arrangement of a country, or how much reading, thinking, and understanding is required for the development of an ability to evaluate a political situation, even without the complication of a sense of personal injury and emotional stress, under which these Russian *émigrés* labored.

After the Revolution, everyone naturally became concerned with these matters; and, unfortunately, the confusion created not only by prejudice, but by events themselves, was made more serious by the deliberate coloring and misinterpretation of news, which became almost the rule after the overthrow of the Romanovs. To be sure, this was only a repetition of what had happened before in connection with other countries passing through similar changes. No wonder the Russian colonies abroad became a pitiful mixture of misery and psychopathology. That of New York was certainly no exception to the rule. It became a "house divided." On the one hand, there were those who had settled in the United States before the Revolution. These were mostly peasants who had become industrial workers; and their political sympathies naturally tended toward the Left. Some of them soon fell under the influence of the reactionaries and became their prey. And on the other hand, there were the new immigrants, victims of the Revolution, bitter and militant. They wanted to crush the Bolsheviks, mostly for selfish reasons, though sometimes pretending that they were concerned with the welfare of their country and its people. Undoubtedly, some of them were sincerely worried about the fate of their mother country.

Numerous societies, parties, and groups sprang up like mushrooms, and soon there was quite a little "civil war" between them. Realizing the futility of their efforts, and having no reason for lining up with any one of them, I found it more sensible to join a few doctors, engineers, and teachers in a project for educational work among the old colonists. We succeeded in founding a school for adults, and in order to please their vanity, called it the Russian Collegiate Institute. Under the presidency of Professor Petrunkevich of Yale, it became popular and continued to function for more than two years. Finally, disagreements arising from the various shades of political opinion made it impractical to carry on the work. But before its disintegration I had left New York for Europe. Besides teaching classes in the school and acting as its dean, I gave a considerable number of lectures before various groups on the history of Russia. These lectures were published by a little printing shop which I had been induced to purchase and which operated for a short time before I went to Europe for the International Committee of the Y.M.C.A.

During the War the American Y.M.C.A. had done a good deal of work among prisoners of war, and one of their activities in this connection had been the publishing of books. After the war was over, part of the money collected for that purpose remained unused. So one of the secretaries, who was in charge of this work in Switzerland, Dr. Julius F. Hecker, conceived the idea of applying some of this balance to a large-scale publishing venture for Russia. His plan was approved. A large number of Russian specialists in various fields, being abroad at that time, were available for the work; and it was decided to concentrate on books of technical character in order to introduce American methods, American machinery, American technique, for the sake of future business. Nothing of controversial character was supposed to attract the interest of this enterprise, which was to be kept clear of any political complications.

Since the cost of production in the United States was prohibitive for the Russian market, and the scheme contemplated the publication of books in large quantities, it was originally planned to establish the printing plant in Russia, if and when the situation there permitted. I was recommended as general manager and became a "secretary" of the International Committee of the Y.M.C.A. in New York. My first duties were to acquire some knowledge of American typographical machinery, to draw up a plan for the production end of our business, and to make recommendations concerning equipment. Therefore, together with my assistant, I visited one factory after another, staying for a few days or a few weeks, and studying their products.

While I was thus employed, a new war was started against Russia by Poland. Late in April, 1920, the Polish troops, without any declaration of war, entered Ukrainia, and occupied Kiev. The aim was to join the remnants of Denikin's army, then under Baron Wrangel. But the Red Army succeeded in repulsing the Poles and not only forced them to retreat from Soviet territory but pursued them to the very gates of Warsaw, in the heart of their own country. These Soviet successes alarmed the French, who quickly dispatched some one hundred and twenty-five airplanes, all kinds of war supplies, and a large number of military experts to direct the operations of the Polish forces. The Russians meanwhile were carried away by their spectacular success and made the mistake of advancing too rapidly on a very large front without allowing time for organization of their rear and the bringing up of reserves. As a consequence, the Poles were enabled to break through the thin lines of the advanced Soviet troops at the Vistula River. Developing this success, they forced the Russians to retreat. Having no reserves on hand and having failed to compensate for the retreat from Warsaw by occupying Lvov—Trotzky having disapproved of that quite natural maneuver—the Soviet troops proved unable to stop the counteroffensive of the Poles. They continued their withdrawal from Polish territory and even retired beyond the Russian border. On October 20, the preliminary treaty of peace was signed at Riga, and the final one was signed in the same city the following March.

The short period of the Soviet-Polish War served to increase my differences of opinion with certain liberal elements in the Russian colony of New York. Some of the former revolutionaries, those who belonged to parties other than the Bolshevik, took the stand that a defeat of the Red Army by the Poles was desirable. They expected a quick end to the Soviet regime and were looking forward to returning home on the heels of the victorious Polish troops. I could not approve of this. To me their stand meant disloyalty to the mother country and betrayal of their own people. More than ever I became convinced that the entire principle of intervention was wrong and absolutely unacceptable to me. It was not a question of a program; I did not belong to any political party and had no reason to stand by any "program." For me it was simply a question of loyalty to my country, which, in my conception, was not limited to the narrow group of my own class. I was sorry to read about the reverses suffered by the Russian troops after their brilliant success in the early stages of the war, and even sorrier to learn that they were forced to retreat from the gates of Warsaw instead of occupying the city, if only to sign the treaty.

Before the end of 1920, General Wrangel was defeated in Crimea, as nearly all the other White leaders had been before him. Only the unspeakable Ataman Semenov and Baron Ungern still roamed on the borders of Russia and in Mongolia. The "Mad Baron," Ungern, was captured and shot in August, 1921. The Japanese continued their activities in the Far East, and the Finns, with their collaborators, in the northwest. During 1921 the *Basmatchi* uprising developed into a small war in Central Asia under the leadership of Enver Pasha, the former dictator of Turkey. The *Basmatchi* were the bands of Moslem brigands from Central Asia who had been organized against the Soviets by their bourgeoisie and the mullahs, or Mohammedan priests; and in order to attract Turks, Afghans, and other Mohammedans, their uprising was proclaimed a Holy War against European imperialism. It, too, was broken by the Red Army.

But, though the armed intervention failed to crush the Bolsheviks and most of the counterrevolutionary Russians were now looking for new lands to settle, the troubles of the Soviets were not over. In 1921 a new ally appeared for those who were interested in the downfall of the regime led by Lenin. This ally was the great famine which swept the southeast of Russia, the result, not only of a severe drought, which was all too familiar to that part of the country, but also of the civil war. Parts of this granary, so recently the theater of operations of the fighting armies, had remained uncultivated. The extent of the famine was terrific, and the resultant sufferings were horrible. Naturally it created an extremely difficult problem for a country already devastated by war, civil war, and intervention. Various forces inimical to the new regime, inside the country and out, became quite active in their attempts at taking advantage of that calamity by staging a *coup d'état*. Hopes for the end of the hated regime again became high. All sorts of plans were in the making. But even the famine did not bring about the results sought by the enemies of the New Russia.

The attitude of the American people in approving the plan of its government at Washington to use the enormous surplus of wheat, on hand that year, for feeding the starving Russian people, was highly appreciated by every honest Russian. Unfortunately, the same cannot be said of all the Russians then abroad; I remember well the shocking reaction of indifference I met with when asking support for the appeal made by the Russian Patriarch, Tikhon, for funds to purchase food for the famine-stricken people. I am sorry to say that it was not even simple to have it published in the American press. Such was the animosity toward the new regime, that people were able to forget that the victims were not merely the Bolsheviks, whom they hated, but the people of Russia.[1]

The splendid services rendered to the Russian people in that period of need by a number of Quakers who went to Russia deserves especially high commendation. At the risk of their own lives, physicians like Dr. Graff, nurses like Anna J. Haines, ordinary good-hearted individuals, like Anna Louise Strong, Dr. Julius F. Hecker, and many

[1] In the address on the "Medical Relief for Soviet Russia," delivered in Metropolitan Opera House, Philadelphia, on January 18, 1921, Dr. Judah L. Magnes (who is now President of the Hebrew University in Palestine) said among other things: ". . .What humane cause has ever appealed to the heart and the mind of the American people without getting a response in abounding measure? The suffering of the millions within Soviet Russia has not brought the usual response from America because, unfortunately, everything has been done to keep the facts from reaching the heart and the mind of the American people. Anti-Russian propaganda has been carried on by Departments of Government, by the press, by preachers, lawyers, and teachers; and it is no wonder that the American people has come to believe that withholding relief from Soviet Russia is one of the great democratic virtues."

others, went to the typhus-stricken areas of the Lower Volga, and demonstrated by their activities there a nobility of which America may be justly proud. Similarly the wonderful work of the American Relief Administration, under the leadership of General (then Colonel) William Haskel, in Soviet Russia during these months of anguish, served not only to alleviate the sufferings of the Russian people, but to enhance the good name of the United States. The Chairman of that humanitarian organization was Mr. Herbert Hoover; yet one is reluctant to accept the claim that credit for this noble undertaking in Russia belongs to the "Great Engineer." In the appeal for medical relief there, Dr. Judah L. Magnes had quoted from Mr. Hoover's reply to his letter asking if he would not consider sending milk for the starving Russian children, as follows: "That so far as the United States is concerned, nothing prevents the Bolshevik Government from devoting their gold to the purchase of American milk for their children." To this Dr. Magnes added: "This, if correct, will, I have no doubt, be good news to Soviet Russia, which is in fact in need of milk for her children. In the sincere hope of being contradicted tomorrow I would nevertheless hazard the guess that even for so humane a purpose as buying milk for rickety children, Bolshevik gold is still taboo for the present Administration in Washington. They have ordered the Assay Office of the United States Mint to refuse to assay gold having even remotely a Russian Soviet origin." [2]

In view of these events the leaders of the Y.M.C.A. were uncertain what course they should take in their Russian venture. At a meeting held in the Headquarters it was decided to wait and see. "Scouting" was the slogan adopted for a while. Early in spring, 1921, it was decided to look for a place in Europe outside of Russia, for the establishment of the printing plant; and as Czechoslovakia was most favorably considered, I was asked to go there with the Associate General-Secretary of the International Committee of the Y.M.C.A., Mr. C. V. Hibbard, and make a report.

On our arrival in Paris Mr. Hibbard wanted to see the Russian

[2] J. L. Magnes, ibid. This publication includes the letters exchanged between Dr. Magnes and Mr. Hoover. The letter quoted above is found on page 22 of that publication.

leaders in order to find out their attitude toward the plan. We called on Mr. Basil Maklakov, the Ambassador of the Provisional Government, who was still in the Embassy, though the regime he represented had already been out of existence for almost four years. Then we went to see Mr. Avksientiev, the President, and Mr. Paul Miliukov, one of the members of the Russian Committee located on the Rue de Pompe, who were still planning a future for Russia without the Bolsheviks. None of these gentlemen had anything against the publishing of technical books in Russian by the American Y.M.C.A.; they even approved of the idea. Similar approval was secured, while in New York, from the Metropolitan Archbishop Platon, after he had been informed that it was planned to print a large edition of the Bible in Russian, and to accept the text recommended by him. Only the Government at Moscow had not been approached as yet.

This desire of the Y.M.C.A. not to offend any among the Russian *émigrés* produced at least one embarrassing result. A certain small booklet on Russian history, written by a very reputable historian named Khudiakov, was published in Russian by the Y.M.C.A. and was vigorously attacked by the same alert and omnipresent "lawyer," whom I have mentioned in connection with the Russian Officers' Society and my passport difficulties in Japan.[3] His chief complaint, it seemed, was in connection with a remark by the editor on the probable attitude of Count Leo Tolstoy toward the Bolshevik regime. Biriukov, the editor, who had been a close friend of the late Count, asserted that Tolstoy would have approved of it. The "lawyer's" objection was taken so seriously that the entire edition was condemned and burned in the style later practiced on a large scale by Adolf Hitler. The same "lawyer," together with a few other reactionaries, also objected to the fact that we of the Y.M.C.A. had decided to print all our books in the new orthography, developed by the Academy of Science under the Czar, introduced by the First Provisional Government after the Revolution, and now retained for practical reasons by the new regime as

[3] It was this lawyer who later became better known as one of those who introduced in the United States the "Protocols of the Elders of Zion." He was also reported to be the inspiration of the *Dearborn Independent* at the time it was fomenting anti-Semitism in America. He also was pleading for admission to the United States of the infamous Ataman Semenov.

well. I succeeded in defending our decision on the ground of historical fact, and the new orthography was left unmolested.

On our return from Europe the choice of Prague was approved as the best site for the publishing house. Geographically it was not far from Russia. The government was sympathetic to the plan, the people were not unlike the Russians in many respects, typesetters who knew the Russian language were readily available, prices were low, and the exchange favorable.

Some seven months elapsed before we finally moved the business to Prague. In the meantime the former Emperor of Austria-Hungary, Karl, made an abortive attempt to return to the throne. Czechoslovakia, as a former part of the Hapsburg Monarchy, bitterly opposed such a restoration and ordered the mobilization of her army. Consequently the Czech kroner was falling, and I suggested to my superiors in the Y.M.C.A. that we should take advantage of this temporary situation, and convert as many dollars as possible into Czech kroners. I did this on my own account at the rate of one hundred and two kroners per dollar; on leaving Prague next year I received one dollar per forty kroners. It was a good bargain, indeed; and, as we shall later see, it served the Y.M.C.A. in an unusual manner.

In the fall of the same year preparations were made for the international conference convoked at Washington, designed to check the undue expansion of Japan. Bakhmeteff, who was still recognized by the United States Government as our Ambassador, asked me to prepare a memorandum on Russian interests in the Far East, and this, naturally, I was glad to do. I am not in a position to say to what extent Bakhmeteff was instrumental in shaping the policy adopted at the Conference toward the Russian aspect of the problem. There was another Russian representative present, in the person of the envoy of the Far Eastern Republic, Boris Skvirsky, who eventually became Counselor to the Soviet Embassy at Washington, after normal diplomatic relations between Washington and Moscow were established in 1933.

The Far Eastern Republic was created in May, 1920, as a buffer state between Japan and Soviet Russia, and lay to the east of Lake

Baikal. It served a useful purpose so long as the Japanese remained on Russian soil. But after their withdrawal there was no longer any need for this artificial state, and by the end of 1922 the Far Eastern Republic was reunited to the mother country. In spite of the fact that Russia was not represented officially at the Washington Conference, her interests were safeguarded to a certain extent. Japan was advised to evacuate her troops from Russian possessions as soon as possible, and did so for all practical purposes before the end of 1922.[4] Only a few Japanese soldiers remained somewhat longer on the Russian part of Sakhalin Island as security for the settlement of their claim for a "massacre" at Nikolaievsk on the Amur, which had been provoked by the Japanese themselves. About that time the Interallied Technical Board under John F. Stevens, which had continued to direct the operations of the Chinese Eastern Railway from Harbin, was also withdrawn.

In December, 1921, after having shipped the machinery for the printing plant that we had purchased in the United States for some one hundred and fifty thousand dollars, we sailed for Europe. The legalization of the enterprise in Prague did not take very long. We bought a large new building suitable for our purpose, placed an order with a contractor for building another house, and started installation of the machinery. My American colleague, Mr. Niederhauser, who was sent from New York to act as the President of the Corporation, wanted to have an audience with the President of the Republic, and this was arranged through the Foreign Office. When we went to see the venerable Thomas Masaryk at the Gradcany Palace, he asked us about our plans, and, having learned that one of the first books to be printed was the Bible, he turned to me and in his perfect Russian said with a twinkle in his eye: "That is one thing, I am sure, that you could omit from your plans."

But the Bible was considered so important, and its printing so urgent, that before our machinery had been installed, and our plant started to operate, the printing of the Bible was entrusted to a Czech

[4] In February, 1922, the Japanese troops suffered a severe beating from the Red Army near Volochaievsk (not far from Khabarovsk).

firm. It was not expected, of course, that the new regime of Russia would be eager for shipments of the Scriptures; but very obviously the administration wanted to make sure that no time would be lost in delivering the Bibles after that regime was replaced by another. Needless to say, these books never were shipped to Russia! Nor did we ship any other books to the U.S.S.R. While still in New York, we had accumulated more than two hundred manuscripts on a variety of technical and agricultural subjects; so before long there was a problem of storage for the printed material. As the general manager, I was anxious to have authorization to start shipping the books. But no such authorization was forthcoming.

While the printing plant was being organized and the machinery installed, we needed a number of helpers. Numerous Russian *émigrés* were in Prague at that time, the majority being former officers who had left Russia after the retreat of the White Armies. Some of them had been admitted by the Czech Government as students in various educational institutions. Practically all were in need of work. I was able to employ a few, and, naturally, was happy to be able to help compatriots and former colleagues who were less fortunate than myself. One of them was even a former officer of the gendarmerie, who served with me on the staff of the Tenth Army during the War.

As a result, I was accused by the Russians from the Left of harboring counterrevolutionaries. On the other hand, it was known, too, that I was friendly with Madame Breshko-Breshkovskaya, besides having committed the unpardonable "crime" of having been associated with Kerensky, who was "anathema" to the officers. And I was known to be friendly with several Social Revolutionaries in Prague, such as the charming old man, Lazareff. But at the same time I kept away from such leaders as Chernoff and those who had co-operated with the Czechs while they were in Siberia. So, as a consequence, I was also accused by those from the Right, of dealing with the revolutionaries. But in this I was not alone. Practically every Russian was suspected of something, accused of this or that, blamed for things of which he might even have no knowledge, cursed for crimes he had never committed, and, certainly, envied for having a better place in the sun than his neighbor.

But in spite of disagreements and quarrels we always had one malady in common. That common malady was homesickness. Everyone expected to return to Russia before very long. This wishful belief was so strong that in Prague, for instance, a law school was established, in which the old Russian laws were taught, as though nothing had ever happened in Russia. The victims of this were the youngsters, who, after they had finished the law school, went to Paris to become taxi drivers.

Among the various Russian organizations then active in Prague was a committee to help the victims of the great famine. My wife was invited to take part in its work and made an attempt to invigorate its anemic existence. It was planned to organize collections all over the country, following the method used in the United States during the War in selling the Liberty bonds and Victory Loans. One of the first affairs planned in connection with this was a gala concert. The interest of certain influential Czechs was attracted, a number of talents promised to participate, programs were arranged, posters distributed, and announcements made. The large hall of the Obecni Dom, where the Prague Symphony Orchestra gave its concerts, was hired. All preparations had been made, and then, a few hours before the concert, several letters arrived from artists with regrets that they would be unable to appear. The hall was practically empty. The box office remained idle. We and two other secretaries of the Y.M.C.A. paid the expenses, and learned another lesson in the so-called "class struggle." It was a clear case of boycotting an attempt to render help to the starving people, just because their government was not to the liking of those who happened to have money and power.

Early in the summer Mr. C. V. Hibbard arrived in Prague and came to see our establishment. After I had shown him what had already been done, we went to my office, where I explained the situation created by the piling-up of books without any prospect of shipping them to their destination. Anxious to see the proper arrangement made, and in the heat of discussion, I put the problem to him frankly, saying that I must be authorized to organize the shipment of the books to Russia, or I could not remain at my post. The answer was that Washington frowned on the entire scheme, and that the State Department was not inclined to approve the sending of our books to Moscow. In the circumstance there was nothing left for me but to resign.

In about two months, my family and I were back in New York, and confronted with the problem of doing something for a living. The transaction with the Czech exchange proved to be very fortunate; for not only had I converted some of my own money into kroners at a favorable rate, but had the Y.M.C.A. convert my annual salary, too. As for the Y.M.C.A., it benefited by this transaction to an unusual extent and paid me a "bonus" for the advice. Soon after my resignation the entire business was discontinued: the plant was sold to some Czechs, and the manuscripts were shipped to Paris. Probably they are still lying in the darkness of some storehouse on the banks of the Seine. The International Committee of the Y.M.C.A. came out of this venture, apparently, with little or no loss.

On my return to the United States I no longer had any illusions about my chances of going home to Russia. It was obvious that the new regime was there to stay, and I was not convinced that it was a regime of which I could approve. But, by now at least I had accumulated enough evidence not to think of it any longer in terms of disdain. At the same time, I had no desire to return while it was in power. So gradually the idea crystallized in my mind that I had lost my mother country and would have to stay abroad. Therefore I had to look around for some job or employment.

Before joining the Y.M.C.A., I had been engaged for a short time in editing a magazine started by an American lawyer of Russian extraction, under the name *Overseas Enterprise*. The purpose of this periodical was to serve American businessmen in their ventures in Russia and Poland. It was published in three languages: English, Russian, and Polish, and was largely devoted to descriptions of the unlimited opportunities that could be found by enterprising merchants in those two largest Slavic countries. It was not published very long, for those opportunities remained ephemeral. But this short experience taught me one valuable lesson. Once, sitting in my office, I overheard the telephone conversation of the man who was in charge of advertisements. He told his listener that our publication was closely connected with the Russian Embassy, and with the Polish Consulate, too, of course. I was rather surprised to hear this, knowing that it was absolutely untrue. So I told my "chief," the lawyer-publisher, about it with unconcealed disgust. Being philosophically inclined, he answered in a way which later impressed me deeply. "You were used," he said, "to have all the dirty work performed for you by others, without being bothered by it, and, probably, even without knowing about it at all; it was the job of those who made possible your sheltered life of privilege. That is why you are disgusted with a little irregularity, a little liberty with facts, a liberty designed to get results in the everyday business world." Unpleasant as it is, I think he was right, not in countenancing this method for getting business, but in his cynical explanation of the division of labor between the privileged person and the one working for him.

Another lesson along the same lines I received after my return to New York. I was asked by a former secretary of the Y.M.C.A. to invest a certain amount of money in his cafeteria business; and I consented, partly to help a friend, and partly because it offered a chance to learn something practical. One of the employees once came to me and advised me in a most friendly manner not to insist on scruples. "You will never get any results, except losses," he told me, "if you continue to stress honesty." Pretty soon I was out of the business. The busboy was right: the only result for me was a loss. But if I lost in money, I gained in practical wisdom.

It was easier to make a living from a small house that we bought and divided into apartments, which we furnished and rented. But it was not enough. Therefore I studied the insurance business and became an "underwriter" with the Union Central Life Insurance Company. The results were quite satisfactory: I was even awarded a "prize" for a large amount of insurance underwritten in a short time. But the work did not satisfy me in other respects; and when a friend of mine offered to introduce me to Senator France, who was interested in Soviet Russia and was planning business relations with Moscow, I became assistant to the vice-president of his corporation. I quickly learned that the Senator's plan was to supply Russia with ordnance. He was leaving for Moscow soon and would try there to get permission for my entry, after which I was to join him. In the meanwhile, I should wait for word from him in Europe. In connection with this scheme I sailed for France in January, 1924. But no instructions were received from the Senator for my going to Russia, and soon I was back in New York. The Senator's trip to Moscow had been fruitless; there was no business in sight in which he could be interested.

About this time a very charming Southern family, whom I had met through mutual friends, invited me to visit them at their home in South Carolina. I availed myself of this opportunity to spend a few days in their hospitable home and was amazed to find how similar the life of the well-to-do people of the South was to that of Russia in the prerevolutionary days. Here was the same detachment from real life; the easy-going, carefree existence, the same assumed superiority of the landowning class. And the colored people seemed to play much the same role in regard to the wealthy whites, as the peasants in the Holy Russia of the Czars had played to their masters. Charming as was the entourage of cultured, refined, well-meaning people, I was certain that it was not healthy for me to become a part of their life. I was sure that in the ever-busy atmosphere of New York I would more readily find the conditions necessary for my acclimatization to the New World.

On my return to New York I was offered work by a good friend of mine, Dr. M——, who in the early days of the Russian Revolution had been active in raising funds in America to send medical equipment to Moscow. He was now representing in the United States the Soviet Public Health Service. My work consisted of making and translating excerpts from the medical magazines published in America and of very simple research on various problems of interest to the Public Health Service at Moscow. The work was much more appealing to me than soliciting insurance, for I had to visit various medical congresses and conferences, exhibits, lectures, and so forth. While doing this work for almost three years, I met a number of physicians, some of them professors of medicine, who came from Soviet Russia to acquaint themselves with the American methods and achievements in their respective fields. From them I learned more about my mother country than I had been able to learn from the press.

Their stories were very different from those I read in the papers or heard from various "experts" after flying visits to a country which few of them had seen before, and which they, certainly, could not understand in a short time. Long before this, I had suspected that much of the information available abroad was unreliable. Everyone knew what the value of "dispatches from Riga" was. The famous special issue of *The New Republic,* which published the comparisons made by its editor, Walter Lippmann, between the *New York Times'* accounts of the situation in Soviet Russia, and the actual facts, played an extremely useful role in redirecting public opinion about the New Russia. More and more truth was penetrating the mass of distortions and slanders. More and more interest was being aroused among outsiders.

How was it possible for one who had been born in Russia and continued to love his mother country to remain disinterested? I, certainly, wanted to know as much as possible about the actual situation there. Gradually I found ways not only to obtain reliable information, but to correlate the ever-growing store of facts obtained from reliable sources. I eagerly began to seize upon every available piece of news coming from the Soviet Union, and the more I learned, the more I wanted to embark upon more serious and systematic study.

CHAPTER XIX

THE WORLD-WIDE CRISIS

(*Good Method for Learning*)

Institute of Politics at Williamstown. A new line of work. Learning to understand better before trying to explain. Foreign Policy Association. Great institution—the Public Library. My first book in English. A trip to China. *The Chinese Soviets.* Lectures all over the country. Reviewing books and writing articles. A new book, this time on Japan.

GRADUALLY THE FOG surrounding the name "Soviet Union" was clearing, and the age when such a book as *Ten Days That Shook the World* by John Reed, published soon after the Revolution, was considered a product of a rebel, gave place to one in which similar evaluations of events could safely begin to come from the pens of "respectable" writers. The revelations made by Walter Lippmann in *The New Republic* found support in a number of books.[1] The testimony given by William C. Bullitt before the Senate Committee on Foreign Relations appeared in print.[2] An account of military intervention in North Russia was published. Books, newspapers, and magazines from the Soviet Union became available at the Public Library and could now be bought in the bookstores. And what these books and documents made public was definitely not in accord with the information spread by certain newspapers. Thus, a picture somewhat different from that generally accepted was forming in my mind, but facts alone were not sufficient; I needed understanding and an interpretation. This I set myself to acquire.

[1] Arthur Ransome. *Russia in 1919.* B. W. Huebsch. New York. 1919.
H. N. Brailsford. *The Russian Workers' Republic.* Harper and Brothers. New York. 1921.
Albert Rhys Williams. *Through the Russian Revolution.* Boni and Liveright. New York. 1921.
Edward A. Ross. *The Russian Soviet Republic.* The Century Co. New York. 1923.
[2] *The Bullitt Mission to Russia.* Testimony before the Committee on Foreign Relations, United States Senate. B. W. Huebsch. New York. 1919.
Fighting Without a War. An account of Military Intervention in North Russia. By Ralph Alberston. Harcourt, Brace and Howe. New York. 1920.

Reading and attending lectures, debates, and discussions served in various ways to open my eyes. To get more information on foreign affairs I joined the Foreign Policy Association and became a regular reader of its publications. For a long time I missed none of their discussions. Without doubt I learned a great deal through the activities of this organization, so ably led by Dr. James MacDonald.

In 1926 I visited the Institute of Politics at Williamstown for the first time and found it so interesting and valuable for my enlightenment, that I became and remained a regular member, up to its premature demise in 1933. Of course, like everything else, the Institute went through considerable modification of its original plans and methods of work. Gradually, under pressure of the world-wide economic crisis, it began to shun controversial topics, and consequently its usefulness waned. Finally, with not entirely convincing excuses, it was decided to close its doors. I know that I was not alone in my regrets at the disappearance of that forum, where opinions were freely exchanged, usually with the participation of highly qualified experts in various fields. This was one of the numerous casualties of the "depression."

If the first sessions of the Institute, which was founded in 1921, were mostly devoted to debates on the heritage of the World War, the stress by 1926 was being laid on the future. Professor A. Mendelssohn-Bartholdy, the eminent German publicist, discussed the European situation in a series of lectures. This was the year when Berlin concluded a new treaty with Moscow; the second after that of Rapallo, which was signed at the time of the International Conference held at Genoa. Dr. Mendelssohn asserted that Germany would never abandon Soviet Russia, that their co-operation was dictated by mutual interest, and that in the future the two countries would become still more closely bound. It was, of course, a rapprochement of two states driven together because both had become outcasts, ostracized by the others at the end of the World War and the Russian Revolution.[3] Another in-

[3] When the amiable Dr. Mendelssohn died several years later, Nazified Germany had already become violently opposed to the Soviet Union and the Führer was shrieking abuse at Russia in his harangues.

teresting subject, discussed by Professor Mauritz Bonn of Germany at the same session was "The New Aspects of the World Economic Situation." But although he expressed certain vague doubts about the economic health of the world, we heard from him no warning of the coming crisis.

One of the various round-table discussions was devoted to the Far East. I was invited to participate both in the discussion and in a General Conference on the same subject. The addresses that I made received wide publicity all over the country. The several points that I stressed evoked keen interest and found a place on the front pages of various papers. First of all I asserted that, contrary to the prevailing opinion, the Soviet Union had abandoned the policies of the Czars. It was not disposed to be aggressive, and could not be considered a menace to peace generally, and in the Far East particularly. I also pointed out that enemies were attempting to create bad feeling in the Far East between Soviet Russia and other Asiatic nations, which eventually might be harmful to themselves. As for China, I urged a "hands off" policy. Foreign intervention there, I warned, would be as futile and dangerous as it had been in Russia.

The following year I missed the Institute, as I spent the summer with my family in Italy and France. But in 1928 I was back at Williamstown again. This time I took active part in a discussion of the "Problems of the Pacific." Our round table was under the able direction of Professor George H. Blakeslee, one of the outstanding American experts on the Far East; and as the co-operation of the Kuomintang and the Communists had been terminated by the creation of the Nanking regime under Chiang Kai-shek during the preceding year, the question of the future of the Communist influence in China was naturally discussed. I expressed the opinion that the behavior of Japan in China and the widespread poverty of the Chinese population made such a revival highly likely. To support my contention, I referred to the resolution passed by the Third International in July of the previous year, forecasting the coming victory of their movement. "As for Soviet Russia, on the other hand," I added, "I have read several documents stating very emphatically that Russia will refrain from taking any active part in fostering Communism in China . . . that policy was one of the points on which Stalin and Trotzky had split." And I concluded this paper by the following statement: "If there is a probability of the return of Communist influence in China, there is no better encouragement for it than by committing the injustice to China of quasi-sympathy toward Japan and of remaining neutral toward her plans of helping herself to Manchuria."

Again the press gave prominence to my statement, with the usual percentage of misrepresentation. One paper carried a scare-head: "A Communist Threat." Another said: "Expresses Fear Communism May Return in China." The *New York Times* used a somewhat milder headline: "Declares Sovietism Yet Lurks in China," but said that my assertion was based "on documentary evidence," without explaining that the "document" in question was a resolution which had been published for everybody's use, and certainly not secret.

I was kept quite busy during this session, for I prepared and read no fewer than seven papers. In addition, I debated with the Japanese publisher and journalist, Zumoto, and criticized his attempts to justify his country's methods in Manchuria by the acts of Czarist Russia in the past. Another advocate of Japan, the late George Bronson Rae, attempted to justify the aggression of his *protégé* by offering a fantastic interpretation of the Sino-Russian treaty of 1896. His contention was that by signing that treaty China became an ally of Russia in case of war with Japan. I had to bring in this text and analyze its meaning, showing the absurdity of such a conclusion. Several lawyers who were present congratulated me on this score, considering that I had made the point very well and had defeated my opponent. Another address of mine described and defined the policy of the Soviet Union in Outer Mongolia, denying that the former cherished any aggressive designs against the latter. All that Russia wanted there was a "buffer" for her own safety. As for Japan, I indicated that she was breaking the Nine-Power Treaty signed at Washington and ignoring the obligation accepted by her under the Kellogg Pact. And still another paper which I read at that session dealt with Soviet-Japanese relations. Its closing paragraph may be of interest even today. It stated:

> Speaking figuratively, what will be there tomorrow? It is hard to predict. But no one can doubt that the fate of the Far East depends to a great extent on the positions taken by Russia and Japan toward each other and by both of them toward the outsiders. It is full time to know that Russia's interests there are of such a nature that she is neither an aspirant for the mastery of the Pacific, nor a candidate for predominance in the Far East. Russia is not a competitor in that respect for the three leading rivals: Great Britain, Japan, and the United States. But she is so situated that she might play a role of greatest importance in the coming drama in that remote theater. She might be a friend to everyone concerned and remain neutral in the contest; she might choose to do otherwise.

When reviewing the full Pacific Problem, on the General Conference, I also quoted the following from *China and the Powers* by Henry K. Norton: "No Japanese statesman in his right mind would seek a war against the United States, with Russia at his back."

My general attitude toward world events at that moment can be seen from the following extract from my address at the final conference of that session:

> The problem of today is the struggle between Capitalism and Communism, but no such war can be won by one who does not stick to facts, does not take them as realities to be dealt with, and does not offer ideas to fight ideas, but stubbornly repeats old ideas without any modification to suit the moment.

One afternoon, practically all the members of the Institute were gathered at the faculty club of the College to hear a radio speech by Mr. Herbert Hoover, then candidate for the Presidency. He dealt with the present-day situation in the United States. The problem of poverty, he declared, was almost completely solved in this country, and he promised that under his administration there would be "two cars in each garage and a chicken in every pot." Some of the listeners were elated by this prospect, especially those whose family tradition kept them on the side of the Republican Party. But a few skeptics smiled ironically. Most of these belonged to the Democratic Party, of course. There were a few also who were not rigid party men, and these seemed disinclined to take Mr. Hoover very seriously. The following year, of course, was 1929, and the skeptics were vindicated. Mr.

Hoover's Pollyanna attitude became less popular even among the Republicans, at least those who took seriously the assurances of Andrew Mellon, "the greatest Secretary of the Treasury after Alexander Hamilton," that everything was simply fine, as justification for wild gambling. They had been assured by Hoover's optimism and paid for it dearly by their losses on the Stock Exchange.

In 1928, following the advice of several members of the Williamstown Institute, I started a new career, that of a lecturer. My principal topic concerned the Far East, but, being asked again and again to speak on Russia, I included that subject in my programs too. This new kind of work gave me a welcome opportunity to learn more about the United States while traveling; and in the years that followed I visited practically every State of the Union, made endless acquaintances all over the country, and became much more acclimatized to American life than could ever have been possible had I stayed most of the time in New York.

To lecture on international affairs, one must be up to date on many matters. To talk on Russia of today, one must learn a great deal, not only about its political, social, and economic structure, but also about its underlying philosophy. It required constant reading. And that is what I had been doing practically all the time since my return to the United States after the short publishing adventure with the Y.M.C.A. in Prague. The Public Library, that wonderful institution of which New York may be proud, had long ago become my headquarters. There I now spent hours and hours of my time. To be able to explain to others I had to learn more myself. I devoured books, made and classified notes, and accumulated files. From my visits to the Williamstown Institute and from the lecture experience, I learned that there were very few people in America who had even an approximately correct knowledge of Russia's role in the Far East. At the same time it was clear to me that the prevailing misinformation was of such a nature that it might result in real harm to the United States as well as to Russia. Obviously it was desirable that this situation should be remedied. So, as by that time I had acquired a sufficient mastery of the English language to dare to write—subject to a little subsequent polishing by a native hand—I decided to try my forces on a book on Russia in the Far East. A number of specialists in that field encouraged me, and in 1929 I began work.

In the spring of 1929 I made my first attempt to revisit my mother country. With the help of a number of American and Russian friends, and after several months of anxious waiting, I received word that my entry visa would be granted. At that time there were no consular representatives of the Soviet Union in the United States. To have the visa affixed one had to go to one of the European countries where such representatives were stationed; and there were plenty of such countries. Since 1920 the new regime at Moscow had gradually received recognition from practically all countries except the United States. The Great Powers signed treaties for trade first and for normal diplomatic relations afterwards. In addition, nonaggression pacts were in force by that time with most of the European neighbors of the Soviet Union.

On my arrival at Berlin I found that no authorization for my visa had yet been received. It took almost three weeks before it arrived. Finally my documents were in order, and I sailed from Stettin to Leningrad, as Petrograd had been renamed after the death of Lenin in 1924. It was an unforgettable experience—this return to the shores of the mother country. It was also a revelation to discover the New Russia and see the really marvelous changes which had taken place in the twelve years since the Revolution. But of all this, more in the next chapter. After more than a month in Russia, during which I visited a large number of places with which I had been familiar in the past, I started on my way back to America instead of going to China, as I originally intended. I wanted to revisit the Far East before writing the book. But events in Manchuria prevented me from fulfilling my plan. Certain Chinese war lords had made an attempt to take over the Chinese Eastern Railway from the Russians. The Soviet officials of that road were arrested by the Chinese without any pretense of legality, and Chinese troops advanced to the Soviet border. When they began encroaching on Soviet territory, the Red Army chased them in such an effective manner that the entire adventure was immediately abandoned and the Moscow terms for the restoration of the *status quo ante* were accepted by the Chinese *in toto*. But I was the loser. I had to cancel my ticket to China, and, instead of going back to the United States via the Pacific, was forced to return by way of Europe.

Soon after my return to New York I was invited by the Institute of International Relations, held at Riverside by the University of Southern California, to lead a round-table discussion on the Far East. Before going to Riverside, I was asked to address at Los Angeles a group of friends of Dr. Rufus B. von KleinSmid, President of the University. My topic was Soviet Russia. Apparently my address led some newspapermen to believe that I was a Soviet official, for obviously in their opinion one could not be favorable to that regime without being part of it. At any rate my picture appeared in the local papers with a caption: "The Red General who will address the Institute." Therefore I started my lecture at the General Conference of the Institute by expressing my gratitude to the local press for informing me of this unexpected and unsolicited promotion. Such "mistakes" in reports on my lectures began to occur more and more often after I visited Soviet Russia. I never protested, for what is the use? The denials never receive the same prominence as the original gossip or detraction. And, besides, it was unreasonable not to expect disapproval in some quarters. First my mere open-mindedness, and afterward my friendly attitude toward the Soviet Union and its affairs were assailed. What else could one expect from those who never wanted to know the truth about the Soviet Union, never wanted to be fair in that respect, and specialized in keeping their readers misinformed about that strange country which was so out of line with their own philosophy?

But by that time there had appeared numerous books describing the New Russia from every conceivable angle. There was no longer any justification for claiming that it was difficult to know the truth about the Soviet Union. Those who wanted to find it had ample means for digging out the facts and drawing their own conclusions. But to those who did not want to see the truth, of course, no book or report by eyewitnesses was important.[4]

The season 1929-30 brought a large number of speaking engagements and much traveling. But the book was, nevertheless, making good progress, and by the end of 1930 the manuscript was completed. A friend of mine suggested that the value of the work would be considerably increased by adding as many documents on Russian diplomatic relations as possible. So I decided to make another trip to Russia, in the hope of gaining access to the Archives of the Foreign Office. In January, 1931, I was again in Moscow. Through a letter of introduction from Mr. Ludwig Martens[5] I was allowed to examine and copy the original treaties.

Although I was in Moscow only two weeks, the trip was a serious drain on my funds. The time spent on it was lost on lecturing, and therefore I made an attempt to receive a grant from one of the Foundations for finishing the book. A friend of mine suggested that a certain professor at Columbia was the right man to sponsor my appeal. With a letter of introduction, I went to see him, and he asked me to leave the manuscript. A few days later the script was returned with a letter informing me that the professor could not recommend it for a grant because it seemed to be "a brief." The explanation was very simple. My evaluation of the League of Nations was not to the liking of the professor, who was active in its support. Yet all that I said about the League was that I doubted its ability to intervene on the side of China in case of a Japanese aggression. Well, it did not take

[4] *Russia After Ten Years.* Report of American Trade Union Delegation to U.S.S.R. International Publishers. New York. 1927.

Vanguard Studies of Soviet Russia. Edited by Jerome Davis. Vanguard Press. New York. 1927-8.

Soviet Russia in the Second Decade. Edited by Stuart Chase, Robert Dunn, and R. G. Tugwell. John Day Co. New York. 1928.

Theodore Dreiser. *Dreiser Looks at Russia.* Horace Liveright. New York. 1928.

Frederick Schuman. *American Policy Toward Russia Since 1917.* International Publishers. New York. 1928.

John Dewey. *Impressions of Soviet Russia and the Revolutionary World.* New Republic Inc. New York. 1929.

Maurice Dobb. *Russian Economic Development Since the Revolution.* E. P. Dutton & Co. New York. 1928.

[5] The former representative of Lenin's regime at Washington and, at the time of my visit to Moscow, the head of the Lomonossov Institute and Editor of the Technical Encyclopedia.

long for the Japanese to start their occupation of Manchuria, or for Geneva to supply a complete vindication of my opinion. Within one year from the professor's letter, Japan was master of Manchukuo, and the League of Nations had demonstrated its real value.

Even without the grant the book was finished. It was not a simple matter to find a publisher, of course; but my friend, Manuel Komroff, the novelist, introduced me to his own publisher, Mr. Thomas R. Coward; Professor Charles P. Howland, of Yale, editor of the *Foreign Affairs* magazine, recommended my manuscript for publication, and it was accepted. Under the name, *Russia and the Soviet Union in the Far East,* the book came off the press just one month before the Japanese invasion was started. This gave it a peculiar news value, and the reviews were much better and more prominent than I could otherwise have expected. It was unanimously approved, in many cases very flatteringly, by the reviewers and various experts; and I was particularly pleased to find that practically all the reviewers stressed the "remarkable impartiality" of the author in dealing with various controversial matters. This did not sound like an accusation of taking sides, or even of writing a "brief." [6]

As after my first visit to Soviet Russia, on my return I attended the session of the Williamstown Institute. By 1930 its agenda were already reflecting the crisis. One of the round tables dealt with the tremendous changes that the Occident was undergoing; and an analysis of Western civilization was offered by Professor C. DeLisle Burns of the University of Glasgow in an endeavor to reach an understanding of those changes and "to discover what we can do about it." Discussing

[6] Here are a few excerpts. ". . . this fact, aside from the scholarly and realistic temper of Mr. Yakhontoff's timely book, makes its appearance of first importance and accords it a unique place among books now available on the Far East" declared the *New York Times.* "Most welcome addition to the literature of the Far Eastern situation . . . admirable bibliography and collection of documents," was the comment of *Foreign Affairs.* "Impartiality of viewpoint" was one phrase used by the *Evening Sun* of Baltimore. "Admirably thorough historical analysis . . . its importance as a source book cannot be overestimated" said the *New York Sun.* "He is plainly a man of wide learning and of impartial mind" commented the *American Mercury,* then still under Mencken. "Reserve and liberality of spirit distinguishes the whole discussion," wrote Professor Harold S. Quigley in *Current History* magazine. "It is an excellent piece of work. I marvel at the author's fairness and freedom of bias" commented Professor Karl C. Liebrick of Syracuse. "A volume which makes a valuable contribution to our knowledge . . . and which should be in every library" wrote Professor George H. Blakeslee of Clark University.

the peculiarities of modern industry, Professor Burns pointed out that "poverty remains a problem." Contrary to the pronunciamentos of Mr. Herbert Hoover, it seemed, indeed, to be quite a serious problem in the United States under his administration, perhaps even more so than ever before.

The recent economic changes in Europe were discussed at another round table, led by Professor Edwin F. Gray, of Harvard. Much optimism was expressed, and one of the participants declared that "the establishment of the Bank of International Settlements will bring a greater degree of co-operation in finance and industry, which means a more stable and secure world order." It is of course easy in 1939 to sneer at such "foresight."

As for the regular round table on the Far Eastern situation, this again was led by Professor Blakeslee; and in one of my addresses I discussed the existence of Soviet areas in China and the activities of their Red Armies. "It would be naïve to consider them of no political and especially social importance," I said, and closed my remarks by stating:

> To understand the situation, one has to depend on something more real and more serious than accusations of omnipresent and omnipotent Russian Bolsheviks. There are now no Russians but "White" Russians in South China; they have no direct influence in the alarming events around Changsha and Wuhan; these are the developments of the Chinese Revolution, undoubtedly reflecting what happened in Russia a few years ago, and apt to continue for years to come.

The most radical innovations at the Institute in 1930 were the presence of a number of Soviet representatives and a series of conferences devoted to the discussion of "The Domestic and Foreign Problems of Russia." As recently as the early summer of that year the inglorious spectacle of an "investigation" of *"Amtorg,"* the Soviet commercial agency in America, had taken place under the chairmanship of Congressman Hamilton Fish. It came out at the sessions of this Committee that the documents on which the accusations were based, were forgeries, and in the fall of the same year Mr. Peter Bogdanov, the Chairman of the Board of the *"Amtorg"* and a number of his associates were invited to Williamstown to address the session on the problems confronting their country. This was, of course, a good example of American respect for fair play. At the same time, one realized that such a chance would hardly have been given them if they had not had Ivy Lee, the famous publicity agent of John D. Rockefeller, as their adviser on public relations. To counterbalance the Soviet side, a number of "experts" on Russia were invited, including the former representative of the *Berliner Tageblatt,* Paul Scheffer, who was barred from re-entering the Soviet Union after one of his visits to Germany. But the Soviet side was backed by such influential views as those of Mr. Paul Cravath, the distinguished lawyer; Mr. Willis Abbott, editor of the *Christian Science Monitor;* Colonel Hugh L. Cooper, the famous engineer who had helped the Russians in the building of their first enormous hydroelectric development on the Dnieper River; and Mr. Karl A. Bickel, President of the United Press. The general impression left with the members of the Institute was undoubtedly favorable to the New Russia. By that time the Soviet Union was already showing a remarkably rapid reconstruction of her economic life, and it was becoming more and more obvious that the new regime was supported by the majority of the people and was making good progress.

In spite of the marked change in the attitude toward the Soviet Union demonstrated at the session of 1930, Professor T. B. Gregory of London, who led the round table on economic trends in the following year, did not even mention the existence of a new economic order, successfully applied in a country covering a vast section of the land surface of the globe. But the program of the Institute for 1932 included a very significant topic: "The Disintegration of the Modern World Order"; and the leader of the round table, Professor Arnold J. Toynbee of London, invited me to speak on the Soviet Union. Here is an excerpt from the report on my speech in the Proceedings of the Institute:

General Yakhontoff said that at the time of the World War Russia was an agricultural country. Following the War, Russia was almost ostracized by the world. It then became a matter of extreme difficulty to re-establish her national economy and particularly to place it upon an industrial basis. It seems probable that if the capitalist nations had not ostracized Russia and refused financial co-operation to help her out of the chaos brought about by the Revolution, she not only would have been able to avoid famine and starvation but she could have directed her reconstruction processes in a more healthy atmosphere and at a slower tempo. The world's adjustment to the new situation could then have been carried on also more normally. This might have spared us much of the distress of the present crisis.

If there had been no interruption of foreign trade, Russia would probably not have started the development of many industries which she is now trying to create. Being forced to build her national economy on an unhealthy basis of complete isolation, i.e., to build so as to become independent and self-sustaining, Russia naturally is indulging in the creation of industries which, under normal conditions, would be economically irrational for her to develop. This artificially created ultranationalism with the isolated, self-sustained national economy of one sixth of the world (occupied by Soviet Russia), has necessarily affected the economic structure of the whole world and has made for instability.[7]

At the round table on Sino-Japanese relations I was asked to discuss a number of topics, including: "The Soviet Union in the Far East." It will be remembered that this was the year when the Japanese aggression in North China culminated in the creation of the puppet state of Manchukuo. I underlined the fact that those were wrong who contended that the objectives of Soviet Russia's diplomacy in the Far East were not essentially different from those of Imperial Russia, that Russia must inevitably press on towards the Pacific. I asserted that Soviet Russia had become a factor for peace, and had even developed a new technique, not only for advocating peace, but for proving its feasibility by refraining from armed clashes even under the severe strain of irritating provocations. To this I added that "if it were not for certain irrelevant obstacles that still make logical conclusions somewhat difficult, we would probably see a cardinal change in American policy in Asia, as the Russian orientation is apparently gaining more and more adherents in the United States." Obviously I was justified in such an analysis. In November of the following year Washington re-established normal relations with Moscow, apparently realizing the importance, if not of co-operating with the Soviet Union in the Far East, at least of having Russia on her side while Japan renewed her march of aggression in China.

[7] Report of the Round Tables and General Conferences at the Twelfth Session. Edited by John Bakeless. New Haven. 1932. pp. 50-51.

In 1933, encouraged by the success of my first book in English, I was planning another one. This time the Soviet movement in China was to be my subject. With a group of Americans entrusted to me by the "Open Road" traveling agency, I went to the Soviet Union. After our tour of that country was ended, I continued alone, via the Trans-Siberian, to China. The week spent on the train was interesting because of the people I met and the changes in the country that I observed, but otherwise uneventful. After I crossed the Soviet border, however, the situation was changed. On arrival at Manchuli, I was met by an extremely hostile group of former compatriots, who had become Chinese or Japanese by their passports and were in the employ of the Japanese-controlled Manchukuo government, as customs officers, policemen, spies, and the like. Trouble started with the examination of my baggage, for one of my valises was full of books, pamphlets, magazines, and other printed material, mostly on China, and in particular on the communist movement. All this material was confiscated as subversive, and not permissible for importation into Manchukuo. Not only the literature in Russian, but even the publications of the American Foreign Policy Association, the Chinese and Japanese Memoranda on the Litton Report, and numerous other official publications and periodicals in English, were frowned upon. Everything was taken out and laid aside on a bench. When the customs formalities were finished, I asked to speak with someone in authority, and was ushered into the office of the railway police. The chief of police was a former Russian colonel, who obviously had known me before. After protesting against the confiscation of my books, I produced a letter of introduction to the Assistant Minister of Foreign Affairs of Manchukuo, a Japanese, who was actually the omnipotent master of that "independent" country. The letter was given to me by the Japanese Consul General at New York, Mr. Horinouchi.[8] This letter and several others that I had to various important officials, clearly stated that I was on my way to China with the intention of studying the Communist movement there, and asked the authorities to render me every courtesy.

[8] In 1939, Mr. Horinouchi became Ambassador of his country at Washington.

The Japanese officer who was present looked at the letter and gave some instructions to his subordinates. The chief of police then asked me why I had not shown the letter earlier. All that it was possible to do, under the circumstances, he said, was to seal my valise with the books and send it, with me, to Harbin, where superiors would decide on further action.

So I was allowed to continue my trip with the books sealed but unmolested. On my way to Harbin I was under strict supervision; and I was continuously asked to show my passport, as were the other passengers, except the Japanese. Even at night this ceremony was repeated several times. On arrival at Harbin, I was met by a group of Russian policemen and their chief, a former general of the Russian gendarmerie, waiting for me on the platform. My baggage was removed, and I was asked to follow. On our arrival at their office, I asked the chief the reason for this procedure: I was on my way through Manchuria without any desire to stop over; my baggage did not contain anything illegal; and, as could be seen from the letters I had on me, I was expected to carry that sort of material. The "general" was very courteous and did not look at the contents of my valise at all after I showed him my letters; he merely asked me to write down the story of my entry into Manchuria and the trouble I had experienced on the border. He even invited me to his office and offered me his own desk. When I had written what he wanted, he explained that he needed the document to supplement his report to the Japanese military authorities. I was free to continue my trip.

On my way back to the train, the Chinese coolie who was ordered by the "general" to carry my valise, said to me in perfect Russian: "Soon we shall show them their place," meaning, apparently, the Japanese and their Russian servants alike. When I returned to the car, the porters and several other workingmen greeted me with friendly exclamations and very hostile remarks about the police. They realized very well that I had been punished for coming through the Soviet Union.

Undoubtedly the reception tendered by my former compatriots was prearranged; most likely the information about my coming had reached them ahead of my arrival. It was fortunate that I had good letters of introduction, including one to the most influential of all the Japanese in Manchukuo. Otherwise I would probably have been "kidnaped," as were many others, or simply pushed off the train and then reported as a victim of an accident. I recorded the episode as another narrow escape, and forgot about it after having crossed the border of Northern Manchuria, where White Russian influence was still considerable, if only under supervision of the Japanese.

At Shanghaikwan, on the border between Manchukuo and China proper, there was an indescribable lack of order, besides a total absence of illumination. In almost complete darkness, I succeeded in buying my ticket for Peiping. With the help of a porter who was a marvel at acrobatics I reached my car. He managed to bring me and all my luggage to the train, pushing through the thick crowd of Chinese fighting their way toward the train through the dark. Nobody asked for my passport or examined my baggage. But with all these signs of disorder and disorganization, still I felt myself incomparably better off than on the comfortable, clean, well-attended train in the Japanese-controlled Manchukuo.

Next morning I was at Peiping. The feeling of safety, and the entire atmosphere of tranquillity of the old capital of the Celestial Empire, and its comfortable Hotel de Pekin were responsible for a somewhat longer stay there than originally planned. I had always been fond of Peking, and only its name seemed to have changed. I remember this stay in Peiping for another reason also; for I was there at the time of the Reichstag Fire Trial at Berlin and was fascinated by the brave stand and intelligence of the main defendant, the Bulgarian, Dmitroff. There, I thought, was a real "he-man," a human being whose courage one could not help admiring.

From Peiping I went to Shanghai, with only a short stopover at Nanking. Through a number of letters of introduction I was able to meet many prominent Chinese. The bankers were not particularly useful, but the professors were. But, though I succeeded in seeing a number of people who were able to enlighten me on the subject I was interested in, I found most of them not disposed to talk openly about the Communists, the Soviet areas, or the Red Armies. At that time Chinese Communism was taboo. Not a single Chinese bookstore had anything on the subject. Even the magazine *China Forum,* published in Shanghai by an American, was not available in any of these stores. However, the American bookstore arranged for me to receive the back numbers of that magazine, and some other literature. It was difficult to get new material, but finally I was able to collect a little, and to check on what I had already found in Moscow and elsewhere. Through the good offices of Lin Yu-tang [9] I met that wonderful human being and courageous fighter for China, Madame Sun Yat-sen. This had not been easy. The great patriot, widow of the "Father of the Chinese Revolution," and sister of Madame Chiang Kai-shek, lived in constant danger of being attacked, "kidnaped," or worse. Her interest in the people at large, her tolerance toward others' opinions, her pronounced disapproval of the dictatorial policy of her brother-in-law, the Generalissimo, were the cause of this abnormal situation. She told me that she read my book, *Russia and the Soviet Union in the Far East,* and approved of it. She was interested in my new plan and kindly gave a few hints on the subject of my study.

In the middle of October I sailed from Shanghai on a Japanese boat for Nagasaki and Kobe, planning to catch another Japanese boat via Yokohama to San Francisco. My valise with books, considerably swollen since the inspection at Manchuli, was shipped "in bond" directly to America. But this arrangement did not work out as I had expected. At Kobe the Japanese insisted on opening all my valises, including the one with the books. I refused to consent to this and decided to return immediately to Shanghai. On my arrival there I was met on the boat by a Japanese who introduced himself as a representative of the Consulate General and asked me why had I returned and if there was anything wrong?

The following morning the local Russian newspaper carried a paragraph to the effect that I had "not been allowed to land in Japan, as an agent of the Soviet Union." The same journal had published a long

[9] Later well known in the United States through his books, *My Country and my People* and *The Importance of Living.*

article on my first arrival to Shanghai, obviously reprinted from a Harbin paper. In addition to a derogatory description of the episode with my books "that were confiscated as subversive," the article gave a fantastic and malicious account of my past. I was accused of plotting the Revolution in Russia, together with General Polivanov and other "Young Turks." I had been a friend of Kerensky's long before the Revolution. I was the author of the famous Order No. I, which was issued immediately after the February Revolution and was considered the cardinal cause of the disintegration of the Army. There was not a word of truth in any of these accusations. I never met Polivanov in my life, and certainly never plotted any revolt either with him or with anyone else. I had never met Kerensky before I was introduced to him at the session of his Cabinet in the Winter Palace, which I have already described. And I certainly had nothing to do with the Order No. I, or any other orders, for the simple reason that I was in Japan at the time of the Revolution, and had no means for exerting any influence over the makers or breakers of laws and regulations. There were other similarly unfounded details, the only reason for which was the violent disapproval by the White Russians of my return to Russia under the regime they hated. My visit to the Japanese Consul General confirmed my suspicion that the Japanese who met me on the boat was an impostor. Let me repeat that the co-operation of the Japanese and the White Russians at that time was complete and worked like a clock.

In a few days I sailed direct to the United States by an American boat, in order to avoid the unduly curious Japanese inspectors. On November 16, I landed at Seattle. The next day I learned that President Roosevelt had signed an agreement with the Soviet Foreign Commissar, Litvinov. The much-delayed restoration of normal relations between the two great republics became a fact. In Portland, Oregon, I told an interviewer that this act meant "a real service to the peace of the world."

After delivering a series of lectures on the Pacific coast and in the Middle West, I returned to New York. By the spring of 1934 my new manuscript was ready, and in the fall the book came out under the title of *The Chinese Soviets*. It was received very warmly by the critics, especially those of the liberal and radical press. In the headline over the review of my book, the *New York Times* expressed certain doubts about my assertion that the Soviets in China were as strong as I had described and that they had a future. This headline was not warranted by the text of the review. The *New Masses* dealt with this case in a biting article by Granville Hicks. Dr. Edgar Snow, in his very kind review, published in one of the English magazines in China, *The Social and Political Science Review,* remarked that my book "may be emerging rather belatedly, for the success of the sixth anti-Red drive . . . the greater part of 'Soviet China' appears to have been shattered." His own famous book *Red Star Over China,* published four years later, very eloquently told that the Chinese Soviets were very much alive and that their existence was of great importance.[10]

The publication of *The Chinese Soviets* resulted in a number of invitations to speak before liberal and radical groups. In the fall I was asked to address the Congress of the American League Against War and Fascism, held at Chicago, and did this gladly. This started me on lecturing among labor groups; American first, Russian afterward. Such surroundings were strange to me, and I enjoyed my new experiences tremendously. The warmth with which those audiences received me was as heartwarming to me as my soldiers' attitude had been when I was in command after leaving the War College. The touching "address" presented to me by the soldiers at the end of my term, designed, executed, and even framed by themselves, has always been one of my most cherished possessions. I certainly appreciated it far more than all the medals and decorations I received from the Russian and other governments.

Unfortunately, my "regular" lecture engagements were considerably affected by my interest in the workers' groups. Invitations from places where my military rank and past experience as officer of the Imperial Army, as diplomat, and finally as member of the Cabinet of Kerensky, carried more weight than what I had to say, became less frequent. At

[10] *The Chinese Soviets* was banned from China by order of the Nanking government. At the time of Edgar Snow's book, Chiang Kai-shek and the Chinese Soviet leaders were co-operating in fighting the Japanese invaders.

the same time my talks before the labor groups became more and more numerous. The explanation given to me by a lady with experience in this field was that some clubs considered it unjustifiable to pay a high fee for lectures which the same lecturer was giving for practically nothing, when addressing the "proletarians."

One speaking engagement I had in that period was rather unusual. It was a discussion held at Town Hall in New York under the title: "Where are they moving?" in which four generals participated—General Pouderoux of France, General William S. Graves of the United States, General Feng Chen Wu of China, and myself. Our chairman was Anna Louise Strong, the noted author and friend of the Soviet Union.

After 1931 my line of work was augmented; to the lecturing were added radio talks, book reviewing, and articles for various periodicals.

In 1935 I was asked by Mr. Thomas R. Coward, my publisher, to write a popular book on Japan. I accepted the offer gladly, and the following spring the manuscript was ready. In the autumn the book was published as *Eyes on Japan*. The reviews this time were very kind indeed; only the reviewer of *The Nation* found that I was too optimistic in my "Pollyanna" belief that a war in the Far East could be avoided. On the other hand, a former compatriot of mine, Count Ignatieff, wrote a year later in one of the Canadian papers that my book proved to be prophetic. Probably both were justified in their evaluation. The book as a whole stressed the bellicose attitude of Japan and pointed out the danger of further aggression. But in its closing chapter it expressed the hope that war could still be avoided. I think the hope was legitimate, even though up to the present it has been betrayed by the Japanese aggressors and the advocates of "do-nothing" policy in other lands. Logic, of course, had nothing to do with the events that the world was witnessing in Asia and elsewhere. The universal economic crisis of 1929 was not over yet. The fascist states were on their march of conquest. Democracies, genuine or otherwise, were more and more definitely demonstrating their readiness to capitulate before the "conquerors."

CHAPTER XX

RUSSIA AND THE SOVIET UNION

(*Revisiting the Mother Country*)

Personal observation of the U.S.S.R. My first trip in 1929. An amazing experience. Back to America. The world-wide economic crisis. Another visit in 1931. Changes continuing. Japan invades Manchuria. The League of Nations. With a group to the U.S.S.R. in 1933. The White Sea-Baltic Canal. Visit to the U.S.S.R. in 1936. Russia and the Soviet Union

---

The Soviet Union is now more than twenty years old, and even many among those who were hostile toward its regime have been forced to concede its tremendous economic growth, its achievements in cultural progress, its growing importance in the realm of international affairs, and its consistent policy of peace. For this reason it seems strange to recollect how completely ignorant and confused were many utterances about that country in the years following 1917. Even as late as 1929, the favorable reports of various writers on the U.S.S.R. and the stories related by numerous tourists continued to be bitterly attacked from various quarters. I read both these accounts and the attacks upon them at the time; but even then it was apparent to me that the truth was less likely to be on the side of those bitter and often obviously prejudiced critics, than on that of such reporters as William Bullitt, Raymond Robins, Albert Rhys Williams, Paul Monroe, R. G. Tugwell, and Lucy Wilson. These people, to say the least, did not denounce everything in the Soviet Union; and they greatly stirred my already deep concern to know the truth about my mother country: I decided to go and see for myself what had actually taken place in what was once the Russian Empire.

After getting my visa, with much difficulty, I sailed from Stettin to Leningrad in June, 1929, on my first trip to the U.S.S.R. To revisit the land of one's ancestors, the land where one was born and reared, the land that one continues to love, whatever the changes in its political and social structure, must always be an unforgettable experience. And this trip will be ever memorable to me, if only for those first few minutes when the boat passed Kronstadt and Peterhof, and entered the Neva River. These places reminded me of the days of my childhood, they were "home, sweet home." But now they offered a first glimpse of something entirely new, something surrounded by a mystery laboriously built up by various storytellers. What I found in five weeks of travel in my native land was a revelation indeed.

Geographically, of course, it was the land of my childhood; but its people were not the people I had left twelve years before. The apathy of the past had been replaced by a boundless energy. The country was being reconstructed and was developing at high speed. Leningrad was no longer the beautiful St. Petersburg of palaces and mansions I had known. There were still many signs of the destruction wrought by the Revolution; many windows were still boarded up; many panes of glass were not yet replaced; many pavements had not been repaired. But on the outskirts of the city I found numerous new factories and workers' quarters which were being constructed. There was none of this old display of elegance which marked the dominance of a leisure class; but instead one saw the people proud of their emancipation and looking forward to a new life.

In Moscow the change for the better was more striking still. If the old capital of the Romanovs, the former St. Petersburg, was more or less neglected, the new one, or rather the restored capital of the pre-Romanov era, was being rapidly rebuilt, and offered a better example of what the new regime was trying to accomplish. Later, my trip took me from Moscow to Nijni Novgorod; then down the Volga River to Stalingrad; by rail to Ordjonikidze; by automobile over the Georgian Military Highway to Tiflis; and then by rail again to Batum; by boat across the Black Sea to Yalta; by auto to Simferopol; by train to Moscow; and via Leningrad back to Stettin. Such a trip certainly gave me a good opportunity to observe the new country; and my impressions were definitely favorable.

Soon after my return to the United States, the economic crisis occurred. A period of depression, with growing unemployment, set in. Gradually the entire world began to suffer from it. By comparison, all I had seen in Soviet Russia, with no unemployment and steadily mounting production, seemed all the more impressive.

My second visit to the Soviet Union, made in connection with the book I was then writing, took place in 1931. It was very short, partly because life had become much more expensive for a tourist than on my first visit. For now the country was concentrating its energy and resources on the fulfillment of the First Five Year Plan, and was spending enormous amounts of money on "heavy industry" to build up the means of production: factories, mills, machinery, equipment, and so forth. Very little could be allotted for the production of consumers' goods, and consequently prices were high. Personally I did not see much of the construction; it was winter, when very little work of this kind is practicable in the North, and besides I had no time to go anywhere outside of Moscow and Leningrad. But I heard that enormous projects of construction were underway all over the country. In rural life, too, a profound change was clearly being brought about through collectivization. Farming machinery was being introduced, land and driving forces were being pooled, and cultivation was carried on by collective effort on a modern basis with plenty of fertilizer, under the supervision of agronomists, and with generous help from the government. The crops were improving, and peasants were gradually coming to accept the new ideas.

Hardly had I returned to the "outside world" than I learned of new troubles in the Far East. Out of the flesh of China a new colony was being carved by Japan in Manchuria. I learned that the League of Nations was showing the first signs of its impotence and decline. The Great Powers, still suffering from the protracted economic crisis, were unable or unwilling to check the Japanese aggression. But this was only the curtain raiser to a long series of aggressions in the period that followed.

In 1933, on my way to China, I visited the Soviet Union again, this time with a group of American tourists. Our trip covered almost the same itinerary as I had followed in 1929, and I was therefore able to make reasonable comparisons. Changes were noticeable everywhere. The country was rapidly growing, its industry was developing at a tempo unknown to any country before. It is true, in Ukrainia the people had suffered the previous year from a famine, about which fantastic figures had been published by William Henry Chamberlin. He used to write very approvingly of the U.S.S.R., while he was correspondent for the *Christian Science Monitor* in Moscow, but his new assignments were to Berlin and Tokyo, places not particularly healthy for those who approve of anything in the U.S.S.R. Certainly, in 1933, when I was in Ukrainia, I saw a land of plenty and heard that the peasants were flocking into the collective farms, realizing that in these lay the real solution of their problem and not in the restoration of the old methods, so dear to the kulaks. Instigated by the latter, they had sabotaged collectivization during the preceding year and had paid for it dearly.

One of the outstanding feats of the Soviet Union in the field of construction is the great canal linking the Baltic with the White Sea. An achievement of no little importance in time of both peace and war, the canal shortens the route between these two seas and makes possible the use of the Soviet navy interchangeably in both. The canal had just been finished when we were in U.S.S.R. in 1933; and, when I read the announcement about the ceremonies in connection with its opening, I was particularly struck by the list of those who were decorated by the government for participation in its building. To every name a *curriculum vitae* was added, and I was astonished to find that the list included a number of former offenders against the law, both political and criminal. And, to tell the truth, I was at first rather shocked by this frankness about the records of those to be decorated, and the nondiscrimination between shady characters and those whose past had not been stained by crime. But on second thought I understood the real significance. This was a reminder that everyone can err and still be useful to the nation. It meant that in the U.S.S.R. everyone has a chance to be rehabilitated. Everyone honestly willing to go straight is given a chance to do so and is welcomed back into the community.

Internationally, the Soviet Union was thriving. Nineteen hundred and thirty-three, it will be remembered, was the year of the Economic Conference at London. It ended in a complete fiasco. The only positive result gained at the time of this gathering, but independent of it, was the signing of a number of treaties negotiated by Litvinov for the U.S.S.R. with practically all of her neighbors, and the acceptance by many Powers of Litvinov's definition of the term "aggressor." Only the aggressors themselves did not accept it. Their eyes were turned toward easy conquests.

Three years later, in 1936, I made a fourth visit to my mother country, this time with my wife and a number of American friends. I think I am right in saying that Mrs. Yakhontoff's impressions were very similar to those of another Russian lady, Irina Skariatina. An aristocrat by birth and former lady in waiting to the Empress, Irina Skariatina reported her very favorable impressions of the Soviet Union in a number of books, which deservedly were widely read.[1]

This time the improvements were everywhere and quite striking. There was no longer a scarcity of any food products; and, although it was still not easy to find wearing apparel in the stores, the crowds on the streets, and especially in the theaters and hotels, were much better dressed than at the time of my previous visits. The economic development was amazing; already the U.S.S.R. was producing more than any country in Europe. This fact was well known to the outside world, and only extremely naïve or malicious persons now talked of the "economic failures" of the Soviet regime. Furthermore, its international status was one of growing influence and strength. All the Great Powers, and practically all the small ones as well, had by now established "normal" diplomatic relations with Moscow. The U.S.S.R. had joined the League of Nations and had nonaggression pacts with all her European neighbors, and mutual assistance pacts with France and Czechoslovakia in Europe, and with the Outer Mongolian People's Republic in Asia. Foreign trade was growing large, and the balance was favorable to the Soviet Union. Its finances were sound, and

[1] Irina Skariatina. *First to Go Back*. Bobbs-Merrill Company. Indianapolis. 1933. etc., etc.

the gold reserve was piling up; for in gold mining the U.S.S.R. had already taken the second place in the world.

That was the year when Sidney and Beatrice Webb published their two-volume definitive work on the Soviet Union, *Soviet Communism; A New Civilization?* The authors, now Lord and Lady Passfield, were certainly pre-eminently competent people to write such a book. Yet, to explain away the enthusiasm of these pioneers in British socialism, certain critics found it possible to assert that they were already "too old." This inspired me to offer in one of my lectures a humorous classification of those whose reports on the Soviet Union were favorable. They must belong, I said, to one of the following groups: 1) the dupes of propaganda, apparently the overwhelming majority of visitors to the U.S.S.R.; 2) the senile, who can neither see nor understand; 3) those who are paid by "Moscow gold," and therefore, of course, unreliable (this group must be extremely large, for Moscow is considered very extravagant in throwing away its money); and 4) those who are simply stupid or dishonest, or both, which certainly may happen. It never seemed to occur to those who would not believe anything good of the U.S.S.R. that there might be a fifth group embracing those who are open minded and alert enough to see the new trends, and honest enough to speak their minds.

On the side of the Webbs there were already such names as Albert Einstein, George Bernard Shaw, Romain Rolland, and a great number of writers, professors, lawyers, trade unionists, and ordinary tourists from all over the world, who had based their evaluation of the Soviet Union on personal observation. Yet there continued to be a demand for interpretations coming from the pens of such "authorities" as Isaac Don Levine, whose love for justice and democracy landed him with the Hearst publications; Eugene Lyons, whose revolutionary sympathies brought him the editorship of the *American Mercury* in 1938, and other similarly "reliable" reporters.

When reading the unreasonable reports on the U.S.S.R. by certain correspondents, one should be reminded of what had been written about the United States by similarly inclined journalists in the past. In *The Rise Of American Civilization* by Charles Beard, we find, for instance, the following paragraph suggesting comparisons with our days:

> Paying respect to the utility of religious emotions, a carefully selected Catholic priest was dispatched to the Continent to work especially in Paris, Madrid, Vienna and Rome. As a stimulus to action the Confederate Secretary of State, Judah Benjamin, informed this clerical diplomat that a recent raid had been made on Richmond for the purpose of committing it to flames, exposing its women to nameless horrors, and putting to death the chief magistrate...and, by way of elaboration, Benjamin added that the fury of the federals "spares neither age nor sex, nor do they even shrink from the most shameful desecration of the edifices in which the people meet for the worship of God." [2]

Does not all this remind one of more contemporary stories about the nationalization of women in Soviet Russia, persecution of religion, and the like, which were offered to the reading public as true descriptions of what was going on in that country?

Many people remember, of course, the special issue of the *New Republic,* then under Walter Lippmann, where the information on Russia published by a leading metropolitan paper was reproduced in parallel columns alongside the actual facts. It made uncomfortable reading for the owners, who quickly dispatched Walter Duranty to the U.S.S.R. Thanks to this, we soon started receiving reliable and illuminating reports that formed a milestone in contemporary journalism. Duranty "covered" Russia for many years; and his reports, republished in book form by the Viking Press in 1934, have stood the test of time as to accuracy.[3] They are something of which journalism may well be proud.

How much the world has changed its opinion not only since the outbreak of the October Revolution, but since Duranty started to report on Russia! Those who predicted that the new regime could not last longer than twenty days have long since learned their error. A decade ago some interpreters considered that the economic order of Russia was creating a vacuum out of the country. But today the new economic order of the Soviet Union has so demonstrated its advantages that the same critics are forced to shift to the other extreme and announce that Russia is a danger to the old economic order in the rest

[2] *The Rise of American Civilization.* By Charles A. Beard and Mary R. Beard. Macmillan Company. New York. 1930. pp. 86-87.

[3] *Duranty Reports Russia.* Viking Press. New York. 1934.

of the world. Those who in 1922 interpreted Lenin's New Economic Policy (otherwise known under the name of NEP) as a retreat from socialism, later shifted their attack to the so-called "betrayal of the revolution" by the "Stalinist regime," because there was still no equality of earnings and because that regime had mercilessly purged its ranks of traitors.

Probably no event of our time has corrupted as many minds as the Russian Revolution of 1917. How many radicals and liberals has it caused to demonstrate the weakness of their ardor for liberty and justice! How many seemingly decent people have thereby become distortionists, misinterpreters, and outright liars! They began by denouncing the Revolution and its aftermath; then drifted into slandering the Soviet regime and deliberately misinterpreting its acts; and finally found themselves simply lying without restraint. Not only individuals, but whole groups and even governments have indulged in all sorts of unthinkable activities, such as the ransacking of the diplomatically immune Soviet Embassy at Peking in April, 1927; the forcible opening of safes (Arcos in London, May, 1927); buying or manufacturing fake documents, such as the Zinovieff letter of 1926; spying, wrecking, and sabotaging in the U.S.S.R. Even the assassinations of Soviet diplomats accredited to various countries, such as Vorovsky at Lausanne, Voikov at Warsaw, and a vice-consul at Canton, came to be looked upon as a matter of course.

When looking at the balance sheet summing up the irrational attitude toward the U.S.S.R. that prevailed in several countries, one is amazed by the high cost, politically and economically, of the silly sport called red-baiting. While accusing Russia of all imaginable sins and inventing all sorts of fantastic stories, people have been all too apt to neglect problems of direct importance to their own country as a whole. Thus, an incalculable material loss has been incurred by the entire world through the economic consequences of dislocating normal trade and foolishly attempting to strangle a country so vast and populous as the Soviet Union by means of a *Cordon Sanitaire* and other devices. Surely the net result of all this has been the abnormal growth of industrial development in one part of the world at the expense of others. For is it not true that owing to this policy Russia was forced to develop her own industries in fields which normally she would have left to the exploitation of others? And is it not obvious that Japan would not have dared to invade Manchuria and other parts of China, and Germany would not have annexed Czechoslovakia, if the lie that "Communism is the greater evil" had not ruled the policies of certain Foreign Offices?

However, nothing serves so effectively to open the eyes of those who want to know the truth as unfair and dishonest treatment of the object attacked. Suspecting distortion and therefore questioning the good faith of stories emanating from certain sources, it was only natural that more and more fair-minded people should want to see the U.S.S.R. with their own eyes and draw their own conclusions. And this applies in a measure even to those who were honestly antagonistic to the Soviet Union owing to the influence of cleverly designed propaganda. Much honest misunderstanding of the U.S.S.R. in the past has arisen from attempts to measure Soviet Russia with yardsticks utterly unapplicable to that country, so different in many respects.

Thus, even without the aid of propaganda it was quite easy for the man on the street not to grasp the profound changes that had occurred in the former Russian Empire, of which he knew little or nothing. For such people, Corliss and Margaret Lamont provided an excellent introduction in their very interesting and informative little book *Russia Day by Day,* which is a record of impressions gained through a visit to the Soviet Union. They quote several pages from a prerevolutionary edition of Baedeker's *Russia* as a preliminary to their own story, leaving it to the reader to make his own conclusions.

The result is very impressive, for the backward country of the Czar's time has become unrecognizable. Its national economy, based primarily on primitive toiling of the soil, has given place to a modern industrial civilization in which agriculture is playing only a secondary role. In volume of production the U.S.S.R. is now second only to the U.S.A. The "dark people" of the Czar's days, with their shockingly high percentage of illiteracy, have now become a nation in which illiteracy has been practically liquidated, where education is compulsory, where the arts have become everybody's concern, and science and technical knowledge and skill are making remarkable strides. And this country where hygiene and sanitation were once almost unknown, and where the majority of the population had no adequate medical service, has become a leader in prophylactic work and in the protection of public health in general.[4]

Everyone who wants to know the truth about the national finances of the U.S.S.R. may find good information in such periodicals as *Journal of Commerce,* or *Business Week,* or *Annalist,* and the like—publications that can hardly be suspected of fostering communism or socialism. The U.S.S.R. has no debts incurred by the Soviet regime and is steadily and rapidly increasing its wealth. The production of its national economy is growing to the extent of 15 to 20 per cent a year, and the budget of over one hundred and thirty billion rubles in 1938 is something to make one's head reel. Yet very few people realize what the financial status of the new regime in Russia was immediately after the Revolution of 1917. In 1915, by order of the Czar, the Minister of Finance, Bark, shipped one third of the Russian gold reserve, which amounted to a little over one billion rubles, to England and France to support the crumbling currencies of the Allies. Another third of that gold mysteriously disappeared from Russia during the foreign "intervention." Practically the entire balance was to be paid to Germany, according to the terms of the Brest Litovsk Treaty, but by the Versailles Treaty it was transferred, not to Germany, but to England and France.

With no industry to speak of, with their whole national economy ruined by war and revolution, with stores exhausted, without money for buying abroad, even if there had been no *Cordon Sanitaire,* the emancipated people had no choice but to embark on a program of reconstruction, and at a tempo that taxed their strength beyond normal limits. And this terrific task was accomplished while scarcity and sometimes even complete lack of food and other necessities of life

[4] *Red Medicine. Socialized Health in Soviet Russia,* by Sir Arthur Newsholme and John Kingsbury. Doran & Co. New York. 1933.
Socialized Medicine in the Soviet Union, by Dr. H. Siegerist. W. W. Norton. New York. 1937.

were bringing the nation to the edge of starvation. The sufferings of the people were pathetic; but yet, in spite of all this, and through superhuman efforts, the people survived and the new regime endured.

Thousands and thousands of new factories and mills have been built since the Revolution, and the total production volume of Soviet industry as a whole has increased tenfold since 1913. Thanks to this, the industry of the Soviet Union was providing about eighty per cent of the entire national income by 1938, though before the Revolution hardly forty per cent was derived from that source. Agriculture in the meanwhile achieved striking results by collectivization. By 1939, only two per cent of the total area cultivated remained in the hands of individual peasants, the rest being used by collective farmers. To a great and increasing extent, Soviet agriculture is mechanized. Grain production, with larger areas cultivated, selected seeds used, fertilizers applied, and expert supervision provided, has been increased at least fifty per cent since prerevolutionary days. This result was achieved while the rest of the world saw an increase of only ten per cent. In addition to this, the U.S.S.R. has increased its cotton cultivation to a point where it is no longer dependent on foreign countries. Indeed, cotton is now exported from the Soviet Union.

With such achievements in industry and agriculture, the standard of living of the population has been materially improved since the Czar's days.

But the most important and far-reaching effect of the Revolution was the cultural improvement of the people as a whole. Culturally, Russia had been frightfully backward. But she is rapidly forging toward a front position among the nations. The number of pupils in the elementary schools had been quadrupled by the time the twentieth anniversary of the Revolution was celebrated. In the high schools and institutions of higher learning the number of students had increased almost tenfold since the year before the Revolution. By 1939 there were, according to Molotov, the Prime Minister of the U.S.S.R., more students in all the institutions for higher learning in the Soviet Union than in those of France, Germany, Italy, and Japan combined.

The publishing activities of the U.S.S.R. have demonstrated a fabulous development. For several years now the U.S.S.R. has been first among all countries as to the number of new titles of books appearing yearly, some of the most popular books being printed in millions of copies. The same is true of newspapers. If before the Revolution the circulation of all dailies in Russia amounted to only two and a half million copies, in 1939 there were some forty million copies printed in various languages.

One has only to look at the records of any international scientific or technical congress to realize how rapidly the Soviet Union is advancing in science and technical knowledge and skill. Believing that "Science is the salvation of mankind," the Soviet regime is doing its utmost to create the most favorable conditions for the promotion of science in its pure form not less than in its practical aspects of fostering the material well-being of the nation.[5]

As for the Soviet aviators, they have set a number of world records. They have spanned the North Arctic, covering the enormous distance between Moscow and California in two successive flights in 1937, and from Moscow to Canada in 1939. Russian scientists spent a whole winter at the North Pole collecting scientific data useful to the entire world.

In the domain of art the Soviet citizens have more than maintained the established high reputation of the Russians and other peoples inhabiting that enormous country. Their theater is probably the most progressive in the world today. Their cinema is acclaimed as superb. Their music, too, is on a very high level, and Soviet contestants won most of the first prizes at the international contests in Europe in 1937 and 1938. Their literature is prolific and full of vitality. But, the most important phenomenon is the participation in creative effort by millions who are seeking self-expression in the various arts; for to this end the State offers every imaginable encouragement and facility. This alone should give the lie to those who assert that in the Soviet Union artists are regimented and "in uniform."[6]

[5] *A Scientist Among the Soviets.* By Julian Huxley. Harper & Brothers. New York. 1932.

[6] Huntly Carter. *The New Theatre and Cinema in Russia.* International Publishers. New York. 1925.

About the opportunity for every child in the Soviet Union to develop his talents and aspirations, the late Dr. Frankwood E. Williams, one of the foremost experts in this field, wrote an excellent book, of first-hand observation, in which he expressed his admiration for the methods applied in the U.S.S.R.[7] And Sidney and Beatrice Webb, in their chapter on "Remaking the Man," have offered the following interesting explanation of the meaning of culture in the Soviet Union, as contrasted with England:

...In the usage of Soviet Communism there is, in the conception of culture, no such connotation of inevitable exclusiveness, of a pleasant aloofness, or of a consciousness of superiority. It is, at any rate, definitely the policy of the Soviet Government—as it is very far from being that of any other government in the world—that the possession of culture shall be made, not necessarily identical or equal, but genuinely universal; that none of the known means of awakening the powers of the child, or stimulating the development of the adolescent, or refining the life of the adult, shall be withheld from, or denied to, any resident in the USSR; and that, as fast as the increasing wealth production permits, these means shall actually be put, for individual use or enjoyment according to their several faculties, at the disposal of literally everybody. Soviet Communists actually believe that, by a sustained effort of self-sacrifice on the part of the older people, the entire generation that is growing up in the USSR can be raised to a high level of culture. There will be some who will see in that very belief, and in the strenuous efforts that it inspires, a real evidence of culture in the best sense of the word.[8]

Turning to the international status of the U.S.S.R., what a change we see! With the Revolution of 1917, Russia promptly became an outcast, ostracized by all. Twenty years later she was not only recognized by all the Great Powers, and all others of any importance, but respected for her economic, political, and military strength. No one will deny that this marked change in the U.S.S.R.'s international position is at least partly due to her great and growing military strength. Her Red Army has become a factor not to be ignored by the warmongers. Yet at the same time her consistent policy of nonaggression has made her the center of all forces striving for the preservation of peace. Was

Dr. Harry Ward. *In Place of Profit.* Charles Scribner's Sons. New York. 1933.
H. W. L. Dana. *Handbook on Soviet Drama.* American-Russian Institute. New York. 1938.

[7] Frankwood E. Williams. *Russia, Youth and the Present Day World.* Farrar & Reinhart. New York. 1934.

[8] Sidney and Beatrice Webb. *Soviet Communism: A New Civilization?* Charles Scribner's Sons. New York. v. 2, p. 924.

it not partly on this consideration that President Roosevelt decided, almost immediately after his first inauguration, to re-establish normal relations with Moscow? Was it not thanks to that wise step of the President that the tension in the Orient somewhat subsided and the American position there temporarily improved?

On December 5, 1936, the Congress of the Soviets approved a new Constitution, evolved after six months' study of its original draft by the people and after the incorporation of various changes, modifications, and additions suggested by the inhabitants of the Soviet Union, and outsiders as well, for everybody was invited to criticize and suggest improvements. Now this Constitution has become the basic law of the country. And even if we must wait a reasonable time before pronouncing judgment on its merits in practice, there is no gainsaying that, as it stands, the Constitution is a most democratic document and a new milestone in political theory.

Especially significant was the decision to pass this new, very liberal law, granting universal franchise and allowing secret balloting, at a time when it became necessary to hold the trials of a number of traitors and saboteurs. This would seem to show that the opposition to the government was negligible in numbers and its chances of overthrowing the regime practically nil.

Lenin realized, of course, that the process of establishing an entirely new and still untested departure in government could not be accomplished at once, without efforts by the remnants of the "Old" to overthrow it. In connection with this, he wrote as follows:

> It is to be expected that the achievements of the new cannot at once give us those firm established, almost stagnant and rigid forms, which were long ago created, have grown to strength, been preserved through the centuries. At the moment of birth the elements of the new are still found in the period of fermentation and utter instability.[9]

Yes, the Soviet Union experienced boundless difficulties in the herculean task of building a new country in the wake of wars and revolutions. It was a tremendous undertaking to transform the backward

[9] Lenin. "Incidental tasks of the Soviet power." (Sketch for an article.) Quoted from the *Text book of Marxist Philosophy*. Edited by John Lewis. London. Victor Gollancz. 1937. p. 311.

agricultural country, that had been the Russia of the Czars, into the advanced modern industrial state we see today. But, hard as it was, the labor was not Sisyphean, even in spite of all the hindrances and all the plots of enemies boring from within or acting from without. They were right, who said, after the Munich "sellout," that the Soviet Union, maligned, slandered, and misrepresented, nevertheless looms ever mightier as the hope of all the peoples of the world for a peace front.

CHAPTER XXI

TWENTY YEARS AFTER

(*The Balance Sheet*)

Tempo of modern life. Heredity and environment. Accumulation of experience. Instinctive and conscious reactions. Rationalizations and generalizations. Poets of gloom. I am an optimist. The old versus the new. Aggressors rampant. Is fascism inevitable? Chicago Congress of the American League Against War and Fascism. Hoover's promises of 1928 and the actualities of the later years. Roosevelt's New Deal. A few comparisons with the Russia of the Czars. Democracy as the hope.

IN THIS EPOCH of high speed and rapid developments in most fields of human endeavor, twenty years is a long span in the life of an adult. And twenty years in postwar America—where I have made my home since 1918—are equal, by the measure of considered experience, to almost twice as many in the Russia of old.

Perhaps the rapid tempo is responsible. The kaleidoscopic changes which the civilized world has witnessed in recent years have undoubtedly produced more intense vibrations of the nervous system than ever before; it may even be said that a great number of the sensations we experience probably flow through our consciousness without leaving a noticeable trace. Most of the events we witness perforce go by without proper evaluation or even understanding, for they come so quickly, so often, and from such unforeseen directions that we lack patience, knowledge, and inclination alike to generalize from what we see and thus gain a better comprehension of the world in which we live. Yet, at the same time, the very magnitude of the events and intensity of the historical developments in our times have persistently forced our mental faculties to a more extensive use. And this, let us hope, may be fortunate for our posterity. In the twenty-odd years that have elapsed since the Russian Revolution of 1917—and very largely because of that Revolution—the world has greatly altered. We have been forced to think about these changes. So thinking, we ourselves have changed. And in our thinking, individual and collective, do we not partly rule the future?

I have tried in this book to probe, describe, and estimate the changes one man has undergone in relation to one of the outstanding social and political experiments of history.

My accumulation of experience during childhood and adolescence was naturally conditioned by environment. I belonged to the privileged class; and my tastes, ideas, and opinions were molded by the habits and the ideology of that class. But there was in me a certain curiosity about the life beyond the limits of my own milieu; and this was cultivated first by reading and later on by contact with people who had wider social interests and vision. Basically, however, I remained under the influence of the class to which I belonged.

Along with the widening of my experiences, and the further accumulation of the wealth of my factual world—as comprehended in direct experience, and interpreted through the glass of acquired formal knowledge—I gradually developed the ability to react consciously as well as instinctively. In other words, I developed a critical capacity and learned to distinguish between various things and events, to analyze, to generalize, and to draw my own, not necessarily orthodox conclusions.

Wars, followed by revolutions, naturally intensified this conscious reaction. At the time of the Revolution of 1917, I was faced with the conflict between class ideology and national interest; and from the very outbreak of that Revolution, to which my colleagues at the Embassy were so strongly antagonistic, I knew instictively as well as rationally that I must soon choose between standing by my class and standing by the people as a whole. Throughout childhood I had been taught that personal desires must be subordinated to those of the family, in the interest not only of the family as a unit but of its individual members. Later, at the State-controlled schools, I learned that the interests of the family were less important than those of the country. And, finally, in adolescence I discovered that international welfare is of more importance than national exclusiveness. I remembered that such was also the teaching of the Church, while the French Encyclopedists, whom some of my teachers and professors had taught me to respect, had advocated those ideas as well. In other words, my mind was now conditioned by Christian ethics and the liberal philosophies as well. So, for me, the choice I made eventually—to stand with my people as a whole, not with my class alone—seemed natural enough. I remembered, too, that the famous phrase, *Après moi le déluge,* was not coined by a representative of the common people, but by a cynical degenerate of the most privileged class, who was not particularly solicitous about the future of his country and its people. I had no inclination to take such a stand, even though the contrary might mean ostracism by my class and scorn by my colleagues; for obviously not everyone could be expected to adopt my attitude.

The decision was made still easier by foreign intervention in the affairs of Russia. To this I was bitterly opposed from the outset, though my attitude was probably dictated more by patriotic feeling, as I understood it, than by any real spirit of internationalism. It would take more time, study, and understanding before I reached that higher level of evaluating events from an international, rather than national, point of view. But gradually, I think, I came to it—partly through reading and through the acceptance of certain theories, but more by reason of enlarging contacts with foreign nations through travel and long residence among peoples other than my own.

Whatever the causes, I did not confront new situations passively. And so my mysterious and still vaguely defined world of actuality was gradually transformed into a more rational and better understood world of political and social phenomena.

As my eyes opened, my curiosity increasingly demanded explanations. A considerable amount of reading resulted in centering my interest on economic, political, and social matters; and in the twenty-odd years that have elapsed since the Revolution of 1917 I have assiduously tried to gain a better understanding of those problems. In other words, I have actually devoted more time to this study, with a more positive interest than was spent on my fundamental schooling before entering upon the military career which my family chose for me. Lecturing and, later on, writing served as additional stimuli in this direction. That is why and how I became a student of matters usually alien to the professional soldier, and rarely attractive to those who are born in wealth, live a sheltered life, and prefer not to think about the possibility of change.

If the Revolution and the armed intervention of foreigners in the affairs of my mother country prompted me to take a four-square stand with the people, it was the wholesale distortions of the news coming from Russia after the Revolution which aroused the desire to revisit my mother country and discover for myself the real situation. And the more I observed on my several pilgrimages to the Soviet Union, the more I studied the various problems which the U.S.S.R. was solving, the more interested I became. Of course, I was prepared to consider favorably whatever I found there, if only because I wanted to disprove what I felt to be distortions of the truth. But the reality I found on these visits also caused me to revise many of my own old ideas about the events in Russia since 1917. Gradually I came to the conclusion that my mother country was on the sure road to a better life. And was that not of incomparably greater significance, I asked myself, than my own comfort and the interests of the class into which I had been born?

From my earliest days, the code of patriotism had been inculcated—at home, in school, and later on in the Army. But I was never directly taught that I should stand with my class against the nation. On the contrary, the technique was indirect, class consciousness being developed by various other methods. The whole structure of life was so arranged as to keep the privileged apart from the rest of the people, with mode of life, manners, and even language all serving to thrust patricians and plebs into two utterly different worlds. In short, the patrician could normally be counted upon to keep quite aloof from the nation at large, and to care little and understand less about the people, except when some individual circumstance or unforeseen clash of interests confronted him with the necessity of taking a stand. And, like the overwhelming majority of officers in Czarist Russia, I was spared the need of making any such choice before the Revolution; for

I was neither a man of business nor a landlord at any time. When the Revolution broke out, of course, I had to choose; but the issue was clear by then, and, with the old order on the defensive, the motive of class selfishness was more obvious. I might follow leaders who, I could see, had fixed ideas about the relationship of the classes and wanted to curb the Revolution in order to preserve their privileges; or I could step aside and follow the dictates of my own conscience. I did the latter, and I think I could have done naught else. Nor have I ever regretted my decision. On the contrary it has been a source of constant happiness to feel that I took the right turning, and that the right track lies clear before me to be followed for the rest of my life.

Naturally, long before the Revolution of 1917 occurred I had seen that some drastic change was desirable, if only because the country was so clearly and steadily deteriorating under the old order. When the Czar abdicated, I no longer had any allegiance but to my country. This, in my conception, was composed of the territory and the people. My own class was only one of its parts, and not a part which had any particular right to dominate, or to act in opposition to the people at large.

The fate of the Provisional Government was a disappointment to me, because I had faith in the people who were behind it. I found the advent of the Bolsheviks quite incomprehensible; and in this my reaction was consistent with the information supplied by those whom I then considered reliable and well informed. And because the information was so misleading, and the propaganda against the Bolsheviks so well organized, lavishly financed, and generally disseminated, I remained for a while in a state of utter confusion. But as the fog began to lift, as the facts—which are proverbially stubborn—began to be known, I seized upon them eagerly, and was consumed with a desire not only to learn all I could, but to check my information by personal visits. Finally, step by step, I came to some slight understanding of the objective truth about the U.S.S.R., and why it was not commonly known.

However, the Russian Revolution was not the only cause of the profound changes that marked the years which followed the World

War. The War itself certainly accelerated the Russian crisis and its aftermath, but it also brought in its wake numerous other difficult problems. The Versailles Treaty, that formally ended the War, actually removed none of its major causes; and, as we quickly learned, it settled nothing properly, if it settled anything at all. The remaking of the map, which was one of the main concerns of the conferees, did not improve the international situation in the slightest. It only added new problems by creating new states, new borders, new rivalries. And to make matters worse the competition between various countries for markets and sources of raw materials was aggravated by the acute poverty of all the belligerents. Pauperized by four years of senseless destruction of wealth which had been accumulated for several decades, they were all striving to improve their status and eagerly looking at foreign markets. Besides, two of the nations which had supposedly fought in the hope of bettering their economic situation, Italy on one side, and Germany on the other, emerged from the Versailles Conference economically much less secure than they had been when the war began. The Peace Treaty did not bring peace. It merely sowed the seeds of discontent and of new strife.

Italy, poor in her natural resources and dissatisfied with the spoils allowed her at Versailles, looked to some new solution for her economic woes. The method advocated by the leaders of the people, who pointed to the example of Russia, was opposed by those who knew that their well-being depended on the old system. But at the same time the latter fully realized that Italy stood no chance of competing successfully with the other capitalist nations, for they were well equipped and she was poor. In other words, they had to devise some artificial means whereby their "have not" country could continue with private ownership and at the same time compete with the rich "haves." The method introduced in Italy under the name of fascism proved rather effective. Civic liberties, the parliamentary system, and trade unions were all abolished in order to bring back the national economy to conditions resembling those of feudalism. Under such conditions, the cost of production could be lowered so as to make competition with other capitalist countries possible. The State could control foreign trade in such a way as to compensate for the losses on certain commodities by better prices obtained for others.

Some years later Germany followed Italy's suit. This was only natural. The economic life of the new German Republic had been made intolerable by the terms of the treaty concluded at Versailles, in an atmosphere of hatred and revenge, and with complete disregard of the obvious consequences. But Germany was unable and even indisposed to establish a new order as quickly as Italy, if only because the government created by the revolution that ushered in the end of the War was to a certain extent a government "of the people, by the people, and for the people." It took fifteen years of suffering, plots, intrigues, exploitation, and general disillusionment to make possible the ascendency of Nazism. But by 1933 the German people lost the struggle, and the fascist idea forced its way into the Reich under the sweet-sounding name of National Socialism, with Adolf Hitler as its soon-to-be-omnipotent leader.

Never, in all probability, has a nation been sunk in a deeper or more appalling despair than was Germany in the months before the Hitler *coup d'état* and the Reichstag fire. One must not make the mistake of underrating the profundity of that despair or the importance of German domestic evils and foreign intransigence in bringing it about. But at the same time it must be remembered that a cult of helplessness was rife in the world at large during the postwar era. "Disillusionment" was the universal catchword, and the lamentations of Herr Oswald Spengler in *The Decline of the West* echoed the pervading gloom. "Only dreamers believe that there is a way out. Optimism is cowardice. We are born into this time and must bravely follow the path to the destined end. There is no other way. Our duty is to hold on to the last position, without hope, without rescue...." So wrote Spengler in Germany. But other poets of despair were raising their voices in other countries too.

Being an optimist by nature, I was neither impressed nor influenced by this brand of pessimism. Russia's example, it seemed to me, offered a justification for hope; for there, in the former Empire of the Czar, one could see a new life developing under the slogans of a younger generation filled with hope, faith in their forces, trust in their leaders, and a passionate desire to create and to enjoy living.

"Against all the pessimism, decline, decay and filth, tragic destinies, self-heroisings, idolization of death, returns to the primitive, mysticism, spiritualism, and corruption" wrote R. Palme Dutt, "the revolutionary proletarian movement . . . proclaims its unshakable certainty and confidence in life, in science, in the power of science, in the possibility of happiness, proclaims its unconquerable optimism for the whole future of humanity. . . ." [1]

This was the main characteristic of Soviet literature of the epoch. The melancholy, disgust with life, and hypochondria which had filled Russian letters in the past had miraculously given place to cheerfulness and self-confidence. Once, indeed, I had the temerity to point this out in somewhat similar terms during a radio talk for N.B.C. on the new trends in Russian literature. As a result, the person responsible for the programs was reprimanded for allowing "pro-Soviet propaganda," and engagements for radio talks by the offending optimist practically ceased.

This, however, did not change my opinion about the old and the new. On the contrary, it served as additional proof that the old was very sick and much in need of nursing; while the young and vigorous new was in the full bloom of health, in spite of efforts to kill it.

History has taught us that changes are inevitable. Everything is dynamic, and all historical conditions must be superseded at some higher stage of historic development. No one can deny this. But at the same time one ought not to minimize or exaggerate the cost of such changes. Those who stubbornly resist the advent of the new have always suffered the consequences, for one cannot safely stick to the point of view of a single class when it runs counter to the general weal and to natural trends. And the endeavor to do so is likely to make mutual understanding between the classes well-nigh impossible. Unfortunately, it is not easy to be detached, to rise above class interest;

[1] R. Palme Dutt. *Fascism and the Social Revolution.* Martin Lawrence Ltd. London. 1934. p. 231.

and that is why we find such widespread lack of reason in the appraisal of revolutionary changes.

In this connection I call to mind a number of incidents in my own experience which serve to illustrate this truth. When I returned from my first visit to the Soviet Union in 1929 and reported my observations to a certain good friend of mine, a Russian refugee, he told me frankly that although he knew me well enough to feel sure that what I said was true he still preferred not to listen because he could not stand hearing anything good about the new regime. Again, when I was in Shanghai in 1933, after my third visit to the U.S.S.R., a number of Russian refugees came to meet me at the home of an old friend of mine, a highly respected gentleman. When they asked me to talk about Russia, I felt it would be better not to, for I sensed what their attitude would be. But they insisted. The result was that some of them soon left the room, others made most irrelevant and quite unpleasant remarks, while a few became so agitated that our host had to change the topic in order to avoid a clash. It was obvious that hatred was so deep that facts had no value, no interest. Reason was unable to keep their minds open. Some of them wanted to see the "cursed Soviet regime" crushed, whatever the method; some of them went even further and added: "whatever the cost."

The majority of these people undoubtedly deserved pity: They had lost their country and had not found a new one because they continued to hope against hope for a return to Russia. In despair they preferred to ally themselves with any who were interested in defeating the Soviets—with the Japanese, Germans, and other foes of the U.S.S.R. By serving in the ranks of various military units, as was the case in China and Manchukuo, or by joining various fascist and other political organizations, some of them became involved in various plots. Many of these conspirators paid for their treason with their lives.

But these extreme examples of betrayal of the mother country were repeatedly condemned by such leaders of the Russian refugees as General Denikin and Professor Miliukov. I do not believe that the majority of them ever approved such acts. Along with the growing belief that the new regime was doing well, that conditions in the Soviet

Union were steadily improving, and that its international position was becoming quite important, many refugees began planning a return home, "even under that new regime." But it proved to be extremely difficult to fulfill such plans. Only a very few of the expatriates were actually allowed by Moscow to come back after years spent abroad while their country was suffering all sorts of hardships. Numerous sad experiences had taught the Soviet authorities that not everyone professing to be a friend was reliable; and, as usual, a multitude of bona fide people had to pay for the misdeeds of a few plotters and criminals. This situation may be expected to continue for a while, for the Soviet authorities can ill afford to relax vigilance so long as fascist aggression is rampant and the leaders of the Anti-Comintern Pact shriek in chorus that the ultimate objective is the elimination of the Bolsheviks. Moscow must remain on the alert and be prepared for every eventuality.

At present, however, fascism seems to threaten other countries more directly than the U.S.S.R. Its proponents are concentrating their wrath on the old democracies, not on the Soviet State. The former are their competitors in the world markets, the latter is not. Nor must we overlook the much-discussed theory that fascism was born out of communism as an antidote, and that the two are fundamentally very much alike. Of course, there is some interdependence between the two, as there is between any two movements which are on the rise at the same approximate period. But it seems that fascism is less directly an outcome of communism than a device to acquire advantages in the struggle between variously situated capitalist countries. In any event, the pretense of the fascists that they are fighting communism looks strangely like a smoke screen for other, far less ideological plans. Their deeds do not match their words. Japan succeeded in grabbing Manchuria with this transparent excuse. Italy and Germany succeeded in establishing themselves in Spain, with Franco as their agent, by a *reductio ad absurdum* of the anti-Red argument. One is inclined to ask what happened to the interests of those who naïvely believed them? The Soviet Union lost no concessions and privileges in China, Spain, Ethiopia, and elsewhere, for it had none to lose; the victims were those Great, and not so great, Powers, whose rulers played with the red herring of appeasement instead of defending the interests of their countries, and stopping the aggressors.

After returning from China in 1934, I was asked to address the Congress of the American League Against War and Fascism, held at Chicago. This was an invitation which I was particularly happy to accept, partly because, just a short while before, I had witnessed at Shanghai the disgusting spectacle of the Conference of the International League Against War and Fascism being barred by the Chinese authorities, acting under Nazi pressure. The result had been that such celebrities as Madame Sun Yat-sen, the widow of Dr. Sun, Lord Morley, a Whip in the British House of Lords, and a number of other prominent delegates from all parts of the globe were forced to meet in hiding. At the same time the Japanese were openly preparing for the invasion of China, the Germans were busy disseminating Nazi propaganda in that country, and the Italian Fascists were co-operating with both. The others, professing devotion to the principles of democracy, were complacently looking on, if not rendering actual assistance to the activities of the fascists of various brands.

After the dismemberment and subsequent absorption of Czechoslovakia by Germany, and the conquest of Spain by the Italo-German interventionists for their puppet, Franco, the danger of fascism to the democracies, including the United States, became more evident than ever. Meanwhile the menace of aggressive and unscrupulous fascist competitors on the world markets made the problem of resisting them acute enough to evoke protests from certain quarters which had so far preferred to deny the existence of any cause for alarm to America. But the protracted economic crisis has made a Pollyanna attitude irrational; faced by a combination of dwindling industries, continued unemployment of millions, and the expansion of the government-subsidized and controlled trade of the fascists, the democracies, including the United States, are now having to make their choice and decide on their future policies. With the fascists—or against them?

Before the advent of Hitler and the beginning of the world-wide economic crisis, when people were still talking of the "period of stabilization of capitalism," Herbert Hoover, in accepting the Republican nomination for President, said:

Unemployment in the sense of distress is widely disappearing.... We in America today are nearer to the final triumph over poverty than ever before in the history of any land. The poorhouse is vanishing from among us....[2]

That was in August, 1928. Four years later the Research Committee into Modern Trends, appointed by the same Herbert Hoover, reported:

In the best years millions of families are limited to meager living. Unless there is a speeding-up of social invention or a slowing-down of mechanical invention, grave maladjustments are certain. The American standard of living for the near future must decline because of lower wages caused by unemployment.[3]

In such circumstances the menace of fascism to the United States became a reality, not only from the outside, as was made clear at the Pan-American Conference held in Peru late in 1938, but also from within, as evidenced by a growing number of pro-fascist organizations such as the German-American Bund, the Silver Shirts, and the like.

President Franklin D. Roosevelt's warnings have come in quick succession since his famous "quarantine" speech at Chicago in October, 1937. In one of his "fireside chats" to the nation, he said in explanation of his New Deal "emergency" program:[4]

....I am thinking not only of the immediate economic needs of the people of the nation, but also of their personal liberties, the most precious possession of all Americans. I am thinking of our democracy and of the recent trend in other parts of the world away from the democratic ideal.

Democracy has disappeared in several other great nations, not because the people of those nations disliked democracy, but because they had grown tired of unemployment and insecurity, of seeing their children hungry while they sat helpless in the face of government confusion, government weakness, through lack of leadership in government. Finally, in desperation, they chose to sacrifice liberty in the hope of getting something to eat.

We in America know that our own democratic institutions can be preserved and made to work. But in order to preserve them we need to act together to meet the problems of the nation boldly and to prove that the practical operation of democratic government is equal to the task of protecting the security of the people.

[2] Quoted from the *Nation*. New York. June 15, 1932. p. 671.
[3] Quoted from R. Palme Dutt. *Fascism and the Social Revolution*. London. 1934.
[4] April 14, 1938.

Not only our future economic soundness, but the very soundness of our democratic institutions depends on the determination of our government to give employment to idle men.

The people of America are in agreement in defending their liberties at any cost, and the first line of that defense lies in the protection of economic security. Your government, seeking to protect democracy, must prove that government is stronger than the forces of business depression.

History proves that dictatorships do not grow out of strong and successful governments, but out of weak and helpless ones. If by democratic methods people get a government strong enough to protect them from fear and starvation, their democracy succeeds; but if they do not, they grow impatient. Therefore, the only sure bulwark of continuing liberty is a government strong enough to protect the interests of the people, and a people strong enough and well enough informed to maintain its sovereign control over its government.

We are a rich nation; we can afford to pay for security and prosperity without having to sacrifice our liberties into the bargain.

Unfortunately, the good intentions of the President were sabotaged by certain powerful groups. The "quarantine" of the aggressors actually led on the one hand to withholding the means of defense from such victims of aggression as Spain and China, and on the other to direct or semidirect help to such aggressors as could trade on a "cash and carry" basis. This resulted, in the case of Japan, in bringing most of the gold of that country to the shores of America, and in the supplying of Japan by American exporters with more than one half of all her war needs. Apparently the "merchants of death" were not impressed by the fact that this was a war not only against China and the idea of democratic intercourse, but against the vital interests of their own country. Are they sure, these "merchants of death," that the bombs which sent the U.S.A. gunboat *Panay* to the bottom of the Yangtze River were not made of scrap iron they had sold to Japan?

Many events in the United States during the last decade have reminded me of the evils of Russia in the years preceding her Revolution of 1917. In both countries the people engaged in the sport of building their own fortunes have had little interest in the future of their mother country. The "high society" of Russia was capable of seeing nothing, hearing nothing, and enjoying itself in a sort of fool's paradise, while the people were starving and suffering from the ills of the regime. "High society" everywhere seems to be the same.

Those Russians who "gloriously" defended the monarchy against the advent of new forces resorted to the same red herrings and accusations of "radicalism" as are used today by self-interested reactionaries all over the world.

But in one respect, at least, the United States seems to me incomparably more fortunate than was the Russia of Nicholas II. For about one hundred and fifty years—or from the birth of their country—the people of the United States have enjoyed democracy, even if sometimes in a modified form. But now, after years of depression, and with the insidious example of the quick fascist method of "solving" economic difficulties, democracy has become seriously endangered, even in the "Land of the Free." For this reason, among others, I am proud of the fact that since 1934, when I was asked to address the Congress of the American League Against War and Fascism, I have tried to miss no opportunity of stressing the danger of these two enemies of the people, fascism and war, in my lectures and writings. I am quite convinced that fascism, which is being based on hatred and glorification of war, is the Enemy Number One of the human race.

Fortunately, to admit that democracy is menaced by fascism, is not the same thing as to concede that the latter's triumph is inevitable. But to suppose that this triumph is impossible just because, for instance, the Constitution of the United States does not allow such an arrangement, would be dangerously naïve. To assert that fascism has no future, because it is a step backward, and has no sound economic basis, does not mean it may not have a momentary success. Abnormal situations can be arranged and forced temporarily upon a nation, if the nation fails to discover the plot in time and to take protective action. Everything depends on the people themselves and, particularly, on the middle class. Nazis and Fascists are aware of this. The technique of Herr Hitler has been to soothe the middle class by picturing a bourgeois paradise under his National Socialist movement. The same, or a similar technique is applied in other lands by the advocates of fascism. One of the methods employed by them is to frighten the middle class with the bogey of socialism, the "horrors" of revolution, and the menace of the bewhiskered "Bolsheviks." Very often this brings quick results; and, before the middle class realizes the deception, it has become as much the victim of fascism as are the workers and the farmers. They never reach the promised paradise; always it is unattainable, for fascism accepts the present class stratification as permanent. On discovering this unpleasant truth, the middle class people must realize that it has no choice but to join the united front of the underprivileged, and then, most likely, work for revolution. The masters of fascist states, the ardent believers in brute force and advocates of violence, will yield only to force and violence.

It is most unfortunate that many people who enjoy the blessings of democracy stubbornly refuse to recognize the impending danger from advancing fascism. It is most unfortunate that many people, misled by propaganda, believe that fascism is concerned only with fighting socialism, communism, and the other "isms." They fail to see that fascism is a "complete reversal of the whole trend of European civilization." The words are those of an American ex-Secretary of State, Henry Stimson. "Fascism," he continues, "has involved a serious moral deterioration; an increasing and callous disregard of the most formal and explicit international obligations and pledges; extreme brutality toward helpless groups of people; the complete destruction within their jurisdiction of that individual freedom of speech, of thought, and of the person, which has been the priceless goal of many centuries of struggle and the most distinctive crown of our modern civilization. Such a loosening of the moral and human ties which bind human society together gives powerful confirmation of the basic unfitness of such a system for organized international life." [5]

After twenty-odd years in the United States, I have learned to respect more deeply than ever before the idea of genuine democracy, as it was visualized by Thomas Jefferson and other fathers of this country, who fought for their people and opposed the additions and modifications of the Constitution in the interests of the privileged. I believe in democracy as it was pictured by the Encyclopedists of France, that is to say, in realistic democracy which allows an economic basis for the free pursuit of happiness. Such democracy remains the hope of the

[5] *The New York Times,* March 6, 1939.

people all over the world, in spite of the fascists, who are trying to turn back the wheels of history and re-establish national economy on the basis of a medieval order with a feudal serfdom.

But life is action, and the great danger today is that democracy may become passive. Genuine democracy must be alert, active, and progressive. Machiavelli may have scorned the "masses" as devoid of judgment and deserving of no particular consideration; and "wise" individuals may overrate their mental capacity and qualifications for leadership, but the people at large form the true basis of a nation. State control over the individual, when it protects the community from abuses by the self-seeking, must be a real guarantee of a better life to the individual himself.

In making up the balance sheet of my "twenty years" spent in America after the Russian Revolution, I can truly say that I am more than ever convinced that happiness of the individual is closely dependent on the happiness of his nation, and that no individual or nation can enjoy true peace and prosperity, while surrounded by the misery and suffering of others.